THE COMPLEAT
PRACTICAL JOKER

THE COMPLEAT
PRACTICAL JOKER

H. ALLEN SMITH

WILLIAM MORROW AND COMPANY, INC.

New York   *1980*

Library of Congress Cataloging in Publication Data

Smith, Harry Allen, 1907-1976
    The compleat practical joker.

    Originally published in 1953 by Doubleday, Garden
City, N.Y.
    Includes index.
    1. Practical jokes.   I. Title.
PN6231.P67S62   1980   817'.02   80-20668
ISBN 0-688-03705-4

Printed in the United States of America

1 2 3 4 5 6 7 8 9 10

BOOK DESIGN BY MICHAEL MAUCERI

The extract from *Flush Times of Alabama and Mississippi*, by Joseph G. Baldwin, is reprinted by permission of D. Appleton-Century-Crofts, Inc.

The extract from *A Treasury of British Humor*, by Morris Bishop, is reprinted by permission of Coward-McCann, Inc.

The extracts from *The American Language: Supplement One*, and from *Happy Days*, by H. L. Mencken, are reprinted by permission of the author.

The essay "How to Talk Double Talk," by Elmer Roessner, copyright, 1939, by Esquire, Inc., is used by permission of the author.

The extract from *Working With Roosevelt*, by Judge Samuel Rosenman, is copyright, 1952, by Harper & Brothers, used by permission.

The extract from *My Life and Hard Times*, by James Thurber, is used by permission of the author.

Publisher's Note

The Compleat Practical Joker, presented here in its entirety, was first published in 1953. Over the years that followed, H. Allen Smith received countless letters and
clippings from readers of his classic work. He found himself
saving newspaper accounts of unusual pranks and corresponding with other authorities. After more than twenty
years had passed he contemplated the need for a new book
incorporating the best of this material and explaining the
major changes and contemporary developments.

Shortly before his death in February 1976, as the self-
appointed High Commissioner of Practical Jokery, H. Allen
Smith wrote a long supplementary essay on the subject
which he may have intended to use as the opening chapter
of a new book. With its original title, "The Day of the
Practical Joker," it is presented following Chapter 24 of
this edition of *The Compleat Practical Joker.* The remainder of the book is a selection of the new stories as they
were rewritten by Mr. Smith in his own antic prose.

William Morrow & Company, Inc.
1980

Preface

Fifteen years ago I wrote a series of six articles for the New York *World-Telegram* dealing with famous practical jokes and their authors. As soon as these articles appeared in print a cascade of mail descended upon the newspaper. The letters fell into two categories. One group denounced me for a cur and a cad, as if I had come out in favor of carcinoma, or transvestitism, or peace. A majority of the correspondents, however, sent in additional practical jokes and these letters I placed in a large red envelope. In succeeding years whenever I heard about a practical joke, or read about one, I made notes and added them to my collection. There was no particular reason for my doing this, save perhaps that I have squirrel blood in me.

Recently I was reading an article about Charles A. Lindbergh, written for an anthology by John Lardner. As a young man Lindbergh was a practical joker, somewhat on the crude side, and in the course of recounting a few of his exploits Mr. Lardner wrote:

". . . they were the sort of practical jokes, complicated, strenuous, and 'virile,' about which a monograph might be written in connection with American life."

Monograph. I wasn't sure about the precise meaning of the word. I looked it up and found that I knew how to write a monograph, that I had, in fact, already written several. I went to my files and dug out the practical jokes. By this time there were three fat red envelopes. I spent an afternoon going through the old notes and clippings and, to be truthful, lost my characteristic poise and got to laughing at some of the fool things I had recorded.

So this is a monograph on practical jokes, though not exactly according to Mr. Lardner's prescription. A monograph on the kind of jokes played by Lindbergh (putting shaving cream in the mouth of a sleeping man; filling a friend's bedside water pitcher with kerosene; stuffing a dead polecat into a friend's pillowcase) would be as dull and witless as the jokes themselves.

My principal aim has been to set down as many amusing jokes as I have been able to find, at the same time recognizing the existence of the prank that is nasty and cruel. In the doing, I have come to a number of conclusions. It seems clear that the United States of America produces more practical jokers per capita than any other nation on earth. England ranks second. The remaining nations do not amount to much.

The energy expended on practical jokes, in this country alone, exceeds the combined energy that goes into the production of napalm bombs, erasers and prayer books. Yet an enormous prejudice has grown up against them and against the people who indulge in them. From one point of view this prejudice is probably justified; from another, it is both ridiculous and, in a sense, hypocritical.

The tendency has been to place all practical jokers in the same category: shallow-headed smart alecks. There are people who are favorably inclined toward swindlers, procurers, and tax evaders who grow livid at the mere thought of a practical joker. These same people oftentimes, under investigation, turn out to be practical jokers themselves or, at least, they howl with laughter when recounting pranks played by their grandfathers or their friends or by celebrities past and present. They may also be worshipers of

William Shakespeare who, in common with many other classical writers, employed the practical joke freely as a literary device; they may relish the story of Ichabod Crane's encounter with the Headless Horseman; they may admire the works and personality of Mark Twain, a practical joker who wrote incessantly about practical jokes; they may love the antics of the Marx Brothers, salute James Thurber as a genius, speak glowingly of Uncle Remus and Abe Lincoln, of Richard Brinsley Sheridan and Sir Osbert Sitwell, of Madame Jeritza and T. Coleman du Pont, of Lord Halifax and George Horace Lorimer. But practical jokers! They should all be strangled! I've always suspected that the man who preaches most vociferously against adultery commits a teeny-weeny bit of it on the side, and not for purposes of research.

Sometimes I think the problem is largely a semantic one. The trouble lies in the designation itself: practical joker. They wince when they hear it and vow they'll have nothing whatever to do with such a depraved person. But call him a prankster and no obloquy attaches to him. It all adds up to the same thing; yet a prankster is a gay and witty fellow, whereas a practical joker is an oaf. Putting it another way, a practical joke is played on you; you play a prank on someone else.

It has been said that the only excuse on earth for a practical joke is the deflating of a stuffed shirt. There are stuffed shirts aplenty in the world but, in my own opinion, there is no such thing as deflating them. By their very nature they stay stuffed forever. I don't, however, intend to deal extensively with motives, for in most cases they are self-apparent. Nor am I going into any long-winded, Freudian analysis of the practical joker—the psychiatrists have done that already, with much talk about inferiority complexes and superman fixations.

I want it understood that I am not a practical joker. I have been involved in them, usually as victim, but I'm not a practitioner. The only joke I can remember having played in the last ten years was a simple one. A letter came from a man in the Middle West who had been reading some of my books. He insulted me at the outset by saying he knew I wouldn't even read his letter. My secretary would read it, but I wouldn't. The remainder of his impertinence was addressed to my secretary and, as he warmed to his task, he expressed the hope that she was young and red-headed and beautiful.

I have no secretary and have never had one. But I invented one now. I wrote to this worm. I pretended I was my secretary. I told him he must have possessed psychic powers, for I was truly young and redheaded and people thought I was not bad to look at. I said he certainly sounded in his letter like a real interesting fellow. The kind of masculine man I (the redheaded secretary) was just dying to meet. Maybe he would be coming to New York someday. If he ever did, please let me know—I'd ask the boss to let me off work for a day *and a night* and meet him in New York and we'd have dinner and go places and *do things*. I signed the letter "Eunice Wagstaff." And mailed it.

Two days later Western Union phoned my house and asked if we had a Eunice Wagstaff around the place. Fortunately I remembered the letter and took the message. My letter had had more than its desired effect. The telegram to Eunice Wagstaff said: "Leaving for New York and you tonight. Meet me tomorrow Hotel B——."

I debated with myself about stopping him. Then I decided that he had it coming. Haven't heard another peep out of him to this day.

—*H. Allen Smith*

Contents

1

Two Pieces of String

It is possible to spend large sums of money in the perpetration of a practical joke and quite often an expensive joke will attain a magnificence above and beyond its cost. On the other hand many of the most effective jokes have involved the expenditure of nothing more than a few words, or a simple piece of string, or less than that.

The most elementary of all practical jokes is the goose. It requires no money, no equipment, and a minimum of preparation and planning, for it is usually a spur-of-the-moment, or moment-of-the-spur, operation.

The only man, to my knowledge, who has made any sort of serious inquiry into goosing is H. L. Mencken. In connection with his study of the American language, Mr. Mencken once appealed to the scholars of the nation to help him find the derivation of the word. He set down his findings in *Supplement One* of his masterwork, *The American Language*. From it I quote:

> One of the most mysterious American verbs is *to goose*. Its meaning is known to every schoolboy, but the dictionaries do not list it, and so far as I know no lexicographer has ever worked out its etymology . . . The preponderance of medical opinion, I find, inclines to the theory that the verb was suggested by the fact

that geese, which are pugnacious birds, sometimes attack human beings, and especially children, by biting at their fundaments. There is also the possibility that the term may be derived from the old custom of examining a goose before turning it out to feed in the fields by feeling of its rear parts: if an egg could be felt it was kept in its pen for the day. . . . The question remains why one person is *goosey* and another is not. Some resent *goosing* no more than they resent a touch on the arm, whereas others leap into the air, emit loud cries, and are thrown into a panic. One of my medical informants suggests that susceptibility is mainly psychic, and may have its origin in an obscure fear (and perhaps an infantile memory) of a sexual attack, but other authorities believe that it is caused by physical sensitiveness and is psychic only by association. Meanwhile, every American knows what *to goose* means, though the term appears to be unknown in England, and there are no analogues in the other European languages . . . There was a time when a craze for *goosing* arose on the Hollywood movie lots, to the consternation not only of its victims but also of their directors, who saw many a scene spoiled. One of its most assiduous practitioners was the late Douglas Fairbanks, Sr. When the other performers in his company became so wary of him that he was constantly watched, he took to hiding behind scenery and properties and operating stealthily with a long fishing-rod. He was finally put down by threats of heavy fines from the front office.

So much for goosing.

As a sort of warm-up for many daffy things to come, I propose now that we examine two masterful achievements, each of which required no more equipment than a piece of string.

The most celebrated of all British practical jokers was

William Horace De Vere Cole, whose career will be considered in later pages. He was a citizen of substance and had a large house in a fashionable section of London. One day he was hanging some paintings in his home when he ran out of twine. He put on his hat and walked to the nearest stringmonger's shop and bought a ball of twine. On his way home he saw an elegant Englishman, a stranger, approaching. The man was so stiffish, so splendidly dressed, that Cole could not pass him by. Quickly he whipped out his ball of twine and stepped up to the gentleman.

"I say," he spoke with some show of deference, "I'm in a bit of a spot. We're engaged in surveying this area in order that we may realign the kerb, and my assistant has somehow vanished. I wonder if I could prevail upon your time for just a few moments."

"To be sure," said the stranger, ever the proper Englishman.

"If," said Cole, "you'd be so kind as to hold the end of this string. Just stand where you are, and keep a tight hold on it, and we'll be finished in a few moments. It's really quite important."

The splendid gentleman took hold of the end of the string and Cole began backing away from him, unwinding the ball. He continued all the way to the corner, turned the corner and disappeared. He proceeded, still unwinding the ball, until he was halfway up the block, at which point the string gave out. He stood for a moment, not knowing quite what he should do now. He had about decided to tie the string to a doorknob when Providence sent him a second gentleman, fully as elegant and polished as the first. Cole stopped him. Would the good sir be so kind as to assist him in an engineering project? Certainly! Cole handed him the end of the string and asked that he simply stand firm and hold it. Then Cole disappeared through an alleyway, hastened to the shop for another ball of twine, and returned to his home to resume hanging pictures.

Cole never knew how long those two men stood holding the string. He could have circled back and spied on them, but he didn't even consider doing it. The more accomplished practical jokers seem to prefer a situation in which the denouement is left to their imaginations. They enjoy sitting down and thinking about what *may* have happened. I was told recently of a prominent New York attorney who had occasion to visit a warehouse in Brooklyn. In the warehouse he saw an antique barber chair which was for sale. He bought it. He remembered that once during a world tour he had spent a couple of days in Calcutta and he knew the name of one of the principal business streets there. He had the old barber chair crated and shipped to an address on that street—an address he simply pulled out of the air. And he spent many enjoyable moments thereafter speculating on the bewilderment of the people who received the chair.

We come now to the second piece of string.

Jim Moran, an American philosopher whose exploits have been examined in several of my previous books, was invited one day to a genteel party in the Beverly Hills Hotel. When Jim walked in he was wearing, in addition to his dinner clothes, a piece of string. It was an ordinary piece of grocer's twine. It was looped around his right ear and knotted, and ran down his cheek and into the corner of his mouth.

No one could help noticing it, but Jim made no mention of it as he went from group to group, shaking hands and making small talk. He discovered immediately that no person in the room would speak of it. Nor would anyone pretend to even notice it. Yet he was well aware that his string was a major attraction. People were whispering about it, speculating about it, and getting nowhere. Jim was his most charming self all through the party, occasionally drinking a cocktail without removing the string from his mouth, and at one point, when he undertook to eat a few canapés, he knew that every eye was on him.

In the end he departed without a single person having spoken of the string.

Jim tried it at other gatherings, both public and private, with the same result. The string was never mentioned. It was one of those things, mysterious to be sure, but extremely private—a thing one simply doesn't notice.

Now and then Jim had occasion to fly from California to New York and back and usually these trips were taken alone. He began wearing his string on the planes. He'd manage to get an aisle seat so that a maximum number of passengers could not avoid seeing the string running from his ear to his mouth. He'd sit calmly reading a book or a magazine, well aware of the stir he was creating among his fellow passengers. He enjoyed speculating on the various explanations they were attempting.

One day, wearing his string, Jim arrived at the Burbank airport to take a plane for New York. A friend came to see him off, a man who had a small fruit ranch in the San Fernando Valley. The friend had a pocketful of kumquats and handed Jim a half dozen of them just before he boarded the plane.

Jim took his aisle seat and opened his book and the plane took off. After a while he became conscious of the fact that he was attracting considerably more interest than usual. A college football team was on board and its members, instead of studying their lessons, were buzzing about that string. One of them was saying that it was probably a new kind of hearing aid. Another had a theory that Moran was a guy who had a habit of chewing on string and tied it around his ear so's he wouldn't swaller it. The argument and speculation went on and on and then the football players decided they had to have the answer. They drew slips of paper out of a hat to determine which boy had to do the asking. The loser was a hulking lad with a butch haircut and he tried to beg off the unpleasant assignment, but the others shoved him down the aisle and so he arrived at Jim's seat. Jim raised his eyes from his book.

"Beg your pardon, sir," the boy said. "We . . . that is, the fellas back here . . . it's none of our business but . . . well, we thought maybe you'd tell us . . . that is, you'd tell us . . . what that string is for."

There it was! The first human being to come right out and ask. And Jim wasn't prepared for it. He's a man, however, with a quick mind. He smiled at the boy.

"Why," he said, "I don't mind telling you at all. If I saw somebody wearing a string like this, I'd be curious too." He was stalling. He shifted in his seat, he put the book down in his lap, he put his hand in his coat pocket and touched the forgotten kumquats.

"It's a very simple matter," he said. "I happen to be a doctor, attached to Johns Hopkins in Baltimore. We of Johns Hopkins call it John the Hop. Well, now, down at John the Hop there are six of us, six doctors, who are engaged in an experiment having to do with diet. We are studying the effects of the various citrus fruits on the gastric juices. Each of us has been assigned a specific fruit and for two weeks we are eating nothing else but that fruit. One chap is on oranges. One is on lemons. One on limes. One on grapefruit. One on tangerines. And I . . . I am on kumquats. For two weeks, I am eating nothing whatever but kumquats." He paused and reached into his coat pocket. "By the way," he continued, "they're very good— would you like to have a couple?" The boy accepted two kumquats.

"Now," said Jim, "we come to the string. You note that it's fastened securely to my ear. Let me explain. This string runs down into my stomach. On the end of it is a little gold bucket. Every four hours I pull that little bucket up, and empty it into a small bottle, and when the bottle's full it goes to the lab at John the Hop. So, you see, the explanation is quite simple."

"Gee, thanks," said the football player, and hurried off to inform his colleagues.

That's all there was to it. Somewhere along the way the

football team left the plane and Jim and his string continued on to New York. He still enjoys thinking about the
probable consequences of that little encounter. He knows
that every one of those football players talked about the
man with the little gold bucket in his stomach. He knows
that those boys came from different sections, different
towns. He assumes that when each boy went home from
college, he told his family about the man on the plane
who had a golden bucket in his stomach and a pocketful
of kumquats. He figures that eventually, in each case, the
family doctor comes in and someone says, "Doc, did you
hear about the Johns Hopkins man Bill met on the plane?
Had a string tied around his ear and on the other end,
down in his stomach, a little gold bucket, and every four
hours he'd pull that bucket up and empty it, because he
wasn't eating anything at all but kumquats, and there were
five other doctors that . . ."

And Jim pictures the family doctor saying, "Good Lord!
Have those people down at Johns Hopkins gone clean off
their rockers?"

2

Is It Funny?

People who conduct academic investigations of American humor, often with hilarious results, usually give great emphasis, in treating of its origins, to the New England Yankee peddler and the Western frontiersmen. There were other influences, but these two types contributed most toward the evolution of our native humor. They were both practical jokers.

For months I have been reading the works of the early American humorists and it has occurred to me that if there were no such thing as a practical joke, our comic literature would be reduced by half, and the remainder wouldn't be very funny. Yet the historians consistently speak of the practical joke with distaste, as being crude and vulgar. The tall tale—that's another matter. They overemphasize its importance. Through folklore the tall tale has been elevated to literature, even though it is a sickly brother to the practical joke. In my own estimation, any given practical joke is five times funnier than any given tall tale. And there is good reason to believe that the telling of tall stories began as out-and-out practical jokes with the greenhorn and tenderfoot as victim.

Constance Rourke, whose book *American Humor* is regarded as the classic work on the subject, assumes a condescending air when she writes of the practical joke, yet she is unable to escape it because it comes leaping at her from every direction.

"Elaborately prepared practical jokes," she writes, "consumed time, created enemies, brought into peril life and limb: yet the Yankee evolved a stock of these that amounted to lore and spread from Maine to Georgia."

In considering American humor of pre-Revolutionary times Miss Rourke recalls the comic side of Israel Putnam and recites a Putnam legend out of the French and Indian War. A British officer, jealous of Putnam, sent him a challenge. Receiving no answer, the officer went to Putnam's tent and found him sitting on a keg, placidly smoking his pipe. The Britisher demanded an explanation.

"Why, you see," said Putnam, "I'm but a poor miserable Yankee that never fired a pistol in my life, and you must perceive, Major, that if we fight with pistols you will have an unfair advantage. Here are two powder kegs—I have bored a hole and inserted a slow fuse in each; so if you'll just be good enough to seat yourself there, I will light the fuses, and he who dares sit the longest shall be called the bravest fellow."

The fuses burned slowly. The British officer was nervous and jumpy, but Putnam sat calmly puffing on his pipe. When the fuses burned down to within an inch of the kegs, the Britisher suddenly leaped up and ran for it. The kegs were full of onions.

Miss Rourke does not call this incident a practical joke. Perhaps it was so genuinely amusing to her that it simply couldn't be a practical joke.

She writes, likewise, of the humorous side of Audubon, with special reference to the Rafinesque joke. Rafinesque, also a naturalist, made his way to Kentucky to visit Audubon in 1818. During the visit Audubon began telling him about certain remarkable fish he had observed in the Ohio River. He made sketches of these fish with detailed descriptions. One of these was the Devil Jack Diamond-

Fish, which grew to a length of ten feet. It had large diamond-shaped scales of stone, which made the fish bullet-proof. When the scales were dried they could be used for striking fire with steel. Rafinesque copied down all this grap in his notebooks and went back East, where he told everyone about the strange fish in the Ohio, even asserting that he had actually seen a Devil Jack Diamond-Fish. Other icthyologists went for the story hook, line and sinker, but eventually they discovered it was all a joke. Not long ago *Life* magazine reproduced some of the sketches as "delightful evidence that Audubon's imagination was as fresh as his paintings." The fact remains that Audubon's fresh imagination all but ruined Rafinesque's scientific reputation.

Constance Rourke seems to have missed Benjamin Shillaber, a Boston newspaper writer of the 1840s. His sketches, later published in books, concerned a Mrs. Partington and a scamp of a boy called "that plaguey Ike," who was plaguey by reason of the fact that he was an incorrigible practical joker. Ike was apparently the forerunner of all the "bad boys" to come in American humor. Historians of humor, other than Miss Rourke, say that Shillaber greatly influenced the work of such men as G. H. Derby (John Phoenix), Artemus Ward and Mark Twain.

George W. Peck's tales about Peck's Bad Boy were enormously popular in the 1880s and brought their author so much fame that he was elected Governor of Wisconsin. There is a significant element in these stories, pointing up the fact that practical joking is not necessarily the prerogative of youth. Chief victim of the boy's jokes was the grocer. One day the boy walked in wearing a flower at his lapel and, in time, the grocer got interested in it, and wanted to smell it, whereupon he got a squirt of water in the face. He went into a towering rage, crying, "You condemn skunk!" and threatening to brain the boy with an ax handle. As soon as he cooled down, however, he displayed an eager interest in the contrivance and gave the boy a half pound of his favorite figs for the privilege of using it to squirt on his customers. Later on the boy takes the flower home and squirts his pa with it. Pa goes into a tantrum, but he too cools off, and insists on taking the gadget with him to a church social, where he squirts it on assorted people and ends up getting a black eye.

Almost without exception, the early American humorists found success by inventing characters who were practical jokers. These have included Major Jack Downing, Sam Slick, Birdofredum Sawin of *The Biglow Papers,* the incomparable Sut Lovingood, and certainly the tricksters in the Uncle Remus stories of Joel Chandler Harris.

In Seba Smith's writings about Jack Downing, I have come across a joke which was written in 1830 and which reappears time and again in our own day. In fact, I myself used a variation of it in a book published in the 1940s, as having occurred at a bar in Hollywood.

Major Downing has just arrived in Portland and, in spite of having been warned of the sharp practices among the storekeepers, enters a shop and asks for some biscuits. The merchant gives him the biscuits and Downing pokes around the store a bit, finally asking the price of a glass of cider. The cider costs the same as the biscuits he has in his hands, so he offers to trade the biscuits for the glass of cider. Then having drunk the cider, he starts to leave, but the storekeeper stops him, saying he hasn't paid for the cider. Downing is indignant. He traded the biscuits for the cider. But, argues the storekeeper, he hadn't paid for the biscuits. Paid for the biscuits indeed, says Downing. He didn't eat 'em, did he? And he walks out, leaving a momentarily confused storekeeper.

A Yankee joke of the non-commercial type, dated 1820, is included in James R. Aswell's excellent book, *Native American Humor.* A rawboned Yankee wanders to New York State, where he finds a group of village loafers engaged in a game of throwing stones into the Hudson. The Yorkers begin taunting the Vermonter, who tells them that t'other day he hove a man clear across a big river back home. He says he could do it again—could even heave a man clear across the Hudson. One of the Yorkers bets him ten dollars. The Yankee seizes the man by the britches and hurls him into the river. The shivering victim emerges from the water and demands his ten dollars. But the Yankee says, "I didn't wager to do it the first time. Just said I could do it, and I tell you I can." With which he grabs the Yorker and throws him into the river again. "Third time never fails," says the Vermonter as his victim struggles ashore again, but this time the Yorker has had enough, and pays over the ten dollars.

Mark Twain did not escape the crotchets of old age, and in his later years, on several occasions, he denounced practical jokers. "During three-fourths of my life," he said, "I have held the practical joker in limitless contempt and detestation; I have despised him as I have despised no other criminal, and when I am delivering my opinion about him the reflection that I have been a practical joker myself seems to increase my bitterness rather than to modify it."

A strong declaration from a man who rode to fame on practical jokes.

Ludwig Lewisohn, in his history of American literature, has written of Western humor:

"This humor . . . is directed against pretentiousness and falseness, against all 'putting on of airs'; its fairly constant intention is the discomfiture of the pretentious and false. It 'takes them down a peg'; it exposes them to the laughter of their fellows. A less admirable aspect of this popular humor is its employment of the device of the practical joke. This device, too, Mark Twain took over. His sketches and stories are all written about a practical joke of some kind. But he is careful . . . to be sure that the objects of the practical joke have lost the reader's moral sympathy."

Twain's earliest newspaper sketches were, in effect, practical jokes on the subscribers, both in his native Hannibal and later in Nevada. The story of the jumping frog, which brought him to national attention, was the story of a practical joke. And anyone who has read extensively in all his subsequent works must know that he saw great humor in practical jokes of every kind and description. And even in his later days, when he was denouncing practical jokes, he still told about them with great relish.

At one dinner, late in his life, he told the story of a certain Major Patterson, owner of a large plantation in Missouri, who was unable to get rid of a squatter. After trying all other methods he could think of, Major Patterson dressed himself in black, put on a mask, mounted a big black horse, and rode to the squatter's shanty. He called out to the squatter to fetch him a bucket of water. He had prepared himself with a large leather bag, hidden under his clothing with an opening near his chin. When the water was brought, the Major tipped up the bucket and pretended to drink it down without stopping. When the bucket was empty, he lowered it and exclaimed: "Ahhhh! That's the first drink of water I've had since I was killed at the Battle of Shiloh!" The squatter was gone from his property before morning.

In his Hartford days Mark Twain told a clergyman that every single word of a sermon he had just delivered was in a book he had at home. The clergyman was aghast at the thought of unconscious plagiarism and remained worried until Twain sent the book over to him—a dictionary.

This book could be filled out with practical jokes which Mark Twain wrote about. For the time being let's be content with just one, for the reason that it has had a present-day echo.

During the tour which resulted in *The Innocents Abroad*, Twain and a companion, a doctor, grew weary of the endless procession of babbling guides they encountered in Europe. They decided to have some amusement out of the guides, either by refusing to exclaim over the wonders they were being shown, or by asking idiotic questions. In Genoa one guide was eager to show these two Americans a letter in the handwriting of Christopher Columbus, knowing they would be thrilled to the marrow by it. When the letter is at last displayed to them, they examine it carefully and ask who this Christopher Columbus may have been. And did he write this letter himself?

"Why," says the doctor disparagingly, "I have seen boys in America only fourteen years old that could write better than that." They tell the guide it is the worst writing they have ever seen, and urge him to get out some good specimens of penmanship if he's got any. They say, later, that they have just come from America and that they have not heard anything about a Christopher Columbus discovering that country. Is he dead? What did he die of? Are his parents living? And they keep it up until the guide is on the verge of madness.

They repeat this pattern with other guides. Mark Twain thought it was immensely funny. I think it is funny. And Joseph H. Meyers, a former teacher of English at Purdue, thinks it is funny. Mr. Meyers, writing in the sedate pages of the *Atlantic Monthly*, tells how he and his wife borrowed the Mark Twain technique in dealing with bothersome guides in Italy. In Milan a guard was detaining Mr. and Mrs. Meyers before Raphael's *Wedding of the Virgin*. Raphael, said the guard, was a great artist.

"Raphael," said Mrs. Meyers, "was an American."

"No, no, no!" said the guard. "Was Italian."

"No, no, *no!*" said Mrs. Meyers. "Was American."

"Certainly he was," Mr. Meyers joined in. "Born in Philadelphia."

"Of course," said Mrs. Meyers. "We knew him personally."

They were soon rid of that nuisance. They varied their technique as they went along, and Mr. Meyers found out that one way of getting rid of unwanted guides was to beat them to the punch. For example as the guide approached, Mr. Meyers would seize him by the arm and say: "Is here

Primavera. Primavera by great artist Botticelli, was real
name Alessandro dei Filipepi. Born 1444 question mark,
died 1510." All of which he was reading off the frame.
"Is famous painting," he'd continue, "Symbolical as anything. Now come, is over here another one, called *Birth of
Venus*, is by same man——" But that was enough; the
guide was gone.

An example of Sut Lovingood's pranks, as chronicled by
G. W. Harris, takes place at an old-style camp meeting
where a certain Parson Bullen is preaching of hell and
damnation. Sut provides himself with a half dozen large
lizards, creeps up to the platform, and while the Parson is
going strong on the subject of hell-sarpents, sends the
lizards traveling up the clergyman's legs. In a few minutes
Parson Bullen appears to be going crazy, screaming that
the hell-sarpents have got him. Piece by piece he jerks off
his clothing until he is standing nude in his shoes, and
then he lights out for the woods. "And Old Bullen never
preached agin," the tale concludes. "He tried to, but he
didn't have a sign of a congregation. No, sir, *they had seed
too much of him.*" (This was one of Abraham Lincoln's
favorite stories.)

During the nineteenth century foreigners on the order
of Dickens and Mrs. Trollope, who came to look at America
and write about what they saw, are said to have been
hoaxed unmercifully by frontiersmen. Captain Frederick
Marryat in *A Diary in America* (1839) wrote:
"The Americans are often themselves the cause of being
misrepresented; there is no country perhaps in which the
habit of deceiving for amusement, or what is termed hoaxing, is so common. Indeed, this and hyperbole constitute
the major part of American humour. If they have the
slightest suspicion that a foreigner is about to write a book,
nothing appears to give them so much pleasure as to try to
mislead him: this has constantly been practiced upon me,

and for all I know, they may in some instances have been successful."

Van Wyck Brooks, describing the times of Melville and Whitman, says that "this was a nation of practical jokers." And B. A. Botkin, foremost of contemporary popular folklorists, says:

"Western humorists have used the practical joke as a form of democratic attack on pretense and affectation. To realists and satirists village japes and monkeyshines are an expression of the sadistic or moronic in American life."

A man who seems to have a more balanced view than any yet quoted is Professor Ben C. Clough (*The American Imagination at Work*). He says:

"Hoaxes and practical jokes, in America as elsewhere, begin with banality; the withdrawn chair, the 'glass-crash,' and the hot-foot are typical. But our land has produced real artists in this field."

The tone of American humor changed sharply in the twentieth century. Most authorities on the subject agree that the change was for the better. Yet one of the nation's most distinguished historians, Henry Steele Commager, is not so sure. In *The American Mind* he suggests that with the arrival of the present century American humor "soured" into sophistication and wit. He writes:

"The shift from Artemus Ward and Petroleum V. Nasby and Bill Nye to Ring Lardner and Peter Arno and Damon Runyon . . . was almost a shift from good humor to bad." Dr. Commager seems to regret the fact that twentieth-century humor is shot through and through with disillusionment.

We might reasonably believe that the new order of pessimistic humorists would have no traffic with practical jokes. We would be wrong. Almost all of the modern humorists have been practitioners of the black art, or have written about it with obvious relish. The late Harold Ross, as editor of *The New Yorker*, came close to being the benevolent dictator of American humor for a whole generation.

Ross loved practical jokes, clever ones and crude ones. He enjoyed showing up at the weddings of friends carrying a shotgun.

The most searing portrait of a practical joker I've ever read is that of Jim Kendall in Ring Lardner's classic short story, *Haircut*. This story has had an immense popularity over the years, appearing regularly in anthologies, and very likely has given many readers a wholesome distaste for practical joking in any form. Jim Kendall was a small town "card" and almost all of his jokes were cruel. As a traveling salesman he would be on a train, passing through a town, and he'd take note of a sign, "Henry Smith, Dry Goods." From a distant point Kendall would send a postal card to Henry Smith saying, perhaps, "Ask your Missus who kept her from gettin' lonesome the last time you was in Cartersville." And he'd sign it, "A Friend." That was Jim Kendall's style of a joke. If I were devil's advocate, speaking for the practical jokers of the world, I would point out that Jim Kendall was a low-down skunk over and beyond his stupid pranking. He spent most of his money on booze and rarely gave his wife more than two or three dollars a week toward the support of herself and their two children. He was inexpressibly mean toward his family, and practiced cruelties on the village half-wit, the boy who kills Mr. Kendall at the conclusion of the story. In short, Jim Kendall is not a classical villain by reason of his being a practical joker; he is just a no-good son of a bitch from the word go.

Ring Lardner spent most of his life around newspapermen and baseball players, and in these two professions practical joking has always been second only to eating and drinking. There is a legend that one Thanksgiving Day in Chicago thousands of citizens appeared at a football field to witness an important game they had read about in their morning paper. They found no players, no officials, no ticket sellers. Lardner had simply made up the story of the impending conflict.

The late Robert Benchley, occupying a place in the front

ranks of modern American humorists, played practical jokes on his friends from time to time. His most famous exploit involved Frank Case, manager of the Algonquin Hotel. Case was invited to dinner on Saturday evening at the Benchley home in Westchester. When he arrived he was shown to the powder room and he was somewhat shocked to find that all the towels came from his hotel, as well as the soap. And at dinner all the tableware, down to the napkins, bore the name "Algonquin." Benchley had conspired to have a whole truckload of the stuff sent up to his house.

The foremost living humorist today is James Thurber and he is seldom better than when he is writing about practical jokes. A bit later we shall make mention of his mother's talent for deliberately confusing or alarming people. He has written affectionately, too, of his brother Roy's exploits back in Columbus. Just as a sample, here is Mr. Thurber on the subject of the family automobile:

One of my happiest memories of it was when, in its eighth year, my brother Roy got together a great many articles from the kitchen, placed them in a square of canvas, and swung this under the car with a string attached to it so that, at a twitch, the canvas would give way and the steel and tin things would clatter to the street. This was a little scheme of Roy's to frighten father, who had always expected the car might explode. It worked perfectly. That was twenty-five years ago, but it is one of the few things in my life I would like to live over again if I could. I don't suppose that I can, now. Roy twitched the string in the middle of a lovely afternoon, on Bryden Road near Eighteenth Street. Father had closed his eyes and, with his hat off, was enjoying a cool breeze. The clatter on the asphalt was tremendously effective: knives, forks, can-openers, pie pans, pot lids, biscuit-cutters, ladles, egg-beaters fell, beautifully together, in a lingering, clamant crash. "Stop the *car!*" shouted father. "I can't," Roy said. "The engine fell out." "God Almighty!" said father, who knew what *that* meant, or knew what it sounded as if it might mean.

The quotation is from Mr. Thurber's *My Life and Hard Times*, which is one of the funniest books in the history of the world. Further along in the same book there is another story in which Roy bedevils the elder Thurber anew:

About three o'clock in the morning, Roy, who was wakeful, decided to pretend that delirium was on him, in order to have, as he later explained it, some "fun." He got out of bed and, going to my father's room, shook him and said, "Buck, your time has come!" My father's name was not Buck but Charles, nor had he ever been called Buck. He was a tall, mildly nervous, peaceable gentleman, given to quiet pleasures, and eager that everything should run smoothly. "Hmm?" he said, with drowsy bewilderment. "Get up, Buck," said my brother, coldly, but with a certain gleam in his eyes. My father leaped out of bed, on the side away from his son, rushed from the room, locked the door behind him, and shouted us all up.

Other members of the family assembled, listened to Mr. Thurber's excited story, then tiptoed to Roy's room and found him fast asleep. It seemed clear that Father Thurber had had a nightmare, until Roy himself explained. His father had awakened *him*, said Roy, and had talked about Buck being downstairs, and how he would handle it. The entire family, of course, believed Roy.

James Thurber himself has been known to indulge in practical jokes. The most classic of all the stories about the antics around *The New Yorker* offices concerns Mr. Thurber and the phone booth. He pulled it off the wall in the magazine's reception room, laid it flat on the floor, climbed into it, powdered his face, and played the part of a corpse for a while, startling quite a few people who dropped in to submit poetry.

I remember an incident involving Mr. Thurber, years ago, at the Columbia Broadcasting System offices. Mr. Thurber had agreed to appear on a fifteen-minute radio broadcast. The day before this event someone went to the program director and said, 'Julius, you've made a bad mistake. This Thurber won't show up—he'll get drunk and disappear, or if he does show up he'll ruin you." The program director was genuinely alarmed. He called in the director of publicity, who was a friend of Mr. Thurber. He told the publicity man to stay with Mr. Thurber all the next day and make certain he didn't drink.

A half hour before broadcast time, Mr. Thurber and his keeper were in a nearby bar, perfectly sober. The publicity man got on the phone and called the program director.

"I couldn't stop him," he wailed. "He was sneaking drinks on me. I couldn't do a thing with him."

"My God, where is he?" howled the program director.

"Wait a minute, he was somewhere around here on the floor a few minutes ago."

At this point Mr. Thurber seized the phone and began babbling drunkenly into it, uttering half-intelligible denunciations of radio in general and CBS in particular. The program director was both furious and frantic until the two men resumed their normal speaking voices and said they'd be right over.

3

The Shame of It

The reason the practical joke occupies such an ignominious position in the scale of human frivolity, several degrees lower than the pun, lies in the fact that it is often practiced by men of little wit and less imagination. In such hands it can be cruel and maleficent.

Several individuals, opposed to practical joking, have spoken feelingly to me of the Hollywood writer and his father. One day the old man came home with a cheap painting he had found in a secondhand store. The son began bringing in his friends, including several wealthy movie people, and these friends exclaimed over the painting and tried to buy it. Their offers rose, day by day, and finally reached fifty thousand dollars. The old man, who had paid ten dollars for it, was frantically eager to accept, but his son forbade it. Eventually the excitement became so great that the old man collapsed from a heart attack and came close to entering the shadders.

This case demonstrates, argues the opposition, that practical jokes should be outlawed. For the sake of argument, let us point out that people have heart attacks at baseball games, so let's abolish baseball; people have heart attacks shoveling snow, so let's do away with shovels; people have heart attacks in bed, so let's all stay up. Further than that, let it be said that the old man's heart attack was brought on by the sin of greed, which is as common among us as the sin of concupiscence. Defense rests.

There is a day set aside for the amateur practical joker—the first day of April. This is the day of the sleeveless errand, the wallet-on-a-string, and the comical phone call. Although there have been some major practical jokes timed for the first of April, as a general thing the skilled operators in the business withdraw from the field and leave the day to the minor leaguers, who proceed to fill the sugar bowl with salt and pass around the exploding cigars.

Dr. Bergen Evans of Northwestern University informs me that when he was a boy April Fools' Day was more exciting than Christmas in his home, for the reason that his father was a great practical joker. The elder Evans once acquired an old brass lamp, shaped like a slender cream pitcher. He hid it away, saving it for The Day. Shortly before April Fools' Day he called in his two sons and read them the story of Aladdin and his Wonderful Lamp, taking care to describe the lamp itself. After that he left his own lamp in a place where the boys would be sure to find it. They did find it, the day before April Fools' Day. They were real excited about it, and thought maybe it would work the same way the lamp in the story worked. The younger brother rubbed it and spoke a wish. He loved bananas, in a day when bananas were a rarity. "I wish," he said as he rubbed the lamp, "I wish I had some bananas." The next morning when he came downstairs, he had to almost wade through bananas, for Father Evans had eavesdropped and then gone out and bought a whole stalk of them, and scattered them all over the house.

All Fools' Day is observed in the British Isles and throughout Europe generally. In Germany and Norway one day is not sufficient—the people of those countries observe it on both the first and the last days of April. Mexico has its All Fools' Day on December 28 and a citizen of that country needs to keep himself especially alert for the whole twenty-four hours. According to ancient custom, anything that is borrowed on All Fools' Day in Mexico need not be returned. I do not know if this applies to banks.

In Scotland the first day of April is associated with a practice called the Hunting of the Gowk, a gowk being a cuckoo. The procedure for hunting the gowk is simple. The victim is given a letter which says, "This is the first of April—hunt the gowk another mile." He is told to deliver the letter to a person some distance away. That person, on reading the note, sends him along to another destination, and the joke continues until such time as the fool awakes to the fact that he is being gowked.

This is what the British call a sleeveless errand, a kind of joke that has been practiced by Anglo-Saxons from the beginning of the eighteenth century down to our own day. Writing in the time of Queen Anne, Joseph Addison complained about the custom, mentioning a man who sent a boy to the shoemaker's for a halfpenny's worth of inkle. Sometimes a child would be sent to the grocer's for a pint of pigeon's milk, or to the bookseller for a copy of a biography of Eve's grandmother. There came a time when the most common form of the sleeveless errand involved the cobbler. A boy would be sent to his shop to ask for some strap oil. The cobbler would give him liberally of the strap, without the oil.

In America the sleeveless errand still flourishes. The victim is sent for a four-foot yardstick, a left-handed monkey wrench, the key to the oarlocks, or the key to the pitcher's box. In the military at the present time new arrivals in camp are sent out to get the cannon report, or a biscuit gun for the mess sergeant, or the rubber flag (on a rainy day). Recruits in the air forces are dispatched for a bucket of prop wash, or a gallon of prop pitch, or a box of replacement RPMs.

Printers are great ones for this sort of joke and a new boy around a printshop is shagged all over town for dotted ink, or paper-stretchers. I have written elsewhere of a harrowing experience I had in my first days around a newspaper. I was sent across town to another printshop to get a nonpareil spaceband, which turned out to be a large and heavy piece of machinery requiring a wheelbarrow for transportation. At about the same time I looked at type lice for the first and last time. "You ever seen type lice?" asks the printer. Of course I haven't, and he escorts me to the stone where a page of type is standing. There is an open space in one of the columns of type, a gap of two or three inches. The type lice are down in there. I bend over, closer and closer, peering in, and then the type is slammed together and water flies into my face. This is all part of becoming a newspaperman, or at least it was in my time.

There seem to be standard practical jokes in almost all of the trades and professions. One mechanic will plug up another mechanic's oil can with putty. Carpenters, for some reason, love to play jokes on each other, and one of their favorites is to remove the license plates from the victim's automobile and replace them upside down. A new interne in a hospital is usually sent to the laboratory to analyze urine samples and is greatly perplexed for a while because the bottles have been filled with tea. Apartment house doormen, who lead an otherwise monotonous existence, enjoy sticking a potato on the exhaust pipe of their victim's automobile; the car will then travel but a short distance and stop, and usually the victim has a difficult time locating the trouble.

Recently I approached an architect friend of mine and asked him what sort of practical jokes were most common in his profession. He was insulted. Architects, he said, are men of considerable dignity. They are educated men and they would not stoop to such degrading practices. We talked of other matters for a while, and then I began telling him about some of the practical jokes in my collection—except that I didn't call them practical jokes; I called them pranks. He was vastly amused by my examples, and then he said:

"Oh, I see what you mean. Well, let me tell you a gag that architects are always pulling on each other."

He said that whenever an architect from one city visits another city, he usually makes a point of playing a joke on some members of his profession with whom he's acquainted. A man from Cleveland, say, goes to Buffalo. He knows an architect in Buffalo named Biggerstaff. He knows that Biggerstaff always has several building projects going at the same time. So he gets Biggerstaff on the phone, disguises his voice, and yells, "Hey, for God sakes get out here, the foundations are all of a sudden beginning to crumble away!" Or, "Hurry out here as fast as you can! All the beams are six inches short!"

I could have told my friend a few practical jokes involving architects.

In the 1870s Alva Smith, a girl from Alabama, married William K. Vanderbilt, who had a hundred million dollars, more or less. In spite of all their money, the Vanderbilts were not considered socially acceptable by New York society. The new Mrs. Vanderbilt, however, was an ambitious and determined woman and she set out to conquer and overthrow the reigning Astors. She commissioned Richard M. Hunt, one of the most famous architects in the world, to design a three-million-dollar mansion at Fifth Avenue and Fifty-second Street. The palace that architect Hunt built for her was a replica of the house of Jacques Coeur, the greatest social upstart of the Middle Ages.

Or, let us examine the famous and fashionable St. Thomas Church on Fifth Avenue. This edifice was designed by Cram, Goodhue & Ferguson. Among the firm's architects assigned to the job was a young man, name unknown to deponent, with a rather perverse sense of humor. He slipped in two decorative details which hadn't been ordered. He worked a dollar sign into the tracery above the Bride's Door of the church, and three moneybags initialed "J.P.M." carved above the choir stalls.

Finally, the inscription above the entrance to the Sterling

Hall of Graduate Studies at Yale. It says, "He was born with the gift of laughter and a sense that the world was mad." For a while after the building was completed in 1932, the academic minds of New Haven, if they thought of it at all, concluded that the quotation had a suitably classical sound. Then someone noticed that the author's name was lacking, and someone else remembered; the line was from *Scaramouche*, by Rafael Sabatini, a work that is considered some distance removed from the classical.

Almost all the big amusement parks have a Fun House, sometimes called the Crazy House. Probably the first of these institutions was devised in 1897 by George Cornelius Tilyou when he founded Steeplechase, the earliest of the Coney Island amusement parks. Mr. Tilyou set the pattern by installing "earthquake floors" which jerked and tilted the customers off their feet, other floors that dropped suddenly out from under the customers, leaving them suspended in space for a moment that seemed an hour, trick mirrors, collapsing stairways, and blowholes. Then as now the blowhole was the big attraction. The moment an unsuspecting lady arrived over the blowhole, a hurricane blast of air shot from it, sending her skirts and underskirts above her head.

The men who operate these Fun Houses say that if it were not for the blowhole, their business would likely fail. This gives rise to the notion that the attraction is not so much a quest for humor, but a desire to look at some thighs and panties. There is a legend that some friends of Lillian Russell once lured her into the Fun House at Coney and jockeyed her into position over the blowhole, resulting in the exposure of enough meat to stock a small butcher shop. I recall an interview in recent years with a man employed at a New Jersey amusement park. His job was to sit on a stool and press the lever which activated the blowhole. He had been performing this chore night after night for several years and he was as bored as an eel sorter in the Fulton

Fish Market. He admitted that occasionally a lady comes along who has had to dress in a hurry and who has forgotten to put on underthings. He admitted that he noticed such ladies when their skirts shot up, but only because it was his job to keep his eyes on the blowhole victims. Apparently there is such a thing in this world as a glut of thighs.

Mankind has preserved, in the chronicle of his glorious achievements, an account of the first time a banana was ever eaten under water.

We know that the late Chester Greenwood of Farmington, Maine, was the first human being ever to wear an ear muff. We know the date he did it.

The books say that the first cow ever milked in an airplane was Elm Farm Ollie, a Guernsey. She was taken aloft in 1930 and milked over St. Louis.

These things are on the record. Yet there appears to be no historical notation concerning the first hot-foot. A dozen years ago I began troubling my mind about the origin of the custom. I went to the most famous hot-foot administrator in the land—Jack Dempsey. In those days it was impossible for Mr. Dempsey to attend a public function without getting down on all fours, even when in full dress, and crawling beneath the tables to perpetrate hot-foot after hot-foot. "I have probably given more hot-foots than any man alive," Mr. Dempsey bragged.

Some people say the hot-foot is as old as the shoe. On the other hand, Westbrook Pegler has contended that Pete Reilly, the Brooklyn prize-fight manager, invented the hot-foot soon after paper matches came into general use.

The story goes that Mr. Reilly attended a dinner of the Fight Managers' Friendly Society. Mr. Abe (Singletooth) Yaeger was in the midst of a stirring oration on "Chivalry and Square Dealing" when Mr. Reilly crept beneath the table and gave him history's first hot-foot. Mr. Yaeger (on the word of Mr. Pegler) cried "Oy!" and then cried "Yipe!"

and poured a pitcher of needled beer over his pained member.

That is Mr. Pegler's story of the first hot-foot. It is a gross and blundering fallacy. The hot-foot did not originate with paper matches. The late Ring Lardner often told how his friends were accustomed to giving him hot-foots in Chicago saloons, using store-bought lumber matches.

Moreover, Mr. Pete Reilly denied the allegation. He was willing that he be accorded a place in history, but not for the actual invention of the hot-foot. His own achievement, he felt, was fully as important. He was the first man, he said, who ever gave a hot-foot to a fighter while the fighter was sitting in his corner between rounds. He couldn't remember the name of the fighter, which was unfortunate, because such a man also deserves a place in history.

"The bell rung," said Mr. Reilly, "before the match burned down to this boy's shoe. He got up and started for the middle of the ring. Then all of a sudden a wild look come in his face, and he yelt with pain and grabbed for his hoof. This left him wide open and the other boy seeing him in pain gave him an annasettic by knocking him stiff."

As a dedicated historian, seeking the origin of the hot-foot, I have gone back to the ancient times pictured by Geoffrey Chaucer in *Canterbury Tales*, specifically to the matters set down in *The Miller's Tale*. This is the story of a carpenter's young and beautiful wife, named Alison; a student of astrology named Nicholas, and a parish clerk named Absalom. The significant action occurs on a dark night when the student and Alison have, by trickery, persuaded the carpenter to leave his bed and sleep elsewhere. Nicholas then takes the husband's place in the bed. He and Alison are kissin' and huggin' and all that sort of foolishness when along comes Absalom, the parish clerk, who also is deeply smitten by the young wife. Absalom stands at the window and pleads with Alison for a kiss, not knowing that she has Nicholas with her. Alison sees an opportunity for a little joke, goes to the window and in the darkness tells

Absalom to step forward and receive his kiss, and then she presents her bare backside to the window. Absalom kisses it at some length, then realizes that he has been tricked and goes away, furiously determined on revenge, no longer stirred by love for Alison. He hastens to the blacksmith shop and obtains a red-hot coulter, which is a small blade belonging on a plow. Now he returns to the window, and once again summons Alison and tells her he has brought her a ring, which he will give her in exchange for just one more kiss. Within the dark room, Nicholas the scholar now decides that it will improve the joke for *him* to receive the kiss from Absalom. Accordingly, he presents his bare bottom at the window and receives, of course, a fiery kiss as Absalom rams home the red-hot coulter.

This was not, of course, a hot-foot. There are, indeed, quite a number of variations, and some that have had tragic consequences.

The Colorado City (Texas) *Clipper*, issue of April 11, 1885, carried the following item:

"W. W. Schermerhorn, an attorney of San Angelo, once a citizen of this town, while under the influence of liquor last week in the saloon of Memph Elliott, had his feet badly burned by some unprincipled party pouring coal-oil in his boots and setting fire to them. The proprietor of the saloon, Memph Elliott, is charged with the crime and the people of San Angelo are very indignant at the outrage. Mr. Schermerhorn has entered suit against Elliott for $4,000."

It seems pertinent that the people who were indignant over this incident were the people of Mr. Schermerhorn's town, San Angelo—not the people of Colorado City, where the incident occurred. We must assume that the latter obtained pleasure, and even laughter, from it.

The business of setting people afire just for the fun of it is not uncommon. Within the last year two men in Bowling Green, Kentucky, were fined for having poured gasoline on the trousers of Joe Clay Simmons, and then set fire to them while Mr. Simmons was wearing them.

Recently there came to my attention an advertisement for a book titled *No Man Like Joe*, by Dr. Harvey E. Tobie, published in Oregon. The book was a biography of Joseph L. Meek, who was described in the advertisement as "Rugged, practical joker, mountain man, squaw man, and sheriff." The practical joker angle appealed to me and I sent off for the book. After a long interval it came and I applied myself to it, ready for a feast of practical jokes. I could only find one incident in it which seemed to qualify. Meek and his cronies were camped somewhere in the Rockies. In a playful mood they decided to "baptize" a lanky, redheaded trapper with the contents of an alcohol kettle. Having poured the alcohol over the trapper's head and clothing, they began prancing about, carrying torches seized from the campfire. One man pranced too close and set the redhead afire. They beat out the blaze with packsaddles "but the beating together with the burning nearly proved fatal and the victim never fully recovered from his baptism of fire."

Twelve years ago a letter came from a gentleman in California chiding me for suggesting that the hot-foot was a modern invention.

"My father," wrote Mr. George W. Spencer, "taught me the trick in the early 80's and assured me that his father showed him how to do it. My father told me that during the Civil War the sport was indulged in by those able to get away with it. I have never been robust enough to do much with it." Mr. Spencer means, I suppose, that he was never robust like Jack Dempsey.

Mr. Spencer wrote that in his youth, in the West, most men wore high, tight leather boots, and it was their custom to sit before an open fire in the evenings. As soon as they all got settled, Mr. Spencer continued, "it was my cue to hide all the bootjacks, without which it was practically impossible for a man to remove his own boots. Next I took a long iron poker and played with it in the fire until my father ordered me off to bed, and while I was arguing with him he carefully laid the poker across the instep or toe of the victim's boot. As there were no bootjacks to be found, the victim usually rushed outdoors, swearing to get even later."

The physical cruelty inherent in many practical jokes is to be deplored. The National Safety Council has on several occasions viewed with alarm. Major industrial establishments have appealed to their workers to cut the comedy, with special reference to goosing on the theory that a goosed worker may leap into the machinery or into vats of molten metal.

If civilized man must have his practical jokes, a good basic rule to follow would be: Don't play with fire or explosives. Roy W. Howard, the newspaper tycoon, has been surrounded all his adult life by men with inclinations to horseplay, but he has consistently frowned on anything resembling a practical joke. His distaste for this sort of play dates back to his cub reporter days on the St. Louis *Post-Dispatch*. According to A. J. Liebling, a colleague crept up behind Howard one day and playfully touched a lighted match to the nape of his neck. "Howard," writes Mr. Liebling, "unfortunately had that morning drenched his hair with a tonic that contained alcohol. A blue flame flickered over him and for a moment he resembled a crêpe suzette *flambée*."

Mr. Howard's newspaper, the New York *World-Telegram*, was nevertheless a hive of practical jokers. They conducted their operations surreptitiously, knowing that the big brass disapproved of their roguish exploits. It was in the dead of night that a certain reporter, inflamed against the copy desk for expunging his finest adjectives, crept into the office and poured a quart of glue into the pneumatic tube which transported copy to the composing room.

When the newspaper *PM* was started its management raided the staff of the *World-Telegram* for editors, writers and reporters. Most of those who made the switch had been infected with the Barclay Street virus and I have been told that life at *PM* was just one practical joke after another, with emphasis on smoke and fire. The hot-foot was raised from the floor to become the hot-seat, though not in the sense of Chaucer (perhaps because no red-hot coulters were handy). An artist at *PM* devised a method of setting off explosions on the undersides of chairs. Wads of cotton impregnated with photographers' flash powder were taped under the chair. Then a thin trail of flash powder was laid away from the chair. When this diabolic mechanism had been prepared, into the office would come the victim, a staff writer eager to get at the job of composing a slashing attack on somebody or something, even if only the horrors of inadequate toilet facilities in Harlem. Lost in his subject, the crusader would apply himself to his typewriter, and some distance behind him the fuse would be lighted. Now the entire staff would become attentive, watching the fuse burn. Then the grand PUFFF! and flash, the howls of the victim as he clawed his way out of the clouds of smoke, and the happy laughter of the people who were once described as "a bunch of young fogeys." In the end justice triumphed. The artist who invented the flash powder hot-seat, was hoist by his own petard. A committee of his victims got together and prepared a hot-seat for him, using a triple charge of powder. The man's pants were almost blown off and as he rushed out to a doctor for anti-tetanus shots, he shrieked that he was going to court and sue everyone in sight.

The playfulness of the *PM* crowd reached a sort of climax on the day when the boss, Ralph Ingersoll, was leaving to inquire into the State of the Union in Moscow. His devoted staff constructed Molotov cocktails and other explosive displays. They stationed themselves at the second-floor windows and as Mr. Ingersoll emerged from the building and prepared to enter a taxi which would take him to the airport, the blitz struck. Exploding bombs were raining on the sidewalk. The cab driver departed his machine in a great hurry and took shelter across the way. And now came the second bombing. Some members of the staff had conspired against the conspiracy. The bombers were all leaning out of the second-floor windows. The other gang was on the roof. At the climax of the blitz, the boys on the roof began dropping paper bags filled with water on the heads of the second-floor bombers. And Mr. Ingersoll flew the Atlantic somewhat wet and smelling of gunpowder.

The counter-revolutionists who used the water-filled bags borrowed their joke from major league baseball players who have, for many years, employed it while on tour to while away the hours they spend in hotel rooms.

During the years when I was on the staff of the *World-Telegram* I did a great deal of interviewing. For some reason that is not clear to me, many of the interviewees were given rather rough treatment. Many times, after my stories appeared in print, I would get telephone calls threatening my life and limb. During one period I wrote a series burlesquing some of the popular columnists of the day. I was telephoned by Ed Sullivan and told that my days were numbered. I was telephoned by Lucius Beebe and told to get right with God. I was telephoned by a relative of Louella Parsons and told that Owney Madden himself was going to take care of me. All of these callers were most convincing and I began skulking through side streets and jerking violently whenever people came up behind me and spoke to me. Then I found out that all the calls had been made by the same man, from a telephone in the opposite end of the city room. There was yet one more column burlesque to appear in print—a violent handling of Nick Kenny. On the day the Kenny column appeared, the telephone call came. Mr. Kenny has a distinctive manner of speaking, like a tugboat in distress. The voice on the phone was remarkably true.

"Listen, you son of a bitch," it said, "I'm gonna get you for this if it's the last thing I do on this ert."

"You and who else!" I yelled back at him, having fun. He went on to describe his exploits as a prize fighter in the

Navy, and how he was going to break my nose and knock out all my teeth, and so on. I howled with laughter.

And it turned out that it *was* Nick Kenny.

Not long ago in California a Mrs. Dorothy Dennis went to court seeking separation from her husband, Colonel Chester I. Dennis. Mrs. Dennis charged that one night her husband appeared in their bedroom with a fearsome-looking contrivance in his hands. He wound it up, then flung it under her bed and yelled "Bomb!" Mrs. Dennis leaped from the bed and ran screeching into the garden, while her husband yelled at her from a window, "Yaw, yaw! You got no sense of humor." Mrs. Dennis considered the Colonel's performance sufficient grounds for separation, even though the "bomb" was only a timing mechanism off a land mine.

In court the judge asked Colonel Dennis what he had to say for himself. He admitted the deed. It was in retaliation, he said, for a trick his wife had played on him. She had fastened a Fourth of July torpedo to the underside of a toilet seat. When the Colonel sat down . . . BAM!

The judge turned to Mrs. Dennis, who was laughing. What about the torpedo? "It was funny, very funny," she said. "Just a joke."

In Beckley, West Virginia, a man named Willard Hanks decided to have some fun with his friends. He provided himself with four sticks of dynamite and began carrying them everywhere he went. He'd toss them in the air and catch them, and pretend he was going to whack them against the furniture, and he really had people quaking. On the third day of his dynamite spree he was cutting up in the home of friends. The dynamite exploded and Willard Hanks was literally blown to shreds.

As this is being written a dispatch comes from London. Albert Hulkes, a window cleaner, had a little gag he enjoyed playing on his wife. He'd stick his head in the oven and just as his wife would arrive at the front door, he'd turn on the gas. Came the day when his ears deceived him. He *thought* he heard his wife at the front door, but that day she was late coming home. Albert was asphyxiated.

The practical joke which is most often used to illustrate the tragic implications of the business is the following:

Two young men, named Joe and Bill, were out hunting on a hot day. They arrived at a farmhouse and Joe went inside to ask the farmer's permission to hunt on his land. Bill remained outside. The farmer told Joe it would be all right, if Joe would do him a favor. "On your way over to the woods," said the farmer, "you'll pass through a field where there's a horse. He's old and sick and needs to be put out of his misery. Shoot him for me, and you can hunt all you want to on my land."

Outside Joe said nothing to Bill about the horse and they arrived at the pasture. As they came close to the old horse, Joe suddenly began acting strangely. He rolled his eyes and wagged his head back and forth. "I think I'll kill that horse," he growled and, raising his gun, put a bullet into the animal's brain.

Then Joe turned, swaying crazily, and said: "Now I think I'll kill you!"

Instantly Bill raised his rifle and shot Joe through the heart.

And concluding the parade of horrors, consider the case of the Chicago newspaperman, an alcoholic named Gibbs. He quit drinking, but he enjoyed hanging out in the saloon with his cronies. For two years he went without a drink, sipping ginger ale at the tavern. Then one day his friends played a joke on him. While he wasn't looking, they poured a stiff slug of whisky into his ginger ale. Gibbs was soon drunk and stayed drunk for twelve days and on the twelfth day went home and killed his wife with a butcher knife.

4

Fun Along Main Street

There is something in the atmosphere of a small town that seems to encourage horseplay among its citizens. I mean its grownup citizens.

Every small town has at least one practical joker; usually there are several. As a general thing they are to be found among the younger business and professional men—doctors, lawyers, storekeepers and sometimes even clergymen. They liven up their days by playing jokes on one another.

Having spent a good part of my life in and around small towns, I have some personal knowledge of these operations. From other sources, I have obtained information relating to small-town cutuppery. For the sake of convenience, I am going to lump some of these jokes together as having occurred in a single community—a town called Skylark.

If you ask around for the name of a local practical joker in Skylark, people will smile and probably mention the name of Fred Hawthorn; they will likely say that Fred Hawthorn is the *only* practical joker in town. That, of course, isn't true. Fred has been blamed for every prank whose true authors have managed to escape detection. Fred owns and operates a hardware store on Main Street when he's not up to some form of deviltry.

One of his most famous stunts dates back twenty-five years. It has been said that the man who contributed most to the practical joke was Alexander Graham Bell and this joke involves Bell's invention. At the time Fred Hawthorn pulled it, the telephones in Skylark were almost all of the stand-up receiver-on-the-hook variety.

One Sunday around noontime Fred telephoned the homes of six of his friends. He is, to be sure, an excellent mimic, so he disguised his voice and said he was from the engineering department of the telephone company.

"I'm calling," he said, "to warn you that some time this afternoon we are going to clean out the telephone lines. We would advise you to cover your telephone—tie a sheet over it, or put a pillowcase over it, or even a large paper bag, because we're going to *blow* out the lines, and if you don't have your instrument covered, there'll be dirt and grease all over the house."

Having made his six calls, Fred waited an hour or so, and then started a tour of the affected households—just casually dropping in of a Sunday afternoon. In every case he found the telephone covered. Not only that—the folks were staying in the same room with it, keeping their distance, but watching it closely, waiting for the hiss or roar or whatever would come when the lines were blown out. Most of them had had phone calls during the afternoon, but they had forborne answering, save in the case of Dr. Gerrity. When his phone rang he took the pillowcase off of it, picked up the receiver and without asking who was calling, roared into the mouthpiece:

"Good-God-don't-call-this-number-don't-you-know-the-phone company's-blowing-out-the-lines-this-afternoon!"

With which he slammed up the receiver and quickly replaced the pillowcase.

Back in those days there was a local lumber merchant named Hostetter, long since bankrupt and moved to another State. Hostetter was quite a prankster in his own right and for a while he and Fred Hawthorn worked as a team, conspiring against other citizens. Eventually, however, they began pecking away at each other.

Fred went on a business trip to Chicago and sent a long telegram, back to his friend Hostetter, signing it with the name of another Skylark businessman, Phil Purdee, who was out of town on vacation. The message said that if Hostetter had any old chunks and splinters of lumber around his place, he should deliver a load of same to the Purdee residence for winter firewood, dumping it at the side door of the house. Hostetter knew immediately that the telegram was from Fred Hawthorn. He took his big truck and two workmen and went out east of town and got an old oak stump—an enormous thing of its kind, measuring four or five feet across. It took a lot of doing but in the end Hostetter and his men deposited the stump on Fred's front porch, squarely in front of the door.

When Fred Hawthorn got back from Chicago he was a little sore about it, but Hostetter wasn't finished with him yet. The Hawthorns were giving a party one afternoon and in the midst of the festivities an elephant appeared. A small circus had been playing the town, and Hostetter hired the elephant and two keepers to pay a call on the Hawthorns. The scheme was to try to get the elephant into the house, but the beast smelled the refreshments or something and refused to go near the door. Instead he paraded around the house several times, being careful to walk in all the flower beds.

The day after the elephant episode Fred and Hostetter met on the street and got to discussing what this sort of foolishness was costing them. In a few moments they were arguing about which had spent the most money. Fred contended that it had cost him more to have the stump removed from his front porch than it had cost Hostetter to hire the elephant. The argument ended with their making a five-dollar bet as to which man was most out of pocket. Fred Hawthorn lost the bet, but had the last laugh. He went to the bank and got five hundred pennies. He put these pennies in a gallon glass jug, filled the jug with sorghum molasses mixed with sawdust, and sent it around to Hostetter in payment of his wager.

It wasn't long after this that Hostetter's business failed and he moved away, leaving a large void in Fred's life. But he carried on alone as best he could. His adventures with Hostetter probably inspired his famous carpet-tack adventure with Mrs. Sophie Landmark. Mrs. Landmark was a little dumpy woman with society ideas and inclinations toward snootiness (she had been to Europe twicet). One day she walked into Hawthorn's Hardware Store and said she wanted a nickel's worth of carpet tacks. "Deliver them," she said, putting the nickel on the counter and walking out. Fred sat and thought about it for a while—Mrs. Landmark's house was a good mile from his store. Finally he went over to see Elmer Nowatney, the contractor, and borrowed a team of horses hitched to a huge flat-bed wagon. Fred drove the vehicle himself, pulling it up in front of his store and going in to get the little packet of tacks, which he placed carefully in the middle of the big wagon bed. Then he drove out to Mrs. Landmark's house. Amidst much whooping and yeeing and hawing at the horses, he packed the wagon over the curb, through Mrs. Landmark's shrubbery, across her front lawn, breaking up her sidewalk and digging big ruts and holes in the turf, until the back end of the wagon was even with the front porch. Then Fred got down, took the packet of tacks, rang the doorbell and when Mrs. Landmark answered, doffed his hat like a gentleman and said, "Here's your tacks, ma'am." He was gone before she could realize that an earthquake had hit her front yard. He expected her to sue, but she didn't—someone told her she'd be the laughing stock of the town if she took the thing to court.

These matters occurred years ago. Nowadays Fred Hawthorn's hair is gray and he's somewhat subdued. He says the field of practical joking is overcrowded today—that almost everyone indulges in them. These days he confines himself, for the most part, to rumor-starting. This is an ancient and sometimes wonderful phase of the practical joker's art.

One of the busiest places in Skylark is Rawson's Cigar Store, dealing in newspapers, magazines, stationery, candy, sporting goods, photographic equipment, novelties, sub-novelties, and so on. About once every month or so Fred strolls in to Rawson's to buy cigarettes and he'll say casually to the clerk, "Quite a fire down there!"

"Where? Where's the fire?"

"Didn't you hear about it?" Fred asks, surprised. "My God, the Millertown depot's on fire. Last I heard the roof was gone and they'd carried two people out unconscious."

Within a matter of minutes people are on their way to Millertown, seven miles away, anxious to see the conflagration.

Sometimes Fred's rumors concern other fires, explosions, the sudden hospitalization of the Mayor with a stroke—almost anything but the dam has broke in Columbus, Ohio.

(One of the great practitioners of this form of joke was H. L. Mencken's father. The elder Mencken, a cigar manufacturer in Baltimore, would walk into a saloon, order a drink at the bar, and then ask the bartender, quite casually, if he had heard about the Brooklyn Bridge collapsing. Before the day was out the story of the bridge's falling would be all over Baltimore, and the local newspapers would be urgently querying New York about it. Other rumors Mr. Mencken started, at one time or another, were that the Dutch were all being driven out of Holland, and that Bismarck was leaving Germany, moving to Baltimore and opening a brewery.)

One more Fred Hawthorn deception needs mentioning. He stopped by the Mayhew house one Saturday afternoon and found no one home. The front door was open so he walked in. He took a piece of wrapping paper and wrote a note, using a pencil. Most of the note was in an illegible scrawl, as was the signature. It was possible, however, for the Mayhews, when they came home and found it, to figure out that someone had called and had *borrowed* something. They couldn't make out what it was that had been borrowed, or who had done the borrowing. They began telephoning all their friends, asking if they had stopped by that afternoon. They even called Fred Hawthorn but he said he had been in his store all afternoon. So now the Mayhews began checking over all their earthly possessions, trying to find out what had been taken. They occupied themselves for days trying to solve the mystery and Fred let them worry over it for two months before he finally told them.

In the town of Skylark are three professional men who started their careers in the same year. They are Dr. Vingo, Dr. Fenway and Dr. Costerholdt. The last-named is a dentist, the other two are general practitioners. These three got out of college and began their practice in Skylark at the same time, and have always been great friends. It happens that all three were married at about the same time and before long the two medical doctors began producing young. Dr. Vingo fathered two children and Dr. Fenway produced three during the first five years of marriage. But Dr. Costerholdt and his wife remained childless. Looking at the situation of his two medical friends, the dentist began to worry. He consulted his friends professionally, usually getting them together at the Elks Club and asking them what was wrong, and what should he do? They joshed him considerably, of course. Then one day at the club Dr. Costerholdt demanded that they treat the matter seriously.

"Look, Bill," said Dr. Fenway to the disturbed dentist, "do you mean to sit there and tell us that *you don't really know* what your trouble is?"

"Of course I don't!"

The two medical men looked at each other questioningly.

"Better go ahead and tell him," suggested Dr. Vingo gravely.

"Well, Bill," said Dr. Fenway, "I'm surprised that you're so ignorant. *It's that X-ray machine of yours.*"

"What do you mean, X-ray machine!" demanded Dr. Costerholdt.

"You work all day around that X-ray machine, don't you?"

"Of course I do. Part of my business."

"Well," said Dr. Fenway, "you ought to know that an X-ray machine causes temporary sterility among men who are exposed to it day after day. Not *all* men, but some men —and it's very apparent that you're one of them."

"Well, what in God's name am I gonna do?"

"Get rid of the X-ray machine," said Dr. Vingo.

"But good Lord, I couldn't run my business without . . ."

"Get rid of the X-ray machine!" insisted Dr. Fenway.

The two medical doctors let it stand at that for several days, until they found out that Dr. Costerholdt had actually ordered the machine removed from his office. Then Dr. Fenway telephoned him.

"Listen, Bill, you dumb cluck," he said, "don't take that X-ray machine out. We were kidding you. You want a baby, I'll tell you how to get one. Get hold of a baby's diaper—one that's been used, not a new one—and hang it over the foot of your bed. You'll get a baby."

Dr. Costerholdt thoroughly shocked his receptionist with the language he spoke into the phone.

Horton McNeill lives in Skylark but works in Millertown, where he is a minor executive with a big company that produces plastic articles. One day Horton took a sports jacket to the plant and had one of the side pockets lined with a soft, pliable plastic material. Some days later Horton walked up to the soda fountain in the Skylark Drugstore and ordered a chocolate soda. There were half a dozen people on the stools at the time. Teddy Wilson, the soda jerk, fixed the soda and placed it in front of Horton. As Teddy was handing Horton his change, Horton suddenly picked up the soda. "I think I'll drink it at home," he said, and poured it into the side pocket of his coat. Then he walked out.

Horton says he pulls the same stunt everywhere he goes.

Charles K. M. Porter died in Skylark about ten years ago. He was a retired businessman, director of the bank, and owner of one of the finest homes in town. All his life he seemed to be a man of little humor, and even had the reputation of being a grouch. He left his money to his three sons, in a will that contained one unusual clause.

"At the rear of the closet in my bedroom," it read, "will be found a sealed box, marked with the single word, 'Secret.' I command that immediately after my funeral, my three sons, in the company of my lawyers, carry this box unopened to the back yard of my residence. Under no circumstances shall it be opened. A fire shall be kindled and in the presence of my sons and my lawyers, the box shall be burned until it is completely consumed by the flames."

The three sons and two lawyers returned to the house from the cemetery and got the box from the closet. It was about four feet square, carefully and tightly wrapped in heavy paper and sealed with wax. Out of respect for the departed, the five men did not even discuss what mysterious thing or things might be inside it. They proceeded to the back yard, making a rather solemn procession of it, and built a bonfire. When the fire was going good they placed the box in the middle of it, and then stood around, watching the flames do their work. Suddenly all hell let loose. The box was full of firecrackers, skyrockets, roman candles and pinwheels.

* * *

And now, as they say on television, before we leave Skylark it is necessary that we return to Fred Hawthorn, the sportive ironmonger.

Just recently Fred moved his hardware store to a new location on Main Street—a brand-new building with spacious show windows and a splendid neon sign running across the top of the façade.

As is customary in Skylark, Fred planned a Grand Opening for a Saturday. There would be favors for the ladies and something in the back room for the men. The Mayor would snip a ribbon at the front door. All this to begin on Saturday morning.

During Friday night Fred's friends, all of whom had been his victims at one time or another, went to work.

When dawn broke on Saturday the new Hawthorn Hardware Store was a sight to behold.

The three golden balls of the pawnbroker's trade hung above the entrance.

Suspended from the new neon sign were two dozen chamber pots.

The entire front of the store was plastered with well-prepared signs, saying such things as:

OPENING DAY—EVERYTHING HALF PRICE

FREE COASTER WAGONS FOR ALL THE KIDDIES

TOILET SEATS EXCHANGED EVEN STEVEN—ONE NEW ONE
FOR ONE OLD ONE.

DOLLAR BILLS ONLY FIFTY CENTS

When Fred Hawthorn saw the mess at 7:45 A.M., he flew into a rage. "There's a limit, goddammit," he said, "to all things!"

5

Is It a Man's Sport?

Among all the living authorities on the practical joke there has been an inclination to argue that the business belongs exclusively to the human male. It is my intention, at this point, to set down such evidence as I have been able to uncover, bearing on the question of whether women ever play practical jokes, and whether animals play them.

People who write extensively about animals often describe them as practical jokers. As a general thing, the writers have been point-stretchers. A bear forces his way into a cabin and wrecks the interior. I don't believe he does it as a practical joke on the owner. He is simply irritated at not finding any food, or at finding too much food, or he has found a bottle of whisky. Bear-writers almost always say bears are practical jokers. In the American West the coyote has a reputation as a practical joker. So have some dogs, some cats, foxes, possums, turtles and even rabbits. It is probable that these animals acquire their reputations from the fact that they appear so often in fable and folklore.

A strong case can be made for the chimpanzee. A detachment of British troops was once encamped on the shore of Lake Albert Nyanza in Africa. One night the drum disappeared from the camp. On the following night the camp was aroused by drumbeats. The noise was traced to its source: an old chimp was perched in the top of a tree close beside the camp, vigorously pounding on the drum with a stick. It was apparent to the soldiers that the chimp had become angry at being kept awake by the drum in the day time, and had decided on repayment in kind.

A zoologist has written an account of how two chimpanzees in the Zoological Gardens at St. Louis tried to play a practical joke on a chicken. The chicken was an intruder at the zoo, just wandered in and began strolling about, looking at the various animals, judging them to be farmers. Finally the chicken arrived before the cage occupied by the two chimps. The record doesn't show that the chimps conferred together on the matter, but they began playing a little game. One of them had a chunk of bread. The other went to the back of the cage and found a pole about six feet long. The one chimp sat by the bars, noisily munching at the bread. The chicken began pacing nervously up and down, cocking her head, hungrily observing this performance. Then the chimp took the piece of bread and sticking his arm through the bars, held it toward the chicken. A chicken is not easily gulled, but this one wanted some of that bread. She paced back and forth, clucking and cocking her head, coming closer and closer. Then as she came within range, Chimp No. 2 suddenly thrust the pole through the bars and tried to knock her head off. This pantomime was repeated again and again until the chicken gave up and wandered off to look at the peacocks.

In Morganton, North Carolina, there is a parrot whose owners are willing to take oath that he is a practical joker. His name is General and he lives in the Wilson home where there are two large dogs. It is the family custom to summon these dogs by a distinctive sort of whistle, best described as two longs. Whenever the dogs hear the two longs, they come on the double for it means feeding time. One evening the dogs were lolling about the kitchen when the signal came from the living room. They leaped to their feet and went pounding in. Nobody there. General sat in his cage, staring in a disinterested manner at the ceiling. The dogs looked in corners and under chairs and then at each other, mightily confused. From then on, for several weeks, General made life miserable for the dogs, uttering that distinctive whistle and then, when they arrived, playing dumb.

I have met General. He didn't whistle up the dogs for me while I was there. He wouldn't even talk to me. The Wilsons said it was because he recognized me for a Yankee. Later on, however, after we had gone away from his cage, he suddenly let go with a trilling sound, followed by the cry: "Dell, answer the telephone!" Mrs. Wilson's name is Dell, and General often tries to fool her about the telephone. Considering that he has no metal parts, he is better at imitating a telephone bell than most humans.

One of the leading crusaders against practical jokes today is a writer named Helen Colton. She urges in magazine articles that practical jokers be told they are not funny, and that they be ostracized if they keep it up. Miss Colton collects practical jokes but only insofar as they result in property damage, bodily harm, or death. In one of her essays I find the following statement: "It's interesting to note that women practically never pull practical jokes."

We have already met the California lady who planted the torpedo under the toilet seat. And while I agree that the great majority of practical jokes are the work of men, the ladies have been responsible for some fine examples.

Mr. Robert Bagar, the eminent music critic, informs me that Maria Jeritza had some fun one night in a performance of *Tosca*. In the final scene she was to stab the villain with a dagger. On this particular night she used a ripe banana. Before she was finished she had banana all over the man. Mr. Bagar also recalls the Japanese soprano who specialized in *Madame Butterfly* and who decided to unnerve the tenor during one of the performances. All through one of his big arias, she stood and stared at his fly. He was unnerved.

James Thurber has written lovingly of his mother's many practical jokes, though Mr. Thurber doesn't call them by that name, preferring to define them as pranks. Among them all I think I like best the incident in the Washington railway station. Mrs. Thurber, then in her sixties, was to be met at the station by an old friend, a woman she had not seen in thirty years. By agreement Mrs. Thurber was to wear a red rose so that her friend could identify her. Arriving at the station, Mrs. Thurber noticed an old woman asleep on one of the benches—a woman twenty years older than herself. She pinned the rose on the sleeping woman, then backed off to observe what might happen. She saw her friend arrive, saw her dismay when she spotted the rose, and enjoyed the scene immensely as her friend shook the old woman awake and cried, "Why, Mame Thurber, how are you? You're looking just fine!"

Miss June Havoc, the sparkling comedienne who is Gypsy Rose Lee's sister, was playing in *Pal Joey* on Broadway when, one night, the stage doorman approached her and said there was a visitor outside. "I wouldn't bother about her," the doorman told Miss Havoc. "She's a nut. Claims she's your mother." But Miss Havoc remembered something and hurried to the stage door and found her mother actually was there. She had rigged herself out in a dirty old polo coat, and whitened her face to give it a sickly, dissipated effect. When she approached the doorman she had staggered slightly, and she was wheezing. "If only," she said to him, "if only I could have just a bowl of soup—please go tell Miss Havoc's it's . . . it's . . . her mother." Miss Havoc had remembered that her mother had pulled the same joke on her other daughter when Gypsy was working at the Twentieth Century-Fox studio in Beverly Hills.

We have the testimony of Consuela Vanderbilt that her mother-in-law, the Duchess of Marlborough, was given to practical jokes, and at an elegant party mixed slices of soap in with the cheese, watching her well-bred guests actually eat the soap rather than be guilty of a breach of manners.

The late Carole Lombard was one of the greatest practical jokers in Hollywood and many of her pranks involved the use of dummies of gorgeous women placed in beds. And Tallulah Bankhead is not averse to an occasional practical joke. She was invited once to a society party in Philadelphia, and arrived with an elderly and distinguished-looking Negro. She introduced him as Dr. Bechet, chief assistant to Dr. Einstein at Princeton. The other guests displayed great interest in Dr. Bechet and cross-examined him about relativity and the atom bomb. He stood up very well under this questioning, but after a while he produced a soprano sax and let go with some first-rate Dixieland. He was Sidney Bechet, one of the top jazz musicians of all time.

One more from the distaff side. Kathleen Norris, author of more novels than there are people in Idaho, was walking along Fifth Avenue one afternoon. She stopped to look at the window display in a department store. Reflected in the window glass she saw a man creeping up behind her. She recognized him as Frank Sullivan, the Saratoga philosopher. She recognized, also, his intentions, which were not altogether honorable. It was clear to her that Mr. Sullivan was going to goose her. Suddenly Mrs. Norris whirled about, and Mr. Sullivan stopped in his tracks.

"Not one penny more!" cried Mrs. Norris. "You and your family have had all the money you'll ever get out of me! You've bled me white!" Her voice grew louder, and a small crowd was beginning to gather. "You've spent it all on drink," shrilled Mrs. Norris, "rather than on your sick wife! I've given you everything I have—and still you hound me for more!"

Mr. Sullivan fled and Mrs. Norris proceeded along her way, ungoost.

6

Chaw Raw Beef

It may well be that some of the violent hatred of practical jocosity is inspired by the adult's knowledge that the
business has always been associated with boyhood and is,
per se, juvenile. A boy seems to play practical jokes instinc-
tively. He usually begins indulging in the sport before he
learns to subtract, sometimes even before he notices about
girls. Down through the years the fictional picture of the
American boy has been that of a small fiend almost constantly engaged in pranks. George W. Peck, Thomas Bailey
Aldrich, Booth Tarkington and above all Mark Twain,
each of these gave us classic portraits of American boys and
those boys were hellions. I am willing to go far out on a
limb and venture the opinion that those boys were more
accurately painted than the boys of Horatio Alger, Jr.,
who played no practical jokes.

Not long ago I was in a group sitting late at night in a
New York restaurant. Among those present were a man
and wife who both are prominent in serious literature.
Knowing these two by reputation I would say it's a sure
thing that, if they were asked their opinion of practical
jokers, they would explode in anger. Yet I remember the
conversation that evening. Someone asked them how their
son, Eddie, was doing.

"Oh, haven't you heard of Eddie's latest!" cried Eddie's mother. Then without much urging her husband, who is a *most* grave and dignified man, told the story of Eddie's latest. It seems that Eddie and his pal, George, both fresh out of college, had gone to one of the tall buildings in Rockefeller Center to get a package. They entered an elevator at one of the top floors, with Eddie carrying the package. All during the downward trip, they talked together in loud whispers, about the package, about the place they were taking the package as well as the place where they got it. They framed their talk so that other passengers in the elevator would get the impression they were Communist conspirators and that the package contained either the nation's most secret military plan or a small-size atom bomb.

Well, sir, I never saw people so amused as this tale of Eddie playing Communist was unfolded. They howled with laughter, and exclaimed, "Absolutely *priceless!*" At the time I remember thinking that perhaps the prejudice against practical jokes is not as deep as it seems. I remembered, too, an experience I had during World War II. I had to drive someone to an army camp and with me in the car were two vacationing college boys. They gave me a horrible fright. Every time we came within earshot of guards and sentries and army officers, those two boys began talking in pidgin German. "Hans," one of them would say, "vot iss diss? You got der diagrams und maps?" And so on and on. I was quite happy when we finally cleared the barrier and got out of the place.

The behavior of boys in the time of Mark Twain's Hannibal days was considerably different than it is today. The boys of Hannibal had more time at their disposal, not being afflicted with movies, radio or television. Dixon Wecter's recent book, *Sam Clemens of Hannibal*, is the story of Mark Twain's life up to the age of eighteen. It shows the boys of Hannibal indulging in almost constant pranking. They turn cats loose in all the rooms of the local hotel. They labor mightily to loosen the big boulder on Holliday's Hill and send it crashing into the town. And they indulge in the "chaw-raw-beef" business which was still going when I was a boy. It was almost impossible to go swimming without having your clothes knotted. The villains would creep up and get shirts and pants and stockings, tie them full of hard knots, dip them in the water and then lay them out in the sun. By the time the swimmer was ready to dress, the knots had grown so tight that it was usually necessary to tug at them with the teeth, while the tormentors, from a distance, chanted, "Chaw raw beef! Chaw raw beef!"

The Hannibal boys suffered one major deficiency—they had no telephones. Much of the modern juvenile pranking is concerned with the telephone. Every town suffers from epidemics of it. It is largely the work of teen-age kids. They pick a number and call it and say, "Does King Street run past your house?" The answer is yes. "Then run out and catch it!" And hang up. Or they ask, "Do you live on Jefferson Street?" Yes. "Well, get out of the way, there's a car coming!" There are endless variations, including the call to the cigar store: "Do you keep Prince Albert in the can?" They do. "Well for the Lord's sake let him out!"

There are, on a more heinous level, the water company warnings: "This is the water company calling. The service in your area is going to be shut down for at least twenty-four hours. We'd suggest you fill the bathtub and all the pans you have with water so you'll not be too inconvenienced."

The lives of schoolteachers have always been made slightly more hideous by the pranks of their pupils. I have a note about a stunt that used to be common in English schools where the teacher's desk occupied a wooden platform a foot or two higher than the floor. The boys would secretly move the desk so that its legs were at the extreme edge of the platform; when the teacher leaned forward, ever so slightly, the desk would go crashing down and usually the pedagogue on top of it. And in the same tradition, the boys sometimes put a pigeon in the desk, so that when the lid was lifted the bird would come rushing out, causing momentary fright and maybe even heart failure. Outside of horsewhipping, the teacher could do little about such jokes since one of the world's favorite axioms is: Boys will be boys.

A boy's talent for practical jokes doesn't reach its full burgeoning, however, until he gets in college. It was at Cornell that Hugh Troy, our country's most accomplished man in the business, began his adventures. And it was at Cornell, just a couple of years ago, that a group of students seized the campus radio station.

Around eleven o'clock one night ten students, wearing masks, walked into the radio station, tied up two announcers, and took over the microphone. For eight minutes they broadcast bulletins that Russian planes had bombed London and Marseilles, that other planes were now over Newfoundland—that the world was once again at war. The bulletins caused panic in some quarters of the campus and girls in the sorority houses were reported to have suffered fainting and hysteria. Some twenty-five students were involved in the plot, and were suspended after they confessed. This stunt was not original, having been pulled on a lesser scale in other schools.

Another group of Cornell students developed a grudge not long ago against the girls in a certain sorority house. They figured out a way to embarrass the girls. They dressed themselves as workmen, with red signs and lanterns and tools. They blocked off a thoroughfare leading from the campus proper to a bridge. The girls, in order to get from the campus to their house, had to cross this bridge; otherwise, it was necessary for them to take a long, roundabout way to get home. The boys timed their roadblock so the girls would be late getting to their house, and find themselves in trouble. Ah youth.

Collegiate jokers often concern themselves with bells.

The early American humorist Henry W. Shaw, who wrote under the name of Josh Billings, was expelled from Hamilton College for removing the clapper from the college bell. There have been other cases in which cords were attached to bells, and strung off across rooftops so that the pranksters could set the bells to ringing during the night. The best of these jokes occurred at Harvard. The clock in one of the university towers began performing in a most unusual manner. It would strike thirteen times at noon. At midnight it was content to strike the customary twelves times, but at noon there would be that extra stroke. The deviation was quickly noticed and an investigation was started. Clockmakers were called in to examine the mechanism. They couldn't make out what caused the thirteen strokes at noon. The bell itself was examined, but there were no cords, or other contrivances, connected to it. The thing went along for quite a while, a great mystery to be sure. It was solved by the villain's being caught in the act. He was a student, living on one of the upper floors of a house near by. Each noontime he sat at the window of his room with a rifle. The clock struck twelve and then, with perfect timing, the student pulled the trigger to create the thirteenth stroke.

Among the legends at New Haven is that of the time Lucius Beebe brought in the famous clergyman from the West. Mr. Beebe conceived the joke after having met a man who was an expert ventriloquist. He had the man dress in somber clothes and arrive on the Yale campus for a visit. Mr. Beebe quickly introduced him to the Yale chaplain as one of the most celebrated preachers of the Far West. The chaplain immediately invited the visitor to preach a sermon in the Yale Chapel. A goodly crowd was there and the impostor acquitted himself well, working himself up to a pitch of excitement. Suddenly he paused, threw back his head, cupped his hands to his mouth and shouted toward the ceiling: "Am I right, Lord?" Back from the rafters came the faint but audible response: "You are right, my son!"

* * *

Stanley Halle has told me of a torment he had to put up with regularly during his undergraduate days at Yale. Quite a few of the students would leave New Haven to spend week ends in New York City. On Sunday night there was a certain train which most of them took out of Grand Central—a train that would just get them under the wire at university curfew time. The boys, as a rule, would be dog-tired and perhaps a little woozy when they boarded the train and most of them would collapse in the seats and go to sleep. The train would move out of Grand Central and pull up at the 125th Street station. Almost invariably, says Mr. Halle, just as it was coming in to the 125th Street stop, someone would yell out, "New Haven!" The cry would rouse the sleepers and they'd stumble out of the cars to the platform, their train would depart, and they'd have to wait another couple of hours before resuming their journey.

Down at Randolph-Macon College in Virginia, a couple of generations ago, the students had a way of entertaining Yankee football invaders. Early of an evening the whisper would go round that there was to be a lynching at a spot outside the town. The Northern boys could witness the affair provided they promised secrecy. Usually they agreed, for it is common knowledge that people like to see other people die violently. There would be a large crowd, then, around a big tree, and the victim, a Negro who supposedly had raped a white woman, would be brought up in a wagon. The rope would be placed around his neck and fastened to a limb of the tree—while he shrieked and trembled and cried for mercy. Then the wagon would be driven out from under him, and he'd pitch around a bit and then hang still. At this point the visitors would be taken back to their quarters. For this exhibition the Randolph-Macon boys had in their hire an amiable Negro who could tighten the muscles of his neck, somehow, so that he could take the "hanging" without harm.

An acquaintance of mine in the book publishing business attended Syracuse University twenty-odd years ago. He remembers, with some pleasure, a dance that was given at his fraternity house. Since the house would be co-ed for that one evening, it was necessary to reapportion the toilet facilities. One large bathroom on the second floor was, accordingly, turned over to the girls and a "Ladies" sign placed on the door. Before the hour for the dance to begin, my friend had an idea. He went out to a pet store and bought three goldfish. There were three toilets in the "ladies' room" and he put one goldfish in each of them. He says that all during the evening the girls kept going to the room, but not a single one of them used the toilets for fear of harming the fish, and he says further that the girls seemed to get livelier and livelier as the evening wore on, and in the end they were fair leaping around. Demonstrates the essential kindliness of women.

The business of dismantling and then reassembling large pieces of machinery in a person's bedroom is said to have originated at the Massachusetts Institute of Technology. The pioneer practitioners of this form of foolishness took an automobile apart and put it back together in a student's room. The stunt has been repeated, in variation, many times since, especially in Hollywood, where a visiting Englishman once arrived at his hotel room to find it occupied by a gang plow.

Biographers of the late William Randolph Hearst usually tell of his adventures at Harvard, where he once encompassed the entire faculty in one of his jokes. On a certain day each member of the faculty received a package—a chamber pot with the recipient's photograph pasted in the bottom.

Alexander Woollcott was to be the butt of fantastic jokes

in his later life, but when he was a student at Hamilton College he was not averse to trying a few himself. He was a member of Theta Delta Chi. During one rushing season, his fraternity was in sharp rivalry with another house in the quest for pledges. Mr. Woollcott attired himself in a fantastic costume and went over and sat on the steps of the rival fraternity house, assuming the air of a drooling idiot, as an advertisement of the type of boy belonging to *that* society.

Two eastern college boys once spent their summer vacation as temporary employees at Yellowstone Park. After a while they became impatient with a certain ranger, a pompous individual whose job was to guide tourists to the famous geysers and lecture to them on the wonders of this unique manifestation of natural force. They came, in fact, to dislike the man heartily and so they put their heads together and came up with a scheme.

There was one geyser which spouted with clocklike regularity and the college boys stationed themselves near it. The ranger would arrive with his party of tourists. The boys had placed themselves beyond a slope where the tourists could see them while they were out of sight of the lecturing ranger. They had a steering wheel and post from an old automobile, and they had stuck the post into the ground. While the pompous ranger lectured, they'd pretend to busy themselves with hidden valves and gauges and so on. They were able to judge the precise moment when the geyser would let go with all its force—it always signaled its intentions with a couple of preliminary puffs of steam. So, at the exact moment, one boy would yell, "Let 'er go, Charlie!" The other would swing the steering wheel vigorously. And the geyser would shoot a hundred and fifty feet into the air. There may still be tourists who believe the Yellowstone geysers are a colossal fraud, operated by an underground steam system.

* * *

Some years ago the alumni association of a leading Eastern college held its annual meeting in a New York hotel. The time came for nomination of officers. A man at the side of the room got up and made a short speech, nominating good old Charlie Andrews for president of the association. He said that there wasn't a finer fellow in the whole organization, nay, in the whole wide world, than old Charlie Andrews, and certainly Charlie Andrews worked harder than anybody else for the organization, and even contributed large sums of money out of his own pocket toward the betterment of conditions, and so on. When he sat down a man at the other side of the room got up and loudly seconded the nomination of Charlie Andrews, paying even greater compliments to the man. Within a very few minutes Charlie Andrews had been elected president by acclamation, and the enthusiasm was high for him. There were shouts of "Speech! Speech! We want Charlie Andrews!"

There wasn't any Charlie Andrews.

Returning to the frontier, and leaving halls of ivy, let us consider the story told by the late Jay Williams, of Washington. He spent his boyhood in South Dakota and among his friends was another boy who had a deathly fear of cyclones. The family maintained a cyclone cellar some distance from the house—one of those dugout jobs with a wooden door that closed over it. It didn't take much of a breeze to send this boy racing for the cyclone cellar. One day the other lads decided to have some fun with him. They picked a windy day, and came scampering along, and told their friend a cyclone was on its way, and then they pretended to scatter for their own homes. Their victim raced to the cyclone cellar, got into it and pulled the door shut. For the next three hours the other boys stood around, throwing clods, tin cans, logs and rocks onto the wooden door. Then they stopped and after a while their victim came out cautiously, expecting to see the countryside swept clear of silos, houses, barns, livestock, and everything else. Jay Williams said it was probably a cruel sort of joke, but that it had its good side. The boy was cured of his fear of cyclones.

7

The Good Old Days

Every American who can count to a hundred by fives has heard of the snipe hunt, wherefore it is unlikely that the sport is practiced much in our atomic era. Yet it was one of the favorite practical jokes of our grandfathers.

The conspiracy usually involved at least half a dozen men who convinced their victim that there was a better way of hunting snipe than with a gun. The party went deep into the woods at night, carrying a burlap bag and several candles. When the proper spot had been selected, the victim was accorded the honor of holding the bag. It was placed on the ground and his job was to stand over it, carefully holding it open. A lighted candle was set on the ground directly in front of the opening. The conspirators then left, explaining that they would go out and form a big circle and slowly beat their way in toward the bag, driving the snipe ahead of them. The candlelight would cause the bird to rush headlong into the bag and the night's sport would be over. So the victim took up his position and the others crept off into the woods . . . and went home and went to bed. I have heard that some ninnies spent the entire night in the woods waiting for the snipe to arrive.

A companion piece to the snipe hunt was the joke involving the brakeman's daughter. This requires a considerable build-up. The victim is usually a fellow who fancies himself to be quite a guy with the ladies. He is told about a house, on the outskirts of town, where a railroad brakeman lives with his beautiful daughter. The girl is described as a ravishing, sex-starved creature whose father, a man of violence, will not permit her to associate with the opposite sex. The brakeman, in fact, has proclaimed that he will kill any man who gets near his beautiful daughter.

The girl, however, has let word get around that she has seen our boy on the streets of the town, and that she is strongly attracted to him, and that she hopes he will call upon her some night when her papa is out on his run.

It comes to pass that on a black night one of the jokers escorts the eager lecher out to the brakeman's house. The house is dark and the two men creep onto the front porch and knock at the door. The door is opened and a girl's voice whispers a welcome and at this instant a man comes around the corner of the house, roaring in anger.

The joker screams: "Run for your life! It's the brakeman!"

A shot is fired as the two men star running. The joker gasps, groans, and sinks to the ground as another shot sounds. The victim doesn't stop running until he is home, under the bed or locked in a closet.

Sometimes the joke is carried on for several days after that, with the conspirators furnishing hospital reports on the condition of the wounded man who is, to be sure, at the point of death.

Readers who would be interested in how this joke worked out when played by a group of New Jersey gangsters are referred to Damon Runyon's short story called, fittingly enough, "The Brakeman's Daughter."

Many years ago there was a town called Little Rest in Rhode Island. Apparently it was a community made up almost entirely of practical jokers. They were constantly at work, playing tricks either on visitors or on one another.

Thus the town got its name—the people who lived there got little rest. Subsequently the community changed its name to Kingston.

In another part of the country a specific practical joke, according to legend, gave a town its name. A whimsical traveler on one of the main trails in the State of Georgia painted, on a large rock, the words, "Turn Me Over." Other travelers heaved and struggled to turn the rock over. On the underside of it they found painted, "Now Turn Me Back That I May Fool Another." They sat down and laughed, or cussed, and then moved on. Eventually, however, a village came into being on the spot, and was called Talking Rock.

When the railroads first came to the West, the locomotive engineers sometimes enjoyed themselves at the expense of the crowds that assembled to watch the arrival and departure of the monsters. A train would pull into a community, with every living creature in fifty miles present to see it. As the gaping crowd gathered around the locomotive the engineer would suddenly let go a blast of steam, then yell: "Watch out, boys, I'm gonna turn 'er around!" That always sent them scattering for the woods.

The American Indian apparently was never a man of humor, but whatever comedy he did have in his soul usually took the form of practical joking. The chief folklore of the American Indian is preserved in the "trickster tales" which were common to most tribes. The tricksters were practical jokers; one of them, for example, would advise the fox to catch fish by putting his tail through a hole in the ice; the ice would freeze, trapping the fox, and this was very funny.

Lorenzo Dow, the rambling evangelist of long ago, joined with several other preachers in a camp meeting down South. Dow grew weary of the manner in which one of his fellow preachers always concluded his sermon on the Joys of Heaven. He always finished with the cry, "Hurry up, Gabriel, and blow your horn!" One evening Dow hired a boy to climb a tree near the meeting grounds and when the preacher cried for Gabriel to blow, the boy in the tree let go with a blast on a hunting horn. Whereupon the preacher, according to legend, fell to his knees and cried toward heaven: "Lord, you ought to know I don't mean *everything* I say!"

Another preacher story, recounted by Boatright in *Folk Laughter on the American Frontier,* involves the clergyman's son who found his father's Bible open on his desk, where he had been preparing his sermon for the following Sunday. The boy pasted two leaves of the Bible together.

On Sunday the preacher stood in the pulpit and read his text:

"And Noah took unto himself a wife"—he turned the page and continued—"and the length thereof was three hundred cubits, and the breadth of it fifty cubits and the height of it thirty cubits."

The preacher paused, wiped his spectacles, read it again, and a third time. Then he said:

"Brethren, I have been reading this Bible for fifty years. I do not remember that I ever read this passage before, but it confirms me in my faith in the works of the Lord, for, truly, brethren, we can say of Noah's wife that she was fearfully and wonderfully made."

A lady of my acquaintance, a civic pillar of the Eastern community in which she lives, has given me a profound shock. She was born and raised on the prairies of Oklahoma, and she told me that she could remember many practical jokes that were popular on her native heath. She volunteered to write them out for me, and eventually sent me several typewritten pages of early Oklahoma jokes. They are almost all unprintable. I thought I knew all of the dirty ones, but she has topped me. She reminds me of one, however, that was so common in the West that it must be mentioned. It involved the "bridal suite" in the town hotel. According to her Oklahoma version, it was the custom of the town jokers to hang a couple of cowbells under the bridal bed. I have heard that in other Western communities, years ago, the device was a trifle more elaborate. The "bridal suite" was directly over the hotel lobby. A hole would be bored in the ceiling and a string run through to the bedsprings. On the end of the string, in the lobby, would be fastened a tiny bell. The jokers then could assemble in front and roar with laughter at the tinkling of the bell. Biographers of Abraham Lincoln say that he enjoyed telling about this type of prank.

In the rousing days of the forty-niners a practical joke was called a Whizzer. This "effervescent phenomenon" is described by Robert Welles Ritchie in *The Hell-Roarin' Forty-Niners:*

"The Whizzer was the high ace in the deck of life as it was dealt over gravel bar and auriferous stream bank. Individuals and towns reaped fame by it. A successful Whizzer not only crowned its originator and perpetrator with glory, but shed an enviable light upon the entire community that witnessed—or suffered—its execution."

Mr. Ritchie relates the origin of an expression, "jack-pine gold," which was common among the miners. It came of a Whizzer perpetrated by a certain Pike Sellers, one of the original discoverers of gold at Downie's Flat. These men, about a dozen in all, spent a hard winter at the camp, digging out gold at a fabulous rate. News of their strike leaked out and in the spring the rush was on. The discoverers were not very happy over the arrival of the eager boomers. Mr. Ritchie tells the story of Pike Sellers:

He was working away at the soft dirt of the stream bank one day when he saw one of the boomers, pack on back, crawling precariously down trail. Pike, unseen himself, scrambled up out of the stream bed and commenced furiously prying with his long knife at the bark slabs on a jack-pine. Just as the stranger came up one of the rough shags of bark became loosened. Pike pushed two fingers behind it and withdrew a fat gold nugget.

Eyes of the stranger popped. Pike tackled another bark slab without so much as a glance over shoulder at the fascinated onlooker. By a simple trick of leger-demain that hunk yielded a second alluring gold pebble.

"My Gawd!"—from the tenderfoot. "I hearn ye was diggin' the yaller stuff outa cracks in the rocks, but I didn't know she grew on trees."

"Gits lodged thar when th' tree's pushin' up through th' soil," indifferently from Pike. "Most of th' nuggets is up higher, but too dam'd much trouble to shin up th' trees. Me, I'm jist satisfied to peck round nigh th' ground."

Under the believing eyes of the newcomer Pike found a couple of more nuggets. Then the former whipped out his bowie-knife and started to work on a nearby jack-pine.

"Hold on thar!" commandingly from the Sellers person. "Yo're on my claim. Rule in this camp ev'ry fella's entitled to ten gold bearin' pines; that thar one belongs to me."

The boomer wanted to know in an excited whine where he could stake himself to a tree. Reluctantly Pike Sellers abandoned his work to stride through the forest to where a jack-pine of smaller growth reared.

"Like I said, she's richest nigh th' top. Ye can climb this one 'thout a ladder iffen yo're so minded." Pike showed a commendable interest in seeing the new-comer make his first strike of jack-pine gold. The latter dropped his pack and, bowie in teeth, com-menced to shin up the rough trunk.

"Higher up's better," bawled Pike when his protégé

had come to the first limbs. "Nothin' but flake gold low down mostly."

Up went the avid tenderfoot, before his eyes the vision of a man prying nuggets from beneath tree bark. Pike let him risk his neck until the luckless light-wit was fifty or sixty feet from the ground.

"That's a likely 'nough place to begin on. Only be mighty keerful not to drop any nuggets. I kain't be held responsible for losses like that."

The searcher after tree gold began to attack the bark with his bowie-knife. Pike Sellers sifted back to the stream bed to bring an audience for the farce comedy he had staged. Thereafter "jack-pine gold" became a synonym through all the Northern Mines.

Pike Sellers reaped enduring fame as the father of a Whizzer.

A dude was always fair game for the practical jokers of the frontier. Big-Foot Wallace, the Texas folk hero, once was a passenger on a Mississippi steamboat when, at Vicksburg, a "dandified-looking little fellow" came aboard. He wore considerable in the way of jewelry and had his spectacles hanging by a black ribbon. His chief offense, however, came at the dinner table. He produced a small leather case and from it took his own silver knife and fork, which he used in place of the implements beside his plate. This behavior excited much indignant comment among passengers and crew. On the following day when the boat stopped at a woodyard, Big-Foot Wallace went ashore to get something, and spent the remainder of the day whittling. At dinner that evening Wallace took the seat opposite the dandy. He waited until the fastidious one produced his leather case and special silverware. Then Wallace hove a gun case onto the table, opened it and took out a wooden knife three feet long and a fork to match it. As Wallace began trying to eat with the huge implements, the entire dining room roared with laughter and approval. The captain was so pleased that he knocked five dollars off Wallace's fare, and the dude disappeared from the boat at the next landing.

The story of the Illinois man who ate the "ister" is included in *The Big Bear of Arkansas, and Other Sketches*, a pre-Civil War book by William T. Porter. As near as I can make out the incident occurred in a St. Louis oyster house.

Late of an evening the Sucker from Illinois walked into the place. He was tall and ungainly and shabbily dressed, an obvious rube. He walked to the bar and stood watching the man who was opening the bivalves and after a while, he said, "Isters?"

"Yes sir," responded the man, "and fine ones they are, too."

"Well," said the Sucker, "I've heered of isters afore, but this is the fust time I've seed 'm, and *pre-haps* I'll know what thar made of afore I git out of town."

He stood and watched as more oysters were opened.

"I never seed anythin' hold on so—takes an amazin' site of screwin' to get 'em out, and ain't they slick and slip'ry when they does come?"

At length he decided he'd have a try at some, and was told that a dozen would cost him two bits.

"Two bits!" he exclaimed. "Now come, that's stickin' it on right strong for *isters*. A dozen on 'em ain't nothin' to a chicken."

There followed a period of bargaining in which it was finally agreed that the Sucker would swap two chickens for a dozen *isters*. Meanwhile a local wag had moved in closer to observe the proceedings.

The gawk from Illinois squared off, preparing to eat his first oyster. He took off his disreputable sealskin cap and laid it aside. He rolled up his sleeves like a man preparing for battle, and kept his eye on that first oyster as if it were going to spring away from him. Then he seized it and bolted it down and stood there for a long moment with a peculiar look on his face.

At this point the wag dropped his knife and fork on the bar with a clatter and stood with an expression of amazement and horror.

"Swallowed alive, as I'm a Christian!" exclaimed the wag.

The Sucker turned and stared at the man, who now asked in tones of astonishment: "Did you swallow it alive?"

"I swallowed it jest as he gin it to me," cried the Sucker.

"You're a dead man!" exclaimed the wag. "That creature is alive, and will eat right through you!"

Now the Sucker went into frenzied action.

"Git a pizen pump and pump it out!" he cried. "O gracious! What'll I do? It's got holt of my innards already! Do somethin' for me! Don't let the infernal sea-toad eat me afore your eyes!"

"Here!" said the wag, seizing a bottle of hot pepper sauce and handing it to the Sucker. "Put some of this on it!"

The Sucker grabbed the bottle, tilted it high and swallowed half its fiery contents. Now he doubled up from the effects of the hot sauce, squealing and twisting and gasping and blowing. Finally, when he had quieted down some, yet with tears streaming over his face, the joker asked him how he felt, and if he had killed the ister.

"I did, hoss," gasped the Sucker. "Oh, my innards! If that ister critter's dyin' agonies didn't stir a 'ruption in me equal to a small arthquake, then 'taint no use sayin' it— it squirmed like a sarpent when that killin' stuff touched it!" He paused, and seemed to consider, and then with finality he announced: "If you git two chickens from me for *that* live animal, I'm damned!" And seizing his sealskin cap, he hurried out of the place.

The "Trial of Sore-Eyes Goodner" took place in an Arkansas town thirty-odd years ago. It was the inspiration of Judge Burton, whose office overlooked the town's main intersection. There is a period of the year when no courts are operating in the vicinity and the lawyers have little to do. During this period Judge Burton was sitting in his office, staring down at the street crossing where a new-fangled stop sign had just been put in place.

Down the street came Sore-Eyes Goodner. He was a town character who got his name from the fact of his eyelids being granulated. He had an ancient wagon and two mules and he made a living hauling firewood. He was driving the mules when Judge Burton saw him approaching the corner. Sore-Eyes apparently hadn't heard about the stop sign, for he let his mules start through the intersection. The town constable was standing near by, and yelled at him, and Sore-Eyes rared back on the lines, but he couldn't get the mules stopped and his rig wound up squarely in the middle of the intersection. The constable waved to him to go on, but up in his office Judge Burton had an idea. This was a boresome period for the judge, and for all the other lawyers. He quickly got a few of them together and they drew up a long and involved and eloquent document. In effect it was simply an indictment of Sore-Eyes Goodner, but it was phrased in such sonorous accents that, when read, it sounded like the Declaration of Independence fused with Magna Carta.

Judge Burton's office was roomy and Sore-Eyes Goodner was brought into it for arraignment. A dozen lawyers were present as the flowery document was read to the prisoner. He didn't know what on earth was happening to him, but whatever it was, he knew it was pretty bad.

The normal procedures of the courts were not followed with exactitude. It was decided that Sore-Eyes Goodner should be brought to trial immediately. He must be given adequate counsel. Judge Burton took a list of all available lawyers and divided it in half. One group would prosecute, one would defend. Moreover, the court ruled that inasmuch as the defendant would be deprived of his ordinary means of making a livelihood during the trial of his case, a fund would be provided to make up this deficit. Then the trial began.

It lasted for three weeks. Word of it spread over that whole section of the State, and people came from miles around to sit in for a spell. It was a field day for the lawyers involved. Each was given an assigned period for speaking, usually half a day at a stretch, and the oratory was wonderful. Each lawyer outdid himself, for this was an opportunity to let down all the floodgates, to splatter the premises with high-flown language. One by one they took their places on the floor and tried to out-speechify each other. Their orations ranged over the whole achievement of man, his glorious history, his splendid heritage. Some of them began with the Garden of Eden and worked down to the invention of the stop sign. Others waved the flag, and cried out against entangling alliances with foreign powers.

Through it all Sore-Eyes Goodner sat, his granulated eyelids lowered, utterly bewildered by the magnificence of the proceedings, rousing himself only occasionally to ask if his mules were being fed. The public demand to attend his trial became so great that a system of charging a dime for admission was installed, thus boosting the fund that would go eventually to the defendant.

By the end of three weeks all the lawyers, both for defense and prosecution, had talked themselves dry, and court time was approaching, so the matter was brought to a conclusion. With some reluctance, Judge Burton issued his verdict. Defendant was acquitted, by reason of the fact that the offense was not his own; the true culprits were his mules. Unfortunately, said the judge, our courts make no provision for the indictment and punishment of mules—a condition which he respectfully called to the attention of the State Legislature.

So it ended, but it is still talked about, for no other court case in the history of that section has ever attracted so much attention as the Trial of Sore-Eyes Goodner.

One of the most famous orators of the old South was Sergeant S. Prentiss of Mississippi. As a leading lawyer of the State, Prentiss followed the circuits. On one occasion he and a friend, Judge Gohlson, arrived in the town of Raymond and put up for the night at the old Oak Tree Inn.

The two men were asleep in the same bed when Prentiss was awakened. Bedbugs were nipping at him. He awoke Judge Gohlson and they held a conference on procedure. They decided to attack, so they got out their pistols, and began banging away at the bed. The shooting aroused the entire house and the landlord, arriving on the scene, flew into a rage. Prentiss promptly ordered him to leave the room, contending that he was only "exercising the right of self-defense—the right which the law of God and the law of man had given him." Then he and Judge Gohlson resumed their shooting until the bedstead and bedclothes were riddled. Finally they succeeded in capturing one of the offending bugs. The two lawyers argued about the disposition of this varmint's case. It was agreed that the bedbug should be "fairly and impartially tried by a *jury of his countrymen.*"

Members of the landlord's family were brought in and compelled to sit as the jury. Other townspeople arrived, and a local attorney was designated to sit as judge. The prisoner was then arraigned and the trial began.

Judge Gohlson, described as one of the most able lawyers in Mississippi, spoke for the prosecution—spoke for two solid hours. Then the silver-tongued Prentiss took over in behalf of the bedbug, and he spoke for four hours. According to Mississippi legend, it was one of the most brilliant orations of his entire career and when it was finally concluded, the jury acquitted the bedbug.

* * *

It remained, of course, for the Westerners to set up the court for a trial that ranks as a classic of its kind. Mark Twain tells the story in *Roughing It:*

General Buncombe was shipped out to Nevada in the invoice of territorial officers, to be United States Attorney. He considered himself a lawyer of parts, and he very much wanted an opportunity to manifest it—partly for the pure gratification of it and partly because his salary was territorially meager (which is a strong expression). Now the older citizens of a new territory look down upon the rest of the world with a calm, benevolent compassion, as long as it keeps out of the way—when it gets in the way they snub it. Sometimes this latter takes the shape of a practical joke.

One morning Dick Hyde rode furiously up to General Buncombe's door in Carson City and rushed into his presence without stopping to tie his horse. He seemed much excited. He told the general that he wanted him to conduct a suit for him and would pay him five hundred dollars if he achieved a victory. And then, with violent gestures and a world of profanity, he poured out his griefs. He said it was pretty well known that for some years he had been farming (or ranching, as the more customary term is) in Washoe District, and making a successful thing of it, and furthermore it was known that his ranch was situated just in the edge of the valley, and that Tom Morgan owned a ranch immediately above it on the mountainside. And now the trouble was, that one of those hated and dreaded landslides had come and slid Morgan's ranch, fences, cabins, cattle, barns and everything down on top of *his* ranch and exactly covered up every single vestige of his property, to a depth of about thirty-eight feet. Morgan was in possession and refused to vacate the premises—said he was occupying his own cabin and not interfering with anybody else's—and said the cabin was standing on the same dirt and same ranch it had always stood on, and he would like to see anybody make him vacate.

"And when I reminded him," said Hyde, weeping, "that it was on top of my ranch and that he was trespassing, he had the infernal meanness to ask me why didn't I *stay* on my ranch and hold possession when I see him a-coming! Why didn't I *stay* on it, the blathering lunatic—by George, when I heard that racket and looked up that hill it was just like the whole world was a-ripping and a-tearing down that mountainside—splinters and cordwood, thunder and lightning, hail and snow, odds and ends of haystacks, and awful clouds of dust!—trees going end over end in the air, rocks as big as a house jumping 'bout a thousand feet high and busting into ten million pieces, cattle turned inside out and a-coming head on with their tails hanging out between their teeth!—and in the midst of all that wrack and destruction sot that cussed Morgan on his gatepost, a-wondering why I didn't *stay and hold possession!* Laws bless me, I just took one glimpse, General, and lit out'n the county in three jumps exactly.

"But what grinds me is that that Morgan hangs on there and won't move off'n that ranch—says it's his'n and he's going to keep it—likes it better'n he did when it was higher up the hill. Mad! Well, I've been so mad for two days I couldn't find my way to town—been wandering around in the brush in a starving condition—got anything here to drink, General? But I'm here *now*, and I'm a-going to law. You hear *me!*"

Never in all the world, perhaps, were a man's feeling so outraged as were the General's. He said he had never heard of such high-handed conduct in all his life as this Morgan's. And he said there was no use in going to law—Morgan had no shadow of right to remain where he was—nobody in the wide world would uphold him in it, and no lawyer would take his case and no judge listen to it. Hyde said that right there he was mistaken—everybody in town sustained Morgan; Hal Brayton, a very smart lawyer, had taken his case; the courts being in vacation, it was to be tried before a referee, and ex-Governor Roop had already been appointed to that office, and would open his court in a large public hall near the hotel at two that afternoon.

The General was amazed. He said he had suspected before that the people of that territory were fools, and now he knew it. But he said rest easy, rest easy and collect the witnesses, for the victory was just as certain as if the conflict were already over. Hyde wiped away his tears and left.

At two in the afternoon referee Roop's Court opened, and Roop appeared throned among his sheriffs, the witnesses, and spectators, and wearing upon his face a solemnity so awe-inspiring that some of his fellow-conspirators had misgivings that maybe he had not comprehended, after all, that this was merely a joke. An unearthly stillness prevailed, for at the slightest noise the judge uttered sternly the command:

"Order in the Court!"

And the sheriffs promptly echoed it. Presently the General elbowed his way through the crowd of spectators, with his arms full of law-books, and on his ears fell an order from the judge which was the first respectful recognition of his high official dignity that had ever saluted them, and it trickled pleasantly through his whole system:

"Way for the United States Attorney!"

The witnesses were called—legislators, high government officers, ranchmen, miners, Indians, Chinamen, negroes. Three-fourths of them were called by the defendant Morgan, but no matter, their testimony invariably went in favor of the plaintiff Hyde. Each new witness only added new testimony to the absurdity of a man's claiming to own another man's property because his farm had slid down on top of it. Then the Morgan lawyers made their speeches, and seemed to make singularly weak ones—they did really nothing to help the Morgan cause. And now the General, with exultation in his face, got up and made an impassioned effort; he pounded the table, he banged the law-books, he shouted, and roared, and howled, he quoted from everything and everybody, poetry, sarcasm, statistics, history, pathos, bathos, blasphemy, and wound up with a grand war-whoop for free speech freedom of the press, free schools, the Glorious Bird of America and the principles of eternal justice! (Applause.)

When the General sat down, he did it with the conviction that if there was anything in good strong testimony, a great speech and believing and admiring countenances all around, Mr. Morgan's case was killed. Ex-Governor Roop leaned his head upon his hand for some minutes, thinking, and the still audience waited for his decision. And then he got up and stood erect, with bended head, and thought again. Then he walked the floor with long, deliberate strides, his chin in his hand, and still the audience waited. At last he returned to his throne, seated himself, and began, impressively:

"Gentlemen, I feel the great responsibility that rests upon me this day. This is no ordinary case. On the contrary, it is plain that it is the most solemn and awful that ever man was called upon to decide. Gentlemen, I have listened attentively to the evidence, and have perceived that the weight of it, the overwhelming weight of it, is in favor of the plaintiff Hyde. I have listened also to the remark of counsel, with high interest—and especially will I commend the masterly and irrefutable logic of the distinguished gentleman who represents the plaintiff. But, gentlemen, let us beware how we allow mere human testimony, human ingenuity in argument and human ideas of equity, to influence us at a moment as solemn as this. Gentlemen, it ill becomes us, worms as we are, to meddle with the decrees of Heaven. It is plain to me that Heaven, in its inscrutable wisdom, has seen fit to move this defendant's ranch for a purpose. We are but creatures, and we must submit. If Heaven has chosen to favor the defendant Morgan in this marked and wonderful manner; and if Heaven, dissatisfied with the position of the Morgan ranch upon the mountainside, has chosen to remove it to a position more eligible and more advantageous for its owner, it ill becomes us, insects as we are, to question the legality of the act or inquire into the reasons that prompted it. No—Heaven created the ranches, and it is Heaven's prerogative to rearrange them, to experiment with them, to shift them around at its pleasure. It is for us to submit, without repining. I warn you that this thing which has happened is a thing with which the sacrilegious hands and brains and tongues of men must not meddle. Gentlemen, it is the verdict of this court that the plaintiff, Richard Hyde, has been deprived of his ranch by the visitation of God! And from this decision there is no appeal."

Buncombe seized his cargo of law-books and plunged out of the court-room frantic with indignation. He pronounced Roop to be a miraculous fool, an inspired idiot. In all good faith he returned at night and remonstrated with Roop upon his extravagant decision, and implored him to walk the floor and think for half an hour, and see if he could not figure out some sort of modification of the verdict. Roop yielded at last and got up to walk. He walked two hours and a half, and at last his face lit up happily and he told Buncombe it had occurred to him that the ranch underneath the new Morgan ranch still belonged to Hyde, that his title to the ground was just as good as it had ever been, and therefore he was of opinion that Hyde had a right to dig it out from under there and——

The General never waited to hear the end of it. He was always an impatient and irascible man, that way. At the end of two months the fact that he had been played upon with a joke had managed to bore itself, like another Hoosac Tunnel, through the solid adamant of his understanding.

If the practical joke represents the spirit of the frontier, then the frontier still exists in Nevada. Early in 1953 the government resumed its atomic bomb experiments in the Nevada desert. The most publicized of these test explosions was the one in which two houses were erected near the point of the blast. Dummies of men and women and children were installed in the houses for the purpose of finding out how human beings would fare in an actual bombing. A day or two before the explosion, groups of prominent citizens were escorted into the target area so they might inspect all these arrangements. One of these groups was made up of religious dignitaries. They were about to inspect the interior of one of the target houses when, by good fortune, a military officer went in ahead of them to find out if everything was shipshape. Everything was worse than that. The officer came out and ordered the inspection held up for a few minutes. He gave no explanation to the clergy but soon took them inside and showed them around.

Someone, just prior to the arrival of the religious group, had rearranged the human dummies in the house—placing them in extremely compromising positions.

8

Whipping the Cat

When an Englishman says he's going to whip the cat, he means that he's getting set to play a practical joke. The phrase is of ancient origin and in the beginning described a joke commonly played on country louts. In Grose's Dictionary of the Vulgar Tongue, published in 1785, whipping the cat is described as first involving a wager with the bumpkin that a cat could drag him through a pond. "The bet being made," says Grose, "a rope is fixed round the waist of the party to be catted, and the end thrown across the pond, to which the cat is also fastened by a pack-thread, and three or four sturdy fellows are appointed to lead and whip the cat; these, on a signal given, seize the end of the cord and, pretending to whip the cat, haul the astonished booby through the water."

In the general meaning of the term, many a cat has been whipped in England down through the centuries.

As this book is being put together, word comes from London that the practical jokers have found a new way of having fun with the fountain at the base of Nelson's column in Trafalgar Square. This time they poured a detergent into the pool, and the water from the fountainheads churned up an immense snowy lather. An earlier joker sneaked an assortment of dyes into the fountain, turning the water into assorted colors.

Also of recent vintage is the joke played on Douglas Fairbanks, Jr., whose father was one of the most incorrigible practical jokers in Hollywood. Fairbanks is quite a society figure in London these days and in 1953, before the coronation, Queen Elizabeth and her Philip created a mild social sensation by accepting an invitation to dine at the Mayfair residence of Mr. and Mrs. Fairbanks. In some quarters of London society this whole affair was looked upon as a sanguinary outrage, for Mr. Fairbanks was not only an American—he was a blawdy eck-tor! According to report, the Fairbankses were under extreme nervous tension when the big day arrived, and then came the phone call—it was the power company announcing that the electricity would be shut off that evening while new cables were being laid in the neighborhood. In *Time* magazine's version, "the lights stayed on, but a doctor rushed over before dinner to administer a sedative to the frantic host."

The most talented cat-whipper in all Britain was William Horace De Vere Cole, a proper scamp who died in the middle 1930s. Cole, the same man with the ball of twine who appears in Chapter 1, was a brother-in-law of one Prime Minister, Neville Chamberlain, and bore a striking physical resemblance to another, Ramsay MacDonald. He originated one of the most famous practical jokes of them all—the digging up of a busy street. As in the case of the ball of twine, the excavation joke was impulsive, an inspiration of the moment.

Cole was having his morning constitutional in the neighborhood of Piccadilly when he came upon a gang of workmen equipped with picks, shovels, pneumatic drills and warning signs. The workmen were standing about, apparently awaiting the arrival of their foreman. Cole stepped up to them.

"What the devil do you blokes mean by loafing around here?" he demanded. "Pick up your tools and come along."

They followed him along Piccadilly. At a point near Bond Street he ordered them to stop, and to rope off a large section of the pavement. Bawling orders right and left, Cole paced off the area that was to be excavated. Along came a couple of policemen who took in the scene at a glance, saluted the officious Mr. Cole, and set to work diverting traffic and keeping the sidewalk crowds moving.

Cole took his chance, being aware of the confusions and cross-purposes of the governmental process, and stayed with his workmen throughout the day. By quitting time they had created something that resembled a volcanic crater in Piccadilly, blocking off the whole street.

Dismissing the gang, Cole told them that they need not return on the following day, that a new crew would finish the job. It was midafternoon of the next day before a policeman became suspicious over the absence of any activity and notified the proper authorities. It took another twenty-four hours to repair the damage and restore the busy street to a condition in which traffic could move.

Some years later Hugh Troy executed a similar street excavation operation in New York. Early one morning Troy led four companions down Fifty-fourth Street to Fifth Avenue. They wore overalls, carried picks and shovels and had provided themselves with red lanterns and "Men Working" signs. Opposite the old Rockefeller residence they set to work ripping up the pavement. By noontime they had dug quite a hole in the street. Troy posted flags and signs and they knocked off for lunch. He led his grimy laborers into the dining room of a fashionable hotel near by. The headwaiter was horrified, of course, but Troy was prepared.

"It's all right," he whispered. "It's a little gag the manager wants us to put over."

After a hearty meal, during which some of the other diners stamped out of the place with their noses in the air, Troy led his men back to the excavation. They worked through the afternoon, widening and deepening the hole, then hung up the lanterns and signs and went home. The municipal authorities did not discover the hoax until evening of the following day and they were so bewildered by it that they never did find out who was responsible.

W. H. De Vere Cole's career as a master prankster began during his student days at Cambridge. He was an excellent actor even in those days.

The dark-skinned Sultan of Zanzibar was visiting in London amid pomp and circumstance. The newspapers were filled with accounts of the endless processions and receptions in the Sultan's honor, and the officials of Cambridge were enchanted when they received a telegram announcing that the distinguished visitor would come to Cambridge for a day.

As the hour for his arrival neared the Cambridge dignitaries, wearing their finest robes and decorations, gathered at the railway station. Off the train came the Sultan—a prepossessing figure in garments of purple velvet and a turban of the snowiest white. After him came the members of his entourage, also splendidly caparisoned.

The Mayor of Cambridge tendered a scroll of welcome and the party retired in dignity to the Town Hall, where champagne flowed as freely as the purple prose of the speechmakers. There followed a drive around the University and then the royal party took a train back to London.

That evening a touching memento arrived in the hands of the Cambridge officials, a gift from the Sultan himself. On the card he had written in his own hand: "The dorsal fin from the Sacred Shark of Zanzibar—a token of everlasting remembrance."

The Sultan got off the train at the next station and, after a thorough washing, became W. H. De Vere Cole. His attendants were other Cambridge students. The costumes were shipped back to the theatrical shop where they had been hired, and the boys returned to the routine of student life. The hoax was discovered at once, for the real Sultan had never left London, but Cole and his cronies escaped detection. Their part in the affair was not revealed until after they had finished college.

As stated above, Cole bore a close resemblance to Ramsay MacDonald, the Labor Party leader. He was of a size with the statesman, had the same mustache, the same shock of hair, and he was capable of mimicking the Scot's speech as well as his mannerisms.

Passing through Kew Gardens one spring day Cole came upon a small crowd of laborers having their lunch. One of the workmen took him for MacDonald and yelled:

" 'Ow about a speech there, Mac?"

Cole went into action at once. He began with platitudes and worked slowly into a denunciation of all the principles for which Ramsay MacDonald stood. He damned the trade unions and praised the Torys and announced that as of that moment he was no longer associated with the depraved and rascally Labor Party. His hearers were at first incredulous, then they began to grumble. Their mass behavior grew more menacing with each period of the speech, which Cole wisely concluded walking slowly backward, out of danger. The affair ended with Ramsay MacDonald in full flight.

Cole's friends were never exempted from his schemes, and knew it. One of his closest friends, approaching matrimony, decided on an elaborate church ceremonial. Cole, he reasoned, wouldn't try to disrupt a sacred proceeding with his pranks.

Within the church the ceremony proceeded without a hitch. Cole himself was the soul of dignity in one of the front pews. Bride and groom finally left the altar and emerged from the church. They stood on the steps while the crowd cheered. Then it happened.

Screaming hysterically, a young woman dashed up the church steps. She was beautiful, voluptuous, and dressed to kill. She flung herself upon the petrified bridegroom, clasped him in her arms, showered his face with kisses and cried in the accents of a stricken soul:

"My beloved! If this thing must be, I want you to be happy, but always remember *our* years together, always remember that when *she* grows weary of you, I shall always be waiting!"

Another cry of deep-searing pain and she was gone—gone to a rendezvous with William Horace De Vere Cole, from whom she collected her fee.

Cole, like all men who build reputations as practical jokers, had to be on the alert for the *quid pro quo*. "I have perpetrated ninety-five major practical jokes during my career," he once said, "and have never once been caught out myself."

In theory this statement was true, for he had always been too wily for the snares of others. He admitted, however, that a Corsican had once got back at him. As a young man, visiting on the island of Corsica, Cole played a practical joke on one of the natives, who promptly shot him in the leg.

It was with considerable trepidation that Cole laid plans for his own marriage. Well in advance of the ceremony, he informed all his friends that he was through with buffoonery. He was now ready to settle down, to foreswear all projects bearing the slightest tinge of chicanery or guile.

Surprisingly, his friends permitted his wedding to pass without a hint of any horseplay. No funny business attended the departure of the honeymoon couple for Italy. Cole meant what he had said, and his friends believed him.

In the bridal suite of a big hotel in Venice, Cole contemplated his own domestic bliss and the felicitous future that lay before him, happily devoid of plots and snares and delusions. It was evening, the thirty-first day of March. Cole and his bride sat before the fire for a time and then she, being weary from a day of sightseeing, decided to retire.

Cole stayed by the fire. Suddenly the thought entered his mind that the morrow would be All Fools' Day. He battled against the old urge, but it came on him stronger than ever. For years he had never passed up this day of days, had never failed to execute some imaginative assault upon peace and dignity on the first day of April.

What could be so wrong about just one more? A nightcap, one might call it. One for the road. A farewell to practical joking. He arose and brought out two large suitcases, emptied them and lined them with paper. Then he took up the fire tongs and the luggage and crept into the night.

His course led him away from the center of Venice to a suburban locale where he knew he would find a stable. To the attendant he explained his requirements, tendering a bank note to seal the bargain. He was permitted entrance to the barns where, with the aid of the tongs, he filled his suitcases with a commodity that is quite commonplace around stables and barns.

Quickly he returned to Venice, to the picturesque Piazza di San Marco. As you know, the city proper has no paved thoroughfares save only those in the great piazza. The rest are canals, and the streets are liquid. A horse in the Piazza di San Marco is just . . . well, it's simply impossible.

Yet on the morning of April 1, 1931, the early-rising citizens who entered the piazza bruised their eyes with rubbing.

Impossibilità! Santa Maria! Miracolo! In the night horses had come! Not one horse, but many, and ridden by angels no doubt! There lay the evidence, all around the square, past the great Cathedral of St. Mark's and the Palace of the Doges. The word spread swiftly over the city and thousands came to stare and to wonder at this great thing that had happened.

Exit William Horace De Vere Cole, with belly laugh.

9

More Blows for the Cat

The late Harry Reichenbach, press agent in the grand style, played tremendous practical jokes as a means of publicizing his clients, who usually were motion picture companies. Mr. Reichenbach enjoyed being paid large fees for this work, but occasionally he'd exercise his talents for the sake of the devil that was in him.

Back in 1917 Mr. Reichenbach became acquainted with a man who ran a small art store in Brooklyn. The art dealer was in trouble. He had imported some copies of a nude painting by a third-rate Frenchman named Chabas, and now he was stuck with them. Couldn't sell a single one. He spoke of his woe to Mr. Reichenbach and Mr. Reichenbach went to work.

He cleared the display window and then set a copy of the French picture, which was called *September Morn*, in the center of the window. Then he went out and hired forty or fifty street urchins, at a dollar per urchin. When the thimble had been rigged, an anonymous phone call was made to Anthony Comstock, the celebrated censor of public morals. An outrageous thing, Mr. Comstock was told. A painting of a nude hussy on public display, and crowds of little children gathering to ogle it and acquire impure notions from it. Mr. Comstock hurried to the scene and was aghast at what he saw—a veritable mob of children pressing around the display window for a look at the naked lady. Mr. Comstock got a warrant and arrested the dealer, the story flared in the newspapers, and within a matter of days the war in Europe was forgotten and the entire nation was talking about *September Morn*. Before it was over seven million copies of the picture had been sold and its fame had become so great that an oil millionaire paid ten thousand dollars for the original which, before Mr. Reichenbach took action, had been worth about thirty-five cents.

Mr. Reichenbach became so famous in his field that he was asked to come to London by a group of British film executives. They gave a dinner at which the American spoke and answered questions. One Englishman got up and mentioned a movie soon to be released, and asked Mr. Reichenbach how he would go about calling public attention to it.

"Well," said Mr. Reichenbach, "the first thing I'd do would be to set up a stereopticon machine and project a huge ad on the walls of Buckingham Palace."

He got no further than that. There were exclamations of "Egad!" and "The man's head wants seeing to!" The meeting was in an uproar of indignation and voices were heard recommending that the bloody bounder be given his sailing papers and hurled out of the country.

Mr. Reichenbach had made a mistake. Subjecting British Royalty to any form of prank is unthinkable. Beyond that interdiction, in England anything goes.

The eighteenth and early nineteenth centuries were the great days for practical joking in England. The celebrated rakes of the eighteenth century devoted all their time, when they weren't drinking or wenching, to puerile pranking. Their favorite game was to seize old women in the streets and put them in barrels and roll them around. From all that I've read about these boys, they appeared to believe that barrels were invented for the purpose of rolling old women, and of an evening in London a pedestrian was in dire peril, such were the numbers of old women in rolling barrels.

Among the playful figures of those times was the Earl of Sandwich—the one who invented the ham-on-rye. He was a man of considerable wealth and when he could find time to get away from the gambling tables, he sometimes indulged in jinks that were fairly high. He was a blasphemous man, as were most of his cronies, and he directed many of his jokes against the clergy. He had a chapel on his estate and some Sundays he'd fill it with dogs and cats and pigs and sheep and then he'd mount the pulpit and deliver a sermon. He kept a baboon which he called his chaplain. One evening he gave a dinner party which was attended by an important clergyman. The baboon was given a place at the table and when the guests were all seated, the Earl asked the beast to say grace. Whereupon the clergyman spoke: "My lord, I intended performing this duty myself, not knowing until now that you had so close a relative in holy orders."

Literary historians are inclined to sigh and wag their heads when they consider the career of Theodore Hook, who died in 1841. Hook was an author, one of the handsomest men of his time, possessing "quick intelligence, and brilliant wit with an unfailing flow of animal spirits." But he threw himself away on "boisterous buffooneries" instead of behaving himself in a manner favored by the literary historians. His exploits ranged from the simplicity of an incident in the Strand to the complexity of the Berners Street Hoax. Strolling one day in the Strand, Hook noted the approach of an old gentleman of Pickwickian proportions and pompousness. With extreme gravity Hook stepped up to the old gentleman and said, "I beg your pardon, sir, but are you anybody in particular?" With which he turned and walked away.

The Berners Street Hoax has been described as the most famous practical joke in English history. It had its beginning in a wager.

One day in 1809 Hook was strolling with a friend, Sam Beazeley, who wrote farces for the theater. They came to Berners Street, a small avenue famous in that time for its serenity. People of social importance lived in Berners Street because it was so quiet. Sam Beazeley remarked on the peaceful aspect of the street. "I'll lay you a guinea," said Hook, "that within one week I can make this the most talked about street in all of London." The bet was taken on the spot and Hook quietly noted the name on the doorplate at No. 54. The house was occupied by a sedate widow named Tottingham.

A couple of mornings later, before breakfast, a wagonload of coal drew up before Mrs. Tottingham's house. A van of furniture followed, then a hearse with a coffin and a train of mourning-coaches. Two important physicians, a dentist, and a midwife arrived in separate vehicles and now traffic was beginning to pile up. Into the street came a wagon carrying a pipe organ and six men to unload it and after them a load of beer in kegs. There followed a cartload of potatoes; plus coachmakers, clockmakers, carpet-manufacturers, confectioners, wig-makers, opticians and curiosity dealers, all bearing samples of their wares. And after them, an assortment of coachmen, footmen, cooks, housemaids and nursemaids, all seeking employment. Now arrived vehicles of greater elegance, carrying the Governor of the Bank of England, the Archbishop of Canterbury, a Cabinet Minister, the Chairman of the East India Company, the Lord Chief Justice, the Duke of Gloucester, and the Lord Mayor himself.

Berners Street was bedlam. Carriages and wagons and carts were jammed together, their wheels locked, horses leaping about, and above all, the shriek and clamor of the indignant tradespeople, who began venting their rage on one another. Wagons were overturned and their contents scattered, some of the dignitaries were jostled and insulted, and across the way from Mrs. Tottingham's, concealed behind a curtain in a lodging house, Hook and Beazeley enjoyed the entire spectacle. The madness in the street continued throughout the day and a good part of the night, but when darkness fell Hook departed from the neighborhood, departed even from London, and hid himself deep in the country until public indignation died down. He had written hundreds of letters, signing Mrs. Tottingham's name, and he had lured the dignitaries to the scene by letters which hinted that the Berners Street widow was preparing to dispose of her fortune.

Very droll! Also dastardly. And the stunt has been repeated time and again, down to our own day. I recall a variation of the joke that was played on a friend of mine, a music critic who lived in Greenwich Village. A few days after Christmas a classified ad appeared in one of the New York papers, saying, "Will pay good prices for used Christmas trees." My friend's name, address and phone number were given. The entire block was soon jammed with people carrying their old Christmas trees, the phone rang constantly, and one of the callers was the Erie Railroad, which had two carloads of surplus trees to dispose of. The victim of this joke, after trying to cope with the Christmas tree avalanche for a couple of days, had his phone disconnected and fled to Florida.

Matching the Berners Street Hoax for confusion and violence was the Great Bottle Joke, perpetrated by highborn Englishmen in 1749. It began as a discussion in a London club, the topic being human gullibility.

"I'll wager," said the Duke of Montague, "that let a man advertise the most impossible thing in the world, he will find fools enough to fill a playhouse and pay handsomely for the privilege of being there."

"Surely," spoke up the Earl of Chesterfield, "if a man should say that he would jump into a quart bottle, nobody would believe that."

The Duke said people *would too* believe it. The wager was made and the distinguished gentlemen set to work composing the advertisement. It said that at half-past six on the following Monday, at the New Theatre in the Haymarket, a Person would appear who performed several most surprising things. Among other things, the person would enter a common wine bottle in full view of the audience, and while inside it he would sing.

The public stormed the theater at the appointed hour. The place was packed, with hundreds outside clamoring to get in. The audience was patient for a while, but when nothing happened and the stage remained bare, it began grumbling and then yelling. Someone threw a lighted candle on the stage and that started the riot. Every seat in the theater was smashed, everything in sight was ripped to pieces and the debris was carried into the street and burned.

Morris Bishop, a professor of Romance languages who is among the contributors to *The New Yorker*, edited a fat, fine book called *A Treasury of British Humor*. Within its pages he gives somewhat reluctant consideration to the practical joke, in explaining his selection of a portion of the biography of E. A. Sothern, by Pemberton. Writes Mr. Bishop:

> Someone could write an interesting volume on the Decline and Fall of the Practical Joke. A good medieval practical joke ended in the loss of a limb by the victim, or even in a witty decapitation. Jonathan Swift's enormous jokes were designed only to drive the butt insane. With the softening of manners in the nineteenth century, the practical joke became a simple device for causing physical and mental pain. Our current jesters aim at producing a bewildered frenzy in the victim, who sees the most fantastic results proceed from apparently familiar causes. A modern

joker seeks to reproduce on the intellectual plane the phenomena of the exploding cigar.

Edward A. Sothern, the celebrated actor, the creator of Lord Dundreary in Our American Cousin, devoted his apparently ample leisure to the prosecution of practical jokes. I choose a few examples from the many given by his adoring biographer. I will say that they are funny, at least to read about.

What Mr. Bishop is trying to say, I think, is that by flogging himself real hard he is able to discern some humor in practical jokes. No, he doesn't quite go that far. He hedges a little. He's not quite sure the practical jokes are funny; they only become funny when he can *read about* them. While we're at it, I'd like to take up the cudgels and cudge a little on behalf of Mr. Sothern's reputation. The imputation, in Mr. Bishop's second paragraph, is that Mr. Sothern didn't work too hard at his profession, preferring to waste valuable time on sordid practical jokes. It strikes me as significant that Mr. Sothern's wasted time got him thirteen solid pages in Mr. Bishop's survey of British humor. And finally, I don't understand what Mr. Bishop means by the Decline and Fall of the Practical Joke. Mr. Bishop teaches at Cornell University and if there is one single spot on earth today where the practical joke flourishes best, it's Ithaca.

As for E. A. Sothern, he always referred to his practical jokes as "sells." He chose for his victims his closest friends or complete strangers—anyone at all who came his way.

He had a way of playing a joke on one victim, then giving the thing a deft twist to turn it on someone else. He once gave a dinner for a dozen gentlemen, one of whom was late in arriving. Sothern and the others were at the table when a servant announced the arrival of the tardy one. "Quick!" ordered the host. "Everyone get down, and under the table. We'll give him a good shock!" All of his guests dropped to the floor and crawled beneath the table. In walked the latecomer. "Where is everyone?" he asked. "Strange thing," answered Sothern. "The moment they heard your name they all got under the table."

The actor's skill with what might be called the cumulative joke is well illustrated by his account of an adventure in a Philadelphia hotel. He was having breakfast in the dining room when he noticed an irascible old gentleman who was muttering and complaining about the service. Questioning the headwaiter, Sothern found out the man was a General, a bachelor, a permanent resident of the hotel and a permanent grouch.

Forgetting the General for the moment, Sothern took some letters from his pocket and, running through them, happened on one that was a prop letter—a letter which was used in the course of a play. It began:

"Young man, I know thy secret—thou lovest above thy station; if thou hast wit, courage, and discretion, I can secure to thee the realization of thy most sanguine hopes."

Sothern glanced over at the crotchety old General, then called a waiter and instructed him to leave the room, then return and hand the letter to the man. When the letter was given to him, the General adjusted his spectacles and began reading it, half aloud. He read it over several times, growing more bewildered with each reading, and then he summoned the headwaiter and demanded to see the servant who had brought him the letter. That worthy couldn't be found, and now the General began to storm and rant. Soon he was kicking the furniture and threatening to punch the idiot who had sent him the insane note.

Meanwhile three ladies joined Sothern at his table and, noticing the General's behavior, asked about him. "Please keep very quiet and don't attract his attention," Sothern warned the ladies. "He's an escaped lunatic, a murderer. The keepers are just outside the door, waiting to seize him, and that letter was sent in as a decoy." The ladies became alarmed and left the table, hurrying through a door at the other end of the room.

Now a waiter captain, witnessing the hurried departure of the ladies, came up to Sothern and asked if they had been dissatisfied with their breakfasts. Sothern told him that the youngest lady in the group was actually the General's daughter, that she had written the letter to him, that she was a dangerous maniac at times and that he, Sothern, had asked the young woman's friends to get her out of the room before she flew into a homicidal fit.

Was this enough? Not for E. A. Sothern. He finished his breakfast and went to the desk in the lobby, where he approached the clerk and asked whether the headwaiter was quite sound in his mind. He told the clerk that the headwaiter quite clearly hated the General. "If I were you," he said to the clerk, "I would test it by going up to the headwaiter suddenly and asking, 'Don't you think you will get yourself into trouble about that letter of the General's?' "

The clerk went at once to the headwaiter and asked the question. The headwaiter began stammering excitedly, completely confused and frightened by the way things were going. The clerk had his back to Sothern, who now began making signs to the headwaiter that he'd better get out of the way, that the clerk was armed with a knife and might become violent at any moment.

At this point the angry General came stomping out of the dining room, headed for the desk, and the entire ground floor of the hotel was in a hubbub—each person thought that all other persons were hopelessly mad, and on the verge of homicidal assault. Sothern quickly paid his bill, grabbed up his bag, and departed. He said later that he never did find out how things came out.

Another of Sothern's victims was a Mr. Philip Lee, an Englishman who had just arrived for his first visit to New York. Talking with the actor, Mr. Lee expressed doubts as to the existence of the wild and delightful American

Bohemian life of which he had heard. Sothern told him that his letters of introduction were all to the wrong people, that he'd arrange for Mr. Lee to meet some of the Bohemians.

A private dining room was engaged for a supper party at which Mr. Lee was to meet these American notables. As he was introduced to them he found nothing extraordinary in their appearance. He took his place next to Sothern at the head of the table and the soup was served. At this point one of the Americans pulled a battle-ax from under his coat and laid it on the table. Another produced a knife with a long blade. One by one the other Bohemians laid out their weapons—dirks, revolvers, billy-clubs, blackjacks.

"For heaven's sake," whispered Mr. Lee. "What does this mean?"

"Keep quiet," Sothern warned him. "They are getting ready to discuss literature." He said that the members of the group had quarreled about the work of a Mr. Weymyss Jobson, that they were inclined to violence in their arguments, that they had all been drinking heavily, and he only hoped they wouldn't choose this supper party as the scene for settling their dispute. Mr. Lee, growing more nervous with each passing moment, suggested that the police be called, but Sothern told him that would be madness—that if Mr. Lee so much as tried to leave the room he'd be shot like a dog. "Moreover," said Sothern, "no satisfaction would ever be given your relatives in a court of justice. Such is the way of this country."

"It's an infernal country, then!" muttered Mr. Lee.

Suddenly a noisy dispute broke out at the other end of the table and one man leaped to his feet, and began shouting:

"Whoever says that the *History of the French Revolution*, written by my friend David Weymyss Jobson, is not as good a book in every respect as that written by Tom Carlyle on the same subject, is a liar and a thief; and if there is any fool present who wants to dispute it, I am his man!"

All the others leaped to their feet, grabbing for their weapons. There was a flash of blades, and then shots were fired and the room quickly filled with smoke. Through the smoke Mr. Lee could see the Bohemians struggling with one another. Suddenly one of them loomed before him, thrust a long knife into his hand, and yelled:

"Defend yourself! This is butchery—sheer butchery!"

Sothern, all this while, sat quietly in his chair, and spoke to Lee:

"Keep cool, and *don't get shot!*"

By this time the whole hotel had been aroused and Sothern had to confess all. His American Bohemians were all actors.

In England, Sothern enjoyed confounding people on public conveyances. Sometimes he enlisted his actor friends in these exploits. Once he and the comedian John T. Raymond were on a train traveling from Glasgow to Birmingham. They entered a first-class non-smoking compartment, already occupied by two stout English gentlemen.

"Do you object to smoking?" Raymond asked of the two gentlemen.

"Certainly not," they responded.

Raymond then addressed the same question to Sothern.

"I do," he answered. "I do most assuredly. It is a piece of impertinence for you to ask such a question."

"I beg your pardon," said Raymond. "I am only an American and quite unused to the customs of this country."

"That's easy enough to see, sir," said Sothern nastily. "You are evidently either an American or a fool. We don't conduct ourselves that way in England."

Raymond made out that he was terrified by this attack, and slunk into the corner of the compartment. But the two English gentlemen were outraged, and began loudly condemning Sothern for his conduct. Sothern gazed at them with supercilious contempt for a while, then calmly took a cigar from his pocket, lighted it, and began puffing away on it. Now the two gentlemen were fighting mad. They demanded that Sothern put the cigar out, they threatened to call the guard, they talked of leaping upon Sothern and giving him a good lesson in manners. Sothern paid them no heed, but continued puffing away, filling the compartment with smoke. At this point the train drew into a station. Sothern got up, favored the two gentlemen with another contemptuous look, seized Raymond by the arm and said: "Come John, we'll change to another carriage here, and leave these ill-mannered fellows to themselves."

On another occasion Sothern was walking in Regent Street with Stephen Fiske. Suddenly Sothern suggested that they walk apart, and that they both enter the Atlas bus. When Fiske got on the bus he found Sothern sitting opposite him. Fiske didn't know what the scheme was, and looked questioningly toward his friend.

Sothern immediately assumed a belligerent expression and said: "Are you staring at me, sir?"

Fiske took the cue and responded: "No. If I wanted to stare at anybody, I'd stare at a better-looking man than yourself."

At this remark Sothern appeared to go into an uncontrollable rage. The other passengers on the bus were a perfect audience for this sort of thing—a number of elderly ladies, two sedate gentlemen who appeared to be clergymen, a farmer from the country. Sothern leaped to his feet preparatory to attacking Fiske. The clergymen and the farmer rushed up and engaged in a violent struggle with him, trying to keep him from fighting. When they got the bellicose Sothern quieted down, he demanded that the bus be stopped and that Fiske step outside and take his medicine. "I prefer to settle it right here in the bus!" shouted Fiske, and Sothern went into an even more violent tantrum. He took off his overcoat and handed it to the nearest old lady to hold.

"No man on earth," he howled, "can speak to me like that and live, with the exception of my good friend John Robinson of Philadelphia."

"My name is Robinson," spoke up Fiske, "and my Christian name is John, and I have just arrived from America, but I don't happen to have the pleasure of your acquaintance, nor do I want it."

Instantly Sothern's manner changed. He climbed over several of the other passengers and clasped Fiske in his arms, saluting him as his old friend from Philadelphia. He announced to everyone on the bus that this was his dearest friend, that this was one of the happiest moments of his life, and that he and John Robinson were now going out somewhere and celebrate. They left the bus arm in arm, having given the old women and the clergymen and the farmer something to talk about for the remainder of their lives.

Sothern was an eternal harassment to tradespeople and his exploits in this direction are best illustrated in an account of his experience with the ironmonger's clerk.

Accompanied by a Mrs. Wood, the actor walked into an ironmonger's shop and said to the clerk, "Have you the second edition of Macaulay's *History of England?*" The clerk smilingly explained that this was an ironmonger's, and mentioned the name of a neighboring bookseller.

"Well, it don't matter whether it's bound in calf or not," said Sothern.

"But, sir, this is *not* a bookseller's."

"It doesn't matter how you wrap it," said Sothern. "A piece of brown paper will do—the sort of thing that you would select for your own mother."

"Sir!" shouted the young man, thinking his customer was deaf. "We do not keep books! This is an ironmonger's shop!"

"Yes," said Sothern, "I see the binding is different, but as long as the proper flyleaf is in, I'm not very particular."

"But sir!" cried the young man. "Can't you see that you've made a mistake and come into the wrong shop?"

"Certainly," said Sothern, "but I'm in no hurry. I'll wait while you fetch it down."

The clerk now went to the rear of the shop to summon the proprietor, who came forward and confronted Sothern.

"What is it that you require, sir?" he asked.

"I want," said Sothern calmly, "a small, ordinary file, about six inches in length."

"Certainly," said the proprietor, and giving his assistant a blistering glance, went and got it.

Sydney Smith, the clergyman who still ranks as one of England's greatest wits, was not averse to occasional practical jokes at his country estate. On one occasion, when guests were due down from London, he fastened oranges on the shrubs bordering his driveway. Another time one of his lady guests suggested that his paddock would be much prettier if it contained a couple of deer. The following morning when she looked out the window of her bedroom, she saw two donkeys wearing impressive antlers.

Like so many others, Smith insisted that he was against practical joking. He said his attitude was the same as that of the Marquis of Hertford. The Marquis had been tormented by pranksters at Sudbourn and finally remarked that there was no way of telling how much melted butter a gentleman could bear in his pockets before losing his temper and flogging someone.

Yet Sydney Smith told his friends that there was one joke he would love to see repeated—a joke played on a certain Mr. O'Brien in London. O'Brien's friends conspired with his servants and one night they boarded up the outside of his bedroom window so not a single ray of light could penetrate to the room. In the morning when he awoke O'Brien rang for his servant, who appeared in nightclothes, yawning and carrying a candle. "Are you ill, sir?" asked the servant. O'Brien apologized, dismissed the servant, and tried to go back to sleep. After two hours of tossing, he rang again, and the servant appeared as before. O'Brien couldn't believe it was still night. "Open the shutters," he commanded, and they were opened. No daylight.

O'Brien was kept in his bed in this manner throughout the day, until, driven by hunger, he got up and went outside, to find that he just barely had time to dress for a late dinner engagement.

This joke, which Sydney Smith admired, was similar to another attributed to Richard Brinsley Sheridan. A Dr. Parr, friend of Sheridan's, believed that an east wind was bad for his health, that he might even die of an illness brought on by exposure to such a wind. Accordingly, whenever the wind was from the east, Dr. Parr would not set foot outside his lodgings. One night Sheridan climbed to the roof of Dr. Parr's house and fastened the weathercock to indicate an east wind. The doctor didn't come out of his house for two weeks—at which time the fraud was exposed.

In London some years ago a man named Pierce Bottom, weary of jokes about his name, spent several days combing through the telephone directories, seeking people who had "bottom" in their names. He found dozens—Bottom, Bottomley, Winterbottom, Throttlebottom, Greenbottom, Sidebottom, Higginbottom, and so on. He arranged for a dinner to be served in the sub-basement of a London building, and sent engraved invitations to all the "bottoms." Most of them showed up, but Pierce Bottom did not, and the guests found that each of them had to pay his own check. The entree was rump roast.

In 1860 many of the most prominent residents of London received fancy invitations to attend a special function. The invitations read: "Tower of London. Admit Bearer and Friend to view the annual Ceremony of Washing the White Lions, on Sunday, April 1. Admittance Only at White Gate."

Scores of carriages converged on the Tower that day, creating great confusion as their occupants tried to locate the White Gate. No white lions were washed that April Fools' Day.

* * *

The present Lord Halifax, formerly Ambassador to the United States, was traveling to Bath in a railway compartment, also occupied by two very prim middle-aged ladies who were strangers to each other. The train entered a tunnel and the compartment was engulfed in darkness. Lord Halifax placed the back of his hand to his mouth and kissed it noisily several times. When the train reached his station he arose, doffed his hat, and said, "To which of you charming ladies am I indebted for the delightful incident in the tunnel?" He left them glaring hatefully at each other.

10

La Mauvaise Farce

Inasmuch as the practical joke has been brought to its finest flower by the exercise of American know-how, most of the examples contained in this compendium are American. Yet, as we shall see in a number of cases, the American practical joker has borrowed liberally from the foreigners. The fake work of art, used as a means of ridiculing cultural fads and fashions, or critics, or parvenu collectors, crops up in American social history time and again. Yet it dates back to Michelangelo. The great Florentine carved a Cupid, broke off one arm, and then buried the statue. Giving it time to season in the ground, he then arranged to have it "discovered." The Cupid became an overnight sensation, for even in the time of Michelangelo a thing that was old was better than a thing that was new. Perhaps Michelangelo's joke was directed against that very supposition. In any event, the Cardinal of St. George bought the statue, paying a goodly sum for it, and Michelangelo let him enjoy it and show it off for a while before finally telling him the truth. The artist restored the missing arm to the Cupid and the Cardinal presumably joined in the general laughter and said he'd keep the statue anyway. The record of this transaction is not complete. The Cardinal, being human, surely must have found a way of getting back at Michelangelo, putting sawdust in his umber or some such thing.

Hierarchs of the Church were not above such playfulness, as witness the case of Marcus Sittich, a nephew of

Pope Paul V and Archbishop of Salzburg in the seventeenth century. The Archbishop built a palace at Hellbrunn Gardens near Salzburg and incorporated into it what *Life* magazine describes as "one of the most fiendish practical jokes in history." It was not very fiendish. The Archbishop's trick was simply to squirt water all over his guests. He had the palace and the grounds booby-trapped with hidden nozzles and sprays. Guests at his lavish dinners, held in the garden, would no more than get into their seats when the showers would descend on all but the host. The pathways through the gardens were lined with sprays and unsuspecting callers at the palace entrances were doused with water coming from a dozen different directions. The palace still stands and the water system still works, today's victims being the many tourists who visit the place.

In the same century the Archbishop's gimmick was reproduced in England with an interesting improvement. A visitor at Wilton House, seat of the Earl of Pembroke, reported: "In the gardens were very curious waterworks . . . There was a looking-glass, in which, if any lady beheld her face, a pipe under her feet was sure to convey the water to her thighs." Livelier, perhaps, than the blowhole of the American amusement parks.

Now let us move from Salzburg to California. Andrea Sbarboro, an Italian immigrant, arrived in San Francisco in the 1850s and in time became a grocer. Twenty-odd years later he was the guiding hand behind the founding of the Italian Swiss Colony at Asti, in Sonoma County, one of the largest wineries in the world. As the Colony prospered, Sbarboro built himself a summer home at Asti, copied after the Casa de Vetri at Pompeii. And he copied, too, the Archbishop's practical joke. The grounds of Sbarboro's estate were a maze of hydraulic booby traps and, like the Archbishop, he loved to drench his guests when they were dining outdoors. There was, of course, much drinking of wine at Sbarboro's parties, and he built a cool grotto which was equipped with hammocks, where sleepy guests could retire for a rest. The moment a guest got into a hammock, a cascade of water descended upon him. Sbarboro had improved on the Archbishop's water system, which required that hidden servants open the valves. Sbarboro's pressure valves let the victims drench themselves. Sbarboro was a great practical joker in other directions, but he was also a serious man at times. When the threat of national prohibition arose, he made an earnest attempt to convince the nation that drunkards would disappear if everyone drank wine. He contended that he could cure chronic alcoholics. He proposed that every person arrested for drunkenness be sentenced to thirty days in jail, and served light wines with his meals. At the end of the term, said Sbarboro, the drunk would never again drink hard liquor. Curious.

Thus Sbarboro borrowed from the Archbishop of Salzburg. And there is a famous case in which Hollywood borrowed from Budapest.

Years ago Ferenc Molnar, the Hungarian playwright, was walking along the street in Budapest when he came to the home of his friend, Viktor Jacobi, the composer. Inside the house Jacobi was playing a song he had just written. Molnar lurked in the street, listening. The composer played the number through several times and Molnar was able to memorize it.

A few days later the two men met and during a lull in their conversation, Molnar began casually humming the tune. Jacobi was aghast. "Where did you hear that?" he demanded. Molnar told him he had heard the song recently in Paris, that it was a big hit there.

"Impossible!" cried Jacobi. "It's a new piece I've just finished!"

Molnar assured him that the song was the work of another man, that it was already the rage in Paris, that Jacobi had unconsciously plagiarized it. He convinced Jacobi that the composer had heard the tune, and forgotten, and then set it down in the belief that it was his own.

Years later in Hollywood this joke was repeated but on a more elaborate scale. It involved two of the leading musical figures in the motion picture industry—Max Steiner and Victor Young.

Steiner had just finished a symphonic composition, which he considered to be one of the finest things he'd ever done. He invited Victor Young to come to his house and hear it. Young arrived on the grounds as Steiner was playing his new composition. Young listened awhile, jotting down the basic theme, and then tiptoed away and telephoned Steiner that he wouldn't be able to come.

On the following day Young was making a recording with his orchestra. When the serious work was done, he had his musicians perform the Steiner opus on a record. Then he went home and hooked his record player up to his radio.

Steiner was invited to dinner at Young's house. During the evening Young turned on the radio to get a newscast, and Steiner froze in his seat—behind the talk of the newscaster an orchestra was playing theme music—his new masterwork! Steiner almost went out of his mind. "I swear to you," he told Young, "that I can't remember having heard it before—but I must have heard it, and stolen it without realizing it!"

If the Russians are claiming the practical joke as their invention the fact has escaped my notice. As a people they are reputed to have a sense of humor, though it seems to me it reaches its finest expression in the merry little game of Russian roulette. The nearest I can come to finding a Russian practical joker is in Vladimir de Pachmann, one of the greatest pianists of all time.

Pachmann was an unconventional man even on the concert stage. He originated a gag which is still in use. He came on stage one evening and found that the piano stool was too low and he couldn't raise it, so he called for a large book. He placed the book on the stool, sat down on it, and tried a few chords. The elevation was still bad. He got up, opened the book, tore out one page and cast it aside, sat down again, smiled to show his satisfaction, and proceeded with his concert.

Pachmann, who was generally considered to be the greatest interpreter of Chopin's works, hated all music critics. In Berlin, where he played many concerts, he hated one critic in particular—a man who worshiped Chopin. One night Pachmann came on stage carrying a pair of socks. He stepped to the footlights, held them aloft, and in pontifical accents announced that they were the selfsame socks George Sand had knitted for Chopin. Then he draped them on the piano, where they remained throughout the program.

On the following day, as Pachmann had anticipated, the hated critic arrived at the pianist's place of residence. Could he, please, see the socks up close? Perhaps even handle them gently? Pachmann got out the socks. The critic seized them and pressed them to his lips, kissing them over and over with his eyes closed. After that the pianist let word get around in Berlin music circles that the socks were actually his own, and that he had worn them for two weeks without having them washed.

During a brief stay in Paris I made random inquiries touching on the French attitude toward practical jokes. One cultivated Frenchman said the institution is almost unknown. "We," he said, "regard the whole of life as a practical joke, and we do not try to improve upon it."

There are others with a contrary view, and they summon the French language as witness. The proper definition of the word *farce* is practical joke, and a *farceur* is a practical joker. A *fredaine* is a prank, and *espièglerie* means a roguish or playful trick. A common expression, *mauvais tour*, is understood to mean a practical joke of the worst kind; *mauvais* means bad, evil, ill-natured, injurious, unpleasant and wrong.

A French lady of my acquaintance, member of an upper-class family, has told me of the embarrassment she suffered in boarding school at the hands of her uncle. She no more than got settled in school than a series of postal cards began arriving from the uncle. They were invariably written in the crude script and language of a hopeless illiterate and they usually concluded with the line, "I hope you grow up to be as smart as your uncle." The cards were read, of course, by almost everyone in the school, and the poor girl's protests that her uncle was actually a brilliant and educated man were to no avail.

In the 1890s Anatole France was a candidate for election to the Académie Française, composed of the so-called "Forty Immortals." Under the prodding of his friends, France campaigned for the seat. One member, an old foof named Henri de Bornier, told France he wouldn't vote for him—his ballot would go to a certain editor who used Bornier's stuff. It turned out, however, that two seats were vacant in the Academy, a deal was made, and Anatole France became officially immortal. He did not forget Bornier.

The Forty Immortals, among other things, busied themselves with revising the dictionary, and at one meeting they were discussing the correct definition of the word *anneau*, or ring. They droned on about finger rings and smoke rings and rings of Saturn.

France was sitting beside the same Henri de Bornier who had refused him his vote, and Monsieur de Bornier was snoring gently as the debate proceeded. Suddenly France nudged him awake and whispered excitedly:

"They have forgotten Hans Carvel's ring!"

"What's that! What's that!"

"Tell them they must not forget Hans Carvel's ring!"

Coming out of his snooze, Bornier thought that some horrible mistake was being made, and cried out:

"Wait! Don't forget the ring of Hans Carvel!"

Most of the Immortals turned to him with puzzled looks,

though a few were beginning to show signs of shock. Anatole France wasn't content.

"They *must*," he whispered, "they *must* include the ring of Hans Carvel!"

"I demand," bellowed Bornier, "that recognition be given the ring of Hans Carvel!"

Bornier never quite lived it down. The story of Hans Carvel's ring appears in the works of Rabelais, and is a classic of obscenity. I would like to repeat it here, in the interests of elucidation and clarity, but that would not be proper. It is available to you in almost any bookstore, even in fine leather binding; it is to be found in the private libraries of many of our most proper families; but for me to include it in this book would be a most improper and vulgar act and would fetch down upon me the condemnation of all right-thinking people.

François Rabelais himself was a man who delighted in practical jokes, especially if there was purpose behind them. On one occasion he found himself stranded and without funds in a provincial village. He needed to get to Paris immediately, but he didn't even have enough money to pay his bill at the inn where he was staying. He did, however, have several bottles of wine. So he lettered out some labels and fastened them to the bottles, saying, "Poison for the King," "Poison for the Queen," "Poison for the Duc d'Orléans," and so on. He arranged to have these bottles discovered in his room. Forthwith he was seized and swiftly transported to Paris by special carriage. The claim that the French have no appreciation for a practical joke is a base canard. As soon as Rabelais explained his act to the Parisian authorities, they complimented him on his ingenuity and turned him loose.

That word "canard" as meaning an extravagant or absurd report had its origin in a practical joke. A hundred years ago, give or take a week, a playful Parisian named

Norbert Corneillissen turned in a remarkable item to the newspapers. He reported that he had owned twenty ducks. He cut one of those ducks up into bits and fed it to the other nineteen. Then he chopped up another and fed it to the flock. This procedure was continued until the last duck had devoured her remaining companion. Corneillisen now pointed out for the edification of science and the general public that one of his canards thus had eaten its nineteen cronies in a wonderfully brief period of time.

This story was reprinted throughout Europe and even got into the American newspapers, and the word "canard" came to designate a preposterous hoax.

Let us now go to the other side of the earth and listen to the laughter of the Living Buddha. The story belongs to Dr. Roy Chapman Andrews. Years ago Dr. Andrews went into Mongolia to visit the palace of the Living Buddha, one of the most sacred individuals ever to walk the earth like a natural man. From all over the realm came pilgrims, just to get a look at him, to scoop up handfuls of sacred dirt on which his feet had trod, and to get his blessing.

A short while before Dr. Andrews' arrival, the Living Buddha had imported a Delco electric plant for his palace. But he had discovered a better use for it than the mere lighting of his house. It was his custom to sit at a certain window of his palace and give his blessing, once a day, to the kneeling pilgrims in the yard below. Now he strung a wire from the palace to the courtyard, and ran it across the yard by a series of small posts. As the pilgrims assembled for the daily blessing, they would be instructed to kneel and grasp the wire with both hands. Then the Living Buddha, seated by the window, would throw the switch. The pilgrims reacted with much the same kind of jerks as worshipers at the old-style American camp meetings. And the Living Buddha had so much fun that he ordained three blessings every day instead of just one.

11

Genius at Work

If you would care to know something about the earlier career of Hugh Troy, I would recommend a book titled *La Jungla de Papel,* published in Barcelona. The fifth chapter in this book (*Capítulo V*) is titled *En Particular de Hugh Troy.* The entire volume is almost unreadable, being written in a sort of gibberish, although the name of the author, H. Allen Smith, reads well and easily, and is a delight to the eye. I have taken the pains to make a rough translation in order to set down here the gist of *Capítulo V.*

We have already seen Hugh Troy as leader of the gang of young men who dug up Fifth Avenue. *La Jungla de Papel* tells of that joke, and of quite a few others. Many of Hugh's exploits date back to his undergraduate days at Cornell. He once purloined the rubber overshoes of an absent-minded professor and painted them to resemble human feet. Then he covered them carefully with lampblack. The next time the professor wore them, the rain washed off the lampblack and the good man appeared to be walking about the campus in his bare feet. When the people who lived next door to the Troys went off to Europe one springtime, Hugh and his brother wired their big cherry tree full of apples.

After Hugh finished college he moved on to New York,

ambitious to make a name for himself as an artist, which he soon did. But most of his spare time was spent in fantastic and imaginative pranking. He is the man who bought a park bench and, with a friend, sneaked it into Central Park. With the approach of the first cop, Hugh and his friend picked up the bench and started walking away with it. They were arrested, of course, but at the stationhouse Hugh delivered an indignant speech touching on human rights and produced a bill of sale showing he owned the bench. He repeated the stunt several times, until the cops got so mad that the game became dangerous.

The manager of a Greenwich Village movie house once offended Hugh in some way, and Hugh got even. He went into the theater one night and quietly released a dozen moths; these creatures flew directly into the beam from the projection room and stayed there, mottling the picture on the screen.

On election night in 1932 Hugh was walking through Times Square when his eye fell on a stack of tabloid extras carrying big black headlines: **ROOSEVELT ELECTED.** He bought a dozen copies and took them home and stored them away in a closet. Three years later, on New Year's Eve, Hugh assembled a group of his friends. They went out and rode the subway trains, each with a copy of that newspaper, and great was the bewilderment of other passengers, seeing three or four different men calmly reading a newspaper which proclaimed that Roosevelt was elected.

Those are some of the Troy exploits to be found in *La Jungla de Papel.* Fourteen years have passed since that account was first put on paper. Today Hugh Troy lives in Washington. He is an eminently successful artist and his murals enhance the walls of famous buildings. He doesn't like to be called a practical joker. He considers himself to be a man with an off-beat imagination and a strong inclination to make life more interesting, both for himself and for other people. He believes that his various stunts have done more good than harm—that he has brought excitement and wonderment to people whose lives were otherwise quite drab.

Not long ago I went down to Washington and spent a long evening with him and he brought me up to date on his doings, and reached back into his past for some of the adventures he had forgotten to tell me the first time we met. He said, incidentally, that he is retired from the business of confusing people—that he doesn't practice jokes any more. Yet he can't avoid *thinking them up*.

Hugh may have become a practical joker through association with Louis Agassiz Fuertes, the famous painter of birds, who lived at Ithaca and who encouraged the young Troy to become an artist. Hugh remembers that Fuertes, driving one day from Syracuse to Ithaca, spotted a highway sign which proclaimed: JESUS SAVES. Fuertes took the sign off its post and put it in his car and a few nights later set it in a prominent position in front of the Ithaca Savings Bank.

Hugh is an extremely gentle person, soft of voice, unobtrusive in a crowd in spite of his size—he's six feet five. There is nothing flamboyant about him; in fact he borders on shyness. His friends say he is one of the kindliest men on earth, and there is an anecdote that supports this evaluation. In his Cornell days he helped score the track and field meets for the newspapers. It occurred to him one day that there always has to be one boy who is last in every event and he thought about how hurt such a boy must feel. So Hugh invented a character named Johnny Tsal, and Johnny Tsal's name went into the press reports of the meets; Johnny Tsal always ran last in every race.

Many of the Troy stunts were of a minor character, but somehow they had a *feeling* about them. Simply because he was entranced by the word, he once made a sign which said, PINKING DONE, and put it on the front of his house. Nobody ever came in to have any pinking done, but a few people rang the bell to ask what pinking *was*. If Hugh was around, he told the inquirers that "it's a trade secret."

He belonged to a skating club and one day thought up a means of increasing his pocket money. He took a cigar box and painted it and fastened it to the wall near the entrance to the clubhouse. Above it he placed a small sign, which said: PLEASE HELP! It didn't say who or what needed help. Just PLEASE HELP! A surprising number of people dropped nickels and dimes into the box, and Hugh cleaned it out regularly.

When Hugh was in his teens he and his brother played a game called Getting Grandma Behind. This was a complicated project, requiring manipulation of the newspapers, by which the boys got their grandmother to thinking it was Friday when it was really Sunday, and so on. Today Hugh remembers another conspiracy against Grandma. They would write a letter to Sears, Roebuck & Company ordering an assortment of merchandise such as a corset, three yards of stovepipe, a teething ring and two pounds of nails. When the package would come, plainly addressed to Grandma, she'd open it and examine the articles and exclaim, "Law, me! What a terrible mistake they've made!" Then she'd wrap it up and send it back and write a letter saying Sears, Roebuck had made a mistake. The boys would intercept this letter and substitute one of their own, saying that the mistake was in the order—what Grandma really wanted was quilt wadding, a hot water bottle, a new handle for her clothes wringer and two pounds of soft steel rivets. So another package came and more letters were written, and before long the letters were flying back and forth between Ithaca and Chicago and the chances are Sears, Roebuck was fully as confused as Grandma.

"Those were exciting times for that dear old lady," Hugh recalls. "I like to think that my brother and I made her later years a little more enjoyable than they would have been otherwise. She got more fun out of that Sears, Roebuck business than she'd ever had before in her life."

At the University, Hugh was in the School of Architecture. There was one professor who was continually complaining about the weakness of the ceiling in the room where he taught. He demanded that the school authorities repair and reinforce that ceiling before it fell in on himself and his students. One night Hugh and a few of his cronies crept into the place, carrying ladders and other equipment. Hugh mounted a ladder and painted a large black, jagged hole on the ceiling. Then the boys piled plaster and splinters and other debris around the floor, and departed. The following morning the professor arrived, took one horrified look at the ceiling and the general wreckage, and went scampering off to the Building and Grounds Office, full of indignant I-told-you-sos. The instant he left, in came Hugh Troy and his friends. The black paint on the ceiling was quickly removed, and the debris cleaned up. And back came the professor with the head of the Building and Grounds Office. It is said that the professor used language somewhat alien to the science of architecture.

There was an enormous pipe organ in Bailey Hall, the auditorium where many of the University's principal functions were held. Hugh considered this massive instrument for a long while before devising a proper handling of it. He had to enlist the organist in the conspiracy. Then he built an extra pipe for the organ, bigger than the biggest of all the other pipes, and covered it with gilt paint and set it up so that it wouldn't look conspicuous. All this work was performed during the night preceding a day when there was to be a large and dignified ceremony in the Hall.

In the midst of the big meeting the organist was to render a number. He got well into it when, apparently, he discovered a certain mechanical difficulty. He'd press down on one key and an awful sound, a sort of bray, would come from the pipes. He pretended to be embarrassed, and started over again, but at the same point he'd run into the horribly faulty note. Finally, without consulting the chairman, he stepped to a rear entrance and returned with half a dozen workmen—actually Hugh Troy and his friends. He pointed excitedly to the pipes, finally singling out the biggest of them all. The workmen flung up a couple of ladders and attacked the big pipe, wrenching it loose. It fell to the floor with a crash, breaking open, and out of it came live chickens, ducks, pigeons, and assorted other fowl, both wild and domestic.

Troy and his gang went to great length and considerable expenditure of money sometimes to have their fun. During the period when Lindbergh and the others were making a big thing out of transatlantic flights, Hugh and his friends created a lot of excitement for one day in Ithaca. The wreckage of an airplane was found in a field near the town. Assorted cheeses were scattered over the field, and also a number of letters and other documents. The papers showed that the plane had flown non-stop from Amsterdam, Holland, bound for Amsterdam, New York, bearing good will and cheese. The boys had done a first-rate job of creating airplane wreckage without an airplane.

The best of all the Troy jokes at Cornell, in my own estimation, was the rhinoceros joke. Visiting one day in the home of the artist Fuertes, Hugh noticed a wastepaper basket fashioned from the foot of a rhinoceros. He borrowed the thing from Fuertes and then waited for the proper weather conditions. On a night when a couple of inches of snow had fallen, Hugh and one of his friends went out on the campus with the rhinoceros foot. They had filled it with scrap metal to give it weight, and they had attached a length of clothesline to either side of it. Now they moved across the campus, each holding an end of the clothesline at a distance of perhaps thirty feet from the rhinoceros foot. Carefully they raised it and lowered it to make rhinoceros tracks at the proper intervals in the snow.

When the campus awoke the next morning the strange tracks were found. Professors who knew about animals were summoned, and they inspected the tracks, and exclaimed over them. "Gad, Whitley!" they cried. "It's a *rhinoceros!*"

The trail of the rhinoceros was followed. It led across the campus and down to the shore of Beebee Lake, from which the University gets its water supply. The lake was frozen over, and the rhinoceros tracks led out across the ice to a point about fifty feet from shore and ended at a large gaping hole. Clearly the vagrant rhinoceros had wandered onto the ice too far, and crashed through and drowned.

There wasn't much to be done about it. The local newspapers trumpeted the story, and almost at once half the population of Cornell quit drinking tap water. Those who continued to drink it swore that they could taste rhinoceros in it. And then, after a few days, Hugh Troy let the word get out that the whole thing was a joke—without, of course, any clue to the identity of the jokers.

Hugh seems to know human nature pretty well. He has definite ideas about art, and the public's appreciation of art. Back in 1935, in New York, the first American showing of Van Gogh was held at the Museum of Modern Art. There was much publicity about Van Gogh in the New York newspapers, but the emphasis was on the lurid character of the artist's life, especially on the fact that he had cut off his own ear. When crowds began flocking to the exhibit, Hugh argued with his friends that most of the customers were sensation-mongers rather than art lovers. He decided to test the question. Using chipped beef, he modeled a grisly and withered ear and mounted it in a blue velvet shadow box carrying a neatly lettered inscription:

THIS IS THE EAR WHICH VINCENT VAN GOGH CUT OFF AND SENT TO HIS MISTRESS, A FRENCH PROSTITUTE, DEC. 24, 1888.

Hugh took the little box to the museum and surreptitiously placed it on a table in a room where the Van Gogh pictures were hung. Then he stood back and watched. The chipped beef ear immediately stole the show—the customers ganged up around it, chattering about it, fascinated by it, ignoring the paintings all around them.

Pomposity in all its varied forms irritates Hugh. One summer Sunday a very rich and famous lady held a benefit "carnival" on her estate at Sands Point, Long Island. Assorted entertainers and artists were "commanded" to appear and contribute their services, and among them was Hugh Troy. On his arrival at the big house, he was escorted into the presence of the great lady. "I am giving two minutes to each of you people," she said imperiously. "You are to paint a picture for the auction. Now your two minutes are up. Kindly leave."

The affair was strictly by invitation, and the only people invited were the cream of the social register crowd. Hugh went out and found the supply of art materials. Then he retired to a quiet spot on the premises to paint. He didn't paint a picture—he painted signs. When he had them finished he carried them out the long driveway to the big stone gate which stood beside a busy highway. He placed the signs all around the entrance to the estate, then hitched a ride back to Manhattan. The signs said:

PICNIC PARTIES WELCOME

BASKET PARTIES INVITED

FREE MERRY-GO-ROUND FOR THE CHILDREN

LEMONADE FOR ALL

What causes a man like Hugh Troy to campaign relentlessly against sham and smugness? Hugh isn't sure, but he recalls that when he was a small boy he received a terrible shock when he discovered that people are often not what they seem. Pearl White was in Ithaca, filming some episodes of *The Perils of Pauline*. The Troy lad worshiped her and did his best to get near her in Cascadilla Gorge, where the scenes were being shot. He was constantly being chased away, however, and then one afternoon he was playing in the front yard of the Troy home on Oak Street. Up the street came the famous red Stutz roadster driven by the great heroine herself. She stopped the car directly in front of the Troy house. The boy stared at her in disbelief—she was smoking a cigar! She hopped out of the roadster, swaggered up the lawn, and said:

"Hey, kid, kin I use yer terlet?"

It was too much; he ran weeping into the house, completely disillusioned by the knowledge that Pearl White had to go just like other people.

Hugh Troy went into the Army in World War II and during those exciting years I often caught myself wondering about him and what he might be doing in the way of confounding the brass. Now I know some of it. He took officers' training and in time was sent to a Southern camp which was largely devoted to giving fledgling officers actual experience in leadership. Almost at once he found himself in rebellion against the enormous amount of paperwork he was required to do. Reports, reports, reports, and more reports. He was required to fill out reports on the most trivial details of camp operation, and these reports, great bundles and bales of them, went in to the Pentagon. He thought it was pretty ridiculous and he wanted to protest, but of course he couldn't go to someone and say, "This is pretty ridiculous." He just sat back and waited for inspiration to strike. It struck. In his company's mess hall he had noticed the flypaper ribbons. They were suspended from the ceiling on either side of the hall—ten on one side of the room, ten on the other.

Hugh devised a special report blank and had it mimeographed. It was in re the number of flies trapped during each twenty-four hour period on the twenty flypaper ribbons. The report included a sketch plan of the mess hall, showing the location of each flypaper ribbon in relation to entrances, tables, lights, windows, kitchen and piano. And each flypaper ribbon was identified by code number. Hugh filled out his first flypaper report, making it as complicated as he was able, showing that during the twenty-four hour period covered by the report, Flypaper Ribbon X-5 trapped and retained 49 flies. Ribbon Y-2 did even better—63 flies. And so on. He slipped this report in with the day's accumulation and off it went to Washington. Every day thereafter he sent in his flypaper report. He never did find out exactly what happened in the Pentagon. But he does know that his innovation had quite far-reaching results. About a week after he had sent in his first report, two of his fellow officers called on him.

"You been catching any hell from Washington," they wanted to know, "about some kind of goofy flypaper reports?"

"Why, no," said Hugh. "I don't quite get what you mean."

"It's about a daily report on flypaper ribbons in the mess halls," said one of the officers. "We've been getting directives out of the Pentagon, raising hell with us, wanting to know where our flypaper reports are, why we haven't been sending them in. Do you know anything about flypaper reports?"

"Certainly," said Hugh. "I send mine in every day."

They protested that nobody had told *them* about any flypaper reports, and Hugh showed them the mimeographed blank. They took copies, so they could have some made up for themselves, and they passed the word along to all the other officers and from that day forward every bundle of reports that went in to Washington from the camp included a census of dead flies on the flypaper ribbons. Hugh thinks it's entirely possible that the Pentagon also raised hell with officers at other posts, and set them to work on flypaper reports, and that in the end the daily flypaper report became standard procedure in the Army of the United States.

Captain Hugh Troy went to the South Pacific with the 21st Bomber Command, 20th Air Force, Major General Curtis LeMay commanding. In the midst of a bombing war General LeMay received word that a government folklorist was arriving on the island for the purpose of gathering native tales, and that he should be accorded full cooperation. General LeMay, somewhat impatient at such doings, thought immediately of Captain Troy and Captain Troy was told to cope with the folklorist and get rid of him as quickly as possible. Captain Troy occupied a tent with three other Intelligence officers and they were brought into Operation Folklore.

Hugh was acquainted with a small native boy named Emmanuel. Both the boy's parents had been killed by the Japs and he lived with his old grandfather. Emmanuel had learned English in the American school and, of course, also talked Chamorro. He was a bright boy and he would do anything on earth for Hershey bars and comic books. Captain Troy struck a deal with him.

The folklorist arrived and stated his needs to Captain Troy. Among other things he said that he understood the chief currency in the islands was whisky—that a man with a supply of whisky could get anything he wanted. Accordingly he had brought along a half case of good whisky and he would be willing to pay at the rate of one bottle for every authentic folk tale Captain Troy could get for him. Captain Troy licked his lips and then spoke of the boy Emmanuel. He said that Emmanuel knew all the important folk tales of the islands, but that the boy spoke nothing but the native tongue. The folklorist said that could be handled—he had with him a technical sergeant who understood the language.

So Captain Troy set up the procedure. The Jap bombers came over each night and during that period there was nothing for the four Intelligence officers to do but lie in their cots and wait for two or three hours till the raid was over. They began calling this period the "Mother Goose Hour." For it was then that, under Captain Troy's able direction, they invented the Chamorro folk tales. Captain Troy, with considerable experience in the production of books for children back home, had a wide knowledge of Mother Goose, Aesop's fables, Andersen, the Grimm Brothers, Uncle Remus, Winnie the Pooh, and so on. He drew on all of these sources in constructing fables and fairy tales for Saipan. Once they had polished up a good folk tale, Captain Troy would meet secretly with little Emmanuel, and drill it into him in English. Then the folklorist, the sergeant-interpreter, and Captain Troy would call upon Emmanuel and his grandfather. The boy played his part beautifully and got five chocolate bars and five comic books for each performance. He would sit at the feet of his grandfather and address his story, in his native tongue, to the old man. The sergeant sat near by, taking it all down, and the scholar from Washington stood with Captain Troy, drinking it all in, unutterably thrilled at the way things were progressing. The boy would finish telling his story, his old grandfather would make a vague sort of guttural sound, and a date would be made for another performance the next day.

Back in camp the sergeant would begin translating at once, and the folklorist was in ecstasies—these tales were absolutely fabulous! They would open up a whole new field of inquiry, for there seemed to be definite European and even some American influences in them. One day Captain Troy asked the sergeant what it was the old grandfather grunted out at the end of each of Emmanuel's stories. The grave-faced sergeant said it was rather difficult to translate literally but that what the old man was saying was, "Horse manure." Apparently the sergeant didn't tell the folklorist.

The thing went on until Captain Troy and his tentmates had all the whisky, and Emmanuel was loaded with chocolate bars and comic books, and then the folklorist flew away, to return jubilantly to Washington with the most magnificent yield of his entire career. If he ever found out the truth, Captain Troy doesn't know it. Nor does he feel much like asking.

The 20th Air Force moved on to recapture Guam. Captain Troy fell in with a group of civilian officers who had been newspapermen and press agents in New York and Hollywood. Between air raids these men, in an effort to keep from going nuts (which many of them already were by nature) indulged in long bull sessions. Out of these interminable conversations a figure slowly emerged. They began talking about Señora Cuevas. This old lady became more real and more interesting with the passing of each day. Every man in the group would contribute something to the legend and before long everyone in the group was almost beginning to believe she really existed.

Señora Cuevas was the widow of the first Governor of Guam. She lived in a three-story gingerbread mansion at the other end of Guam. The house stood between the two main runways of the airfield, and was an exact replica of the house where Señora Cuevas had been born in Hoboken, New Jersey. She was a member of the class of 1895 at Cornell and, in truth, had founded the celebrated Cornell Women's Mandolin and Glee Club. She had come out to Guam as wife of the first Governor, who had built the mansion for her, and then her husband had been assassinated. She refused to leave the island, insisting upon staying and performing good works among the natives—even when Guam was in the hands of the Japs. She had, for one thing, donated the furniture for the clubhouse of Guam's conservative social club, the A. R. P. H. A. F. S.—The Agana Royal Palms Halloween and Foxtrot Society. Her ambition was to organize a school to prepare young native boys of good family for Andover and Yale. Unknown to most people, she was a scientist of exceptionable ability.

The natives worshiped the old lady and when the Japs came, they didn't dare abuse her, knowing there would be mass uprisings in her defense. The Japs did, however, find out about the secret laboratory under her big house. They brought in one of their American-trained biochemists and compelled Señora Cuevas to admit him to the laboratory. She pretended to co-operate with him, but all she did was give him confusing formulae and in the end send him away with acid burns from his hips to his eyebrows.

When the island was retaken the seabees had to build an airstrip big enough to handle B-29s and the only available site was on her property. They said they'd have to demolish her mansion, but she talked them out of it and the runways were built on either side of her land. She became a sort of foster mother to all the American airmen. Sometimes their ships would knock the chanticleer off the weather vane on top of her house, but she never got angry so long as the engineers replaced it. She had a small Spanish-style chapel on her grounds and she got the Air Force to install a miniature control board near the altar through which she could keep track of every plane that was out while she prayed for its safe return. And her Saturday night parties became famous. The part of her cellar that wasn't laboratory was well stocked with drinkables and she was liberal with them. She would permit generals and colonels to attend her soirees, but only on condition that they passed the drinks to the enlisted pigs.

There was much more in the way of detail to her story, but the most significant thing about her was her scientific triumph, even though it came too late in the war to do any good. Her experiments were concerned with the sex life of the coral polyp. She realized that the chief handicap to fighting a war in the vast Pacific was the scarcity of landing fields. So she experimented endlessly with polyps and eventually produced a miraculous liquid which accelerated the reproductive activities of these polyps tremendously. Casks of this liquid could be taken out to any point in the South Pacific and spread over the surface of the sea. Within *three days*, such was the stepped up activity of the polyps, a coral island would rise out of the sea, smooth-surfaced and ready for planes to land and take off. But alas, the atom people beat her to the punch, and brought the war to an end before she could get her discovery into action.

Such was the marvelous story of Señora Cuevas and men of the Air Force all over the world knew about her and talked about her. When the war was over, she continued as a tradition of the Air Force, and even the high brass in Washington sometimes sat around and retold the stories about her.

In the post-war years Hugh Troy lived at Garrison, New York. His house overlooked the Hudson River and was directly across from West Point. And up there on the Hudson, Señora Cuevas once again made her presence felt, saving the personnel at West Point from acute discomfort. Hugh got mad at West Point. The buglers, blowing reveille, woke him up at daylight on those mornings when the wind was in his direction. He decided to get even with the Military Academy. He was working out a scheme involving a huge amplifier, and a recording of reveille. He would get up and turn this machine loose and blow reveille a half hour earlier than schedule, and wake the whole damned Academy up. But he never got to it. He was busy working out the mechanical details when he happened to pick up a copy of the *Reader's Digest*. He read the article called *The Most Unforgettable Character I Ever Met*. He thought of Señora Cuevas way out on Guam. Promptly he sat down and began writing the fabulous story. He wrote it as truth, and made a good thing of it, and shipped it off to the *Digest*. Soon he had a letter from one of the editors—they loved it, they'd take it, a fat check would be along soon. But could Mr. Troy make them some sort of an illustration showing the Cuevas mansion? Hugh went to work, and painted a masterpiece. The rococo mansion stands in the center of the picture and on the front steps, waving, is the figure of a little old lady in black bombazine. Overhead two huge bombers are passing, and portions of two others, being serviced, are seen on the runway in the foreground. The Cuevas property is surrounded by an iron picket fence, and a cast-iron deer stands on the lawn. Back of a swaying palm tree stands the little chapel and in the distance, mountains. Hugh drove down from Garrison and delivered the painting, and the *Digest* editor was overjoyed. The two men were walking down a long, cool corridor, headed for the entrance, when along came another editor.

"Hugh Troy!" he exclaimed. "What the devil are *you* up to?"

This second editor knew all about Hugh Troy and within an hour the story of Señora Cuevas was being checked in Washington. The first few air force officers who were approached said certainly they knew about the Señora. Certainly she was real. But then some unknown individual spilled the garbanzos.

Hugh sent back the check and the *Digest* sent back the manuscript and the painting. The *Digest* turned its back on her, but I still believe that Señora Cuevas stands close to immortality.

Hugh Troy, as the most imaginative and ingenious of all practical jokers, rarely is victimized himself. He says that one of the few times he has ever been hoaxed, the joker was not a human being, but a punch bowl. He was once assigned to usher at the fashionable wedding of a friend in New York City. There was a bachelor's wingding the night before, featuring a huge punch bowl. Hugh got to bed late in a Park Avenue hotel and woke late the next morning. He rushed through the business of getting himself into his cutaway, and then ran all the way to St. Bartholomew's Church. The guests were just now arriving so Hugh began ushering. He was being his most polite and elegant self when another usher came up to him.

"Say, who the hell are *you?*" asked the young man.

"I'm Hugh Troy."

"I didn't know," said the other usher, "that you knew Bill and Helen."

"Bill and Helen?" Hugh repeated. "Who's Bill and Helen?"

"Only the people that are getting married."

Then it dawned on him. He was involved in the wrong wedding. *His* people were getting married at St. Thomas Church. He made it just in time to witness the beginning of the ceremony, and too late to do any ushering.

12

The Mental Hot-Foot

Jim Moran insists that he does not play practical jokes. "I administer," he says, "mental hot-foots." We met Jim earlier in this book as the man with the string around his ear and the little golden bucket in his stomach. He was engaged then, under his own definition, in giving people a mental hot-foot.

I have written extensively about Moran in the past and in my own opinion some of his mental hot-foots come quite close to being practical jokes. Others, however, are not practical jokes at all, but come under the heading of philosophical investigations.

He went to Alaska, years ago, and actually sold an icebox to an Eskimo. He fed whisky to a hoot owl to test the wisdom in the expression, "Drunk as a hoot owl." He released a bull in a china shop without damage to a single saucer. He searched for and found a needle in a haystack on a street corner in Washington. He restaged the Battle of Bunker Hill with Colonial soldiers and British troops in uniform, to prove that Prescott was a fool to cry, "Don't fire until you see the whites of their eyes!" He changed horses in midstream, using a river in Nevada, during one of our recent presidential campaigns, to demonstrate that it was perfectly feasible to do so.

None of these exploits could properly be called a practical joke. But when he showed a purple cow to Gelett Burgess one December afternoon in 1940, he was edging into our field of inquiry. Mr. Burgess, who wrote the verse, *I Never Saw a Purple Cow*, was in his New York hotel room when he was asked on the phone to step down to the lobby. Arriving there, he found Jim Moran and after introducing himself, Jim asked him to wait just a moment. Then Jim stepped into the street and led the *purplest* cow in all history into the lobby. He jockeyed the animal up to Mr. Burgess and said:

"There!"

Closely related to the golden bucket adventure is Jim's mental hot-foot involving the empty book. He once acquired this book, bound in maroon and containing about two hundred pages, all blank. Riding transcontinental trains, it was his custom to stroll into the club car, settle into an easy chair, order a drink and then open the book. He usually tried to locate himself so that other passengers could, without too much neck craning, see the blank pages. Then he'd pretend to read, going through emotional upheavals, sometimes bursting into fits of laughter, sometimes scowling as he turned the pages. The other people in the car would look at him, then glance at the book and see blank pages. Jim would concentrate on his reading for a while, let the book drop into his lap wide open, and pretend to think, shaking his head slowly from side to side as though he had just come upon the most remarkable statement ever printed. He kept up this little game throughout his journey and for some reason the other passengers left him strictly to himself, even refusing to sit at the same table with him in the diner.

There is, also, the case of the rubber mask. Ten years ago Jim got involved in a project which required his driving an automobile all over the United States. He traveled alone and the endless hours of driving began to bore him. One day in a novelty shop he bought a rubber mask depicting the face of an idiotic character. He arranged the mask so that it would fit on the back of his head, leaving his vision unobstructed. Driving along the highway, he'd wait until he saw another motorist getting ready to pass him. Then Jim would lean out the window, with the idiot face looking back. The effect on the approaching motorist must have been shocking. He'd see this leering goon, seated at the wheel of a speeding car, but leaning out and staring straight back with no regard for the highway ahead.

During one period Jim was engaged in passing away the time on salary in the Fred Waring offices. Theoretically he was Waring's press agent. One morning he was sitting at his desk running an electric razor over his face when he remembered that he had to call the radio editor of the newspaper *PM*. He picked up the phone and called the number and during the short time it took to get his man, thought of a way of having some fun. He held the mouthpiece a foot or two away from his face and called out:

"Jerry?"

"Yes."

"This is Jim Moran. Guess where I am!"

"You sound like you're at the North Pole," said Jerry.

The electric razor was still running and now Jim began moving it in and out, toward the mouthpiece and then away from it.

"Listen, Jerry!" he cried. "I'm in a United States Army bomber forty thousand feet above La Guardia Field. Can you hear me?"

"Go ahead," said Jerry. More business with the razor.

"Now get this," Jim continued, "we're up here watching the Air Force demonstrate a wonderful new ship-to-ground telephone system. This is the second call made on it. The first was to the President in Washington. We drew lots and I got to make the second call, and I decided to call you. Maybe you can beat the whole town on the story. Can you still hear me?"

Jerry was growing excited. This was something. Second to the President! He could hear the drone of the giant motors, rising and falling.

"Who's up there with you?" he shouted, beginning to jot down notes on this history-making event.

"Oh, lots of people. Big brass. And old Quent Reynolds is here. I can see old Quent, sittin' up there toward the front. You want to talk to old Quent?"

"Sure!" cried the excited Jerry. "Put him on!"

Jim sat in the Waring office moving the electric razor in and out for half a minute or so, then:

"Jerry! You there? I'm sorry but old Quent can't talk to you."

"Why not?" demanded Jerry.

"Well, to tell you the truth, he's asleep."

Jim then pretended to read from an air force handout which described the new communications system in technical jargon, and finally, with the razor still working in and out, announced that he had to stop—that the New York *Times* was yelling for the phone.

Over in the *PM* offices the radio editor discarded the column he had been writing and began hammering out his big exclusive. Meanwhile Jim Moran called back and got the city desk and tipped the boys off to what had happened. They fell in with the joke, and set copy boys to running Jerry's story to the desk a paragraph at a time, contributing even more to the radio editor's excitement. Then when the whole magnificent tale had been written, they let Jerry know that he had been bamboozled by an electric razor. He has not spoken to Jim Moran to this day.

One of the most persistent myths of modern practical jocularity concerns the spilling of jewels on Fifth Avenue. I have read a dozen versions of it. It has been attributed to Harpo Marx, Groucho Marx, Frank Tinney, Brian C. Hughes, Robert Benchley and even Hugh Troy. Each man who tells it, or writes about it, offers it as gospel. The joker goes into Tiffany's (or Cartier's) and looks at a number of cases of expensive gems. Then he says he is not quite ready to buy. He starts for the door and suddenly spills a whole bagful of jewels over the floor—all dime store stuff. Sometimes the gems are dropped in the store, sometimes on the sidewalk outside. The proprietors of both stores say it never happened.

The mental hot-foot which Jim Moran gave the patrons of Ciro's restaurant in Hollywood did happen, however. There are photographs to prove it. Jim planned it with great care, spent considerable money on it, and brought it off to perfection.

In 1947 the Crown Prince of Saudi Arabia, His Royal Highness Emir Saud, spent a month touring the United States. Accompanied by a retinue of guards and servitors, robed and hooded and wearing jeweled daggers, the Crown Prince spent several days in Hollywood and the newspapers made a lot of fuss over him. From the time of Douglas Fairbanks on the glittering folks of the movie capital have always gone hog-wild over any kind of royalty.

Jim Moran schemed his scheme. First he studied the manners and habits of Arabian royalty, and informed himself on protocol, and dietary laws. He examined photographs of the royal party and drew up his requirements in the way of costumes, which he got from one of the big wardrobe companies. He enlisted the services of three actors, two to be his servants and one to be his traveling companion. He was fortunate in getting an actor who could actually speak the Crown Prince's language to serve as the companion.

Jim checked the itinerary of the real prince and found out that the royal party was to leave town on a certain evening—he didn't want to run the chance of getting crossed up with Emir Saud himself. On that evening Jim and his three companions got themselves into their robes and whiskers, and had their faces stained. A reporter and a photographer from the Associated Press were called in and briefed on every move that was to be made. And Jim got together his jewels—a double handful of dime store gems plus one magnificent amethyst, which cost him thirty dollars and which might have passed for a diamond worth more than a Metro musical.

Meanwhile a phone call had been made to the management of Ciro's. The Crown Prince and party desired to dine at the restaurant that evening. The Prince required a certain table and its location was specified. The management of Ciro's gave every assurance that the table would be held—that everything possible would be done to make the Prince's visit a memorable one.

That evening a huge limousine pulled up at Ciro's and out of it first came the two servants. Arms folded, they marched in, surveyed the scene, checking details, conferring with the management. Then, everything seeming to be in order, the Prince and his companion entered and walked swiftly to their table. The Prince and companion sat down at the table; the two servants stood behind them.

Ciro's that night was loaded with important customers, mainly from the film colony, and most of them just simply abandoned their manners and stared. Jerry Wald and his orchestra were on the bandstand and whenever they were playing, the dancers, important people of Hollywood, gravitated toward the Prince's table, shoving and almost gouging to get up close and stare. The Prince and his men ignored them.

During a lull in the proceedings the Prince spoke sharply to one of the servants, who bowed low and then walked to the bandstand. In a thick accent he told Jerry Wald that His Royal Highness would enjoy hearing *Begin the Beguine*. No sooner said than done. The orchestra played the number and when it was over, the Crown Prince nodded his appreciation. Then from his belt he took a goatskin pouch and opened it and spread the jewels out on the table, poking through them, looking for a particular one. He settled on a stone (the thirty-dollar amethyst) that looked like a whopping diamond. He handed it to the servant, muttering something, and the servant went again to the bandstand and presented the gem to Mr. Wald. A loud buzzing of conversation passed through the room—everyone had witnessed every detail of the drama. Five or ten minutes later the Associated Press reporter ducked into the men's room, and the attendant there said to him:

"Lawd a mercy! That Mista Wald won't never have to lead no dance bands no more long as he lives. That King out there give him a diamon' big as a hen's aig! That Mista Wald's fixed for life!"

At last the Crown Prince decided it was time to leave. He clapped his hands together. One of the servants adjusted his robes. He and his companion stood up. The dance floor was clear, so the royal party started across it, toward the entrance. All eyes in the place were on them. Suddenly there was a rattling clatter—the goatskin pouch had fallen open and all those jewels had spilled out on the glistening floor. The royal party paused, and the servants started to bend down and pick up the jewels. But His Royal Highness barked a command, waved his hand imperiously, and the four Arabians continued toward the door, leaving the jewels. They had bounced and scattered in all directions and now, almost instantly, Ciro's turned into a mad scramble. Down on the floor went some of the greatest names in Hollywood, both male and female. Chairs and tables were knocked over and some of the waiters joined in the scramble.

The Crown Prince and his people didn't even turn around to look. They marched out of the place, got into their limousine, and departed allegro. Mission accomplished.

A man of Jim Moran's imagination is bound to dream up more mental hot-foots than he can ever carry out. He has worked up the details of another stunt, involving the tonier night clubs and restaurants of Hollywood, but apparently he never expects to put it into execution. This time he needs one companion and certain equipment, including an ambulance.

A call comes to Romanoff's famous restaurant. The caller is the secretary to Smedley J. Vincent. Mr. Vincent is a member of the famous Vincent family of Philadelphia, wealthy beyond estimate. Mr. Vincent is suffering from a rare disease and has been told by his doctors that he has only six months to live. Being a gourmet, he has decided to spend those six months roving the world, seeking out the finest restaurants on earth, and satisfying his great love for good food. He has come to Hollywood for the purpose of tasting the gastronomical delights of the Romanoff kitchen. He wants to dine there this evening.

The secretary explains that Mr. Vincent is required to wear an apparatus through which he receives oxygen, that he travels in his own ambulance, and that he is always accompanied by his doctor. And money is no object to him. It is requested that a special parking place be reserved, close by the entrance, for the ambulance; and that everyone be requested *not* to stare at Mr. Vincent because of his oxygen apparatus.

So the ambulance arrives and out of it comes Mr. Vincent and his doctor, a white-haired man, brisk and efficient. Mr. Vincent himself has, strapped to his back, a large box-like affair. Fastened over the upper part of his face is a half mask made of inflatable rubber, and tubes lead from the box on his back to the mask. The mask itself puffs in and out, constantly.

Mr. Vincent and his doctor are escorted to a table. The mask covers his nose, but not his mouth, and he is able to talk, and to discuss the menu, and accept recommendations about food. His dinner is brought, and rare wines, and there is much fussing over him by the help, and of course all the customers are watching him, for the mask gives him a science-fiction look that approaches the horrible.

Mr. Vincent begins eating his dinner with great relish, talking with the doctor. And then midway of the meal, he stiffens, and begins gasping. The doctor leaps up, manipulates some dials on the box, and seizing a small handle which projects from it, begins pumping furiously. Slowly Mr. Vincent sags forward into unconsciousness, his face in his plate. The doctor swiftly tests his pulse, bows his head a moment, and exclaims, "Alas, he is gone! But he died happily—eating good food—as he wanted." He turns and calls for assistance and before the goggle-eyes of the other customers, the body of Mr. Vincent is carried out and loaded into the ambulance and driven away.

Swiftly the ambulance races to another famous restaurant, where the same sort of arrangements have been made. Mr. Vincent and the doctor enter, and repeat the little tableau, with Mr. Vincent dying in his plate and being carried out. And from there to still another place, and a fourth.

The beauty of this operation, to Jim Moran's mind, is the confused aftermath. An actor, or producer, meets another actor, or producer, and begins telling excitedly about the strange character who dropped dead "before my very eyes in Romanoff's," and the second actor or producer says "Good God, you've got the place wrong—I saw it happen in Ciro's!"

Well, Jim Moran says he's not a practical joker—that he merely administers mental hot-foots. Not long ago he told me about a contrivance he had seen in action in one of the Hollywood radio studios. This thing, invented and manufactured by a Texan, was a weight-lifting machine. It was a long box-like affair, standing about a foot off the floor, with a platform in the center for the feet. As a test of strength, a man stands on the platform, bends forward, seizes a handle, and pulls upward with all his might. Beside the handle, directly in front of the man's face, is a dial which registers his strength. Jim tried it himself. He was appearing on a radio show which required several days of rehearsal and on his first day in the studio, he was shown the strength-testing machine.

"I always fancied myself as being fairly strong," he said, "and so I got on it, and bent over and took a good grip on that handle, and then gave it all I had. Great God! The things that happened! A plank came up from behind and hit me a helluva belt right in the pants. At the same instant I got an electrical shock from the handle that almost took my hands off at the wrists. At the same instant a .45 revolver went off inside the box, and a stream of water shot up from that dial and hit me square in the face. All at once! They had to take me home and put me to bed. Most unnerving thing that ever happened to me in my life. They kept this machine around for wise guys, especially some of the Hollywood hams who come in and talk big and make life miserable for everyone else. Those are the very kind of people who'll bite on a thing like that—a chance to show off their powerfulness. I saw several of them get it after that. It really unnerves people—it shatters them. They remain sheeplike, and sort of numb, for a week. They don't talk biggety for quite a while."

13

Talk and Double Talk

The science of dido-cutting was greatly enhanced when, in 1876, Alexander Graham Bell invented the telephone. At the same time much misery was added to the world. There are occasions when it is possible to believe that the instrument was discovered for the sole benefit of a single class of citizens—the practical jokers.

There are hundreds of minor league jokers who employ the telephone to confuse people, from the man who always answers by saying, "Harvey's Livery Stable," to the puerile wise guys who announce that the water or power is going to be shut off.

Several weird telephonic methods have been employed during recent years for making a man believe he has momentarily lost his marbles. These might be called shaggy telephone jokes. Lee Barker remembers a publishing executive who sometimes sat at his desk, depressed by the presence of his firm's books on the worst-seller lists, and then picked up the phone and called one of his associates in an adjoining office.

"Wiggins?" he'd say.

"Yes, this is Wiggins."

"This is Shikes. I wanted to ask you about the new ads on that antiques book."

"Well," says Wiggins, "I've got the layouts here on my desk and I can show them to you."

Shikes immediately turns irritable. "Wiggins," he says, "how many times have I got to tell you not to bother me with such trivia? Dammit, I'm up to my ears today in work, and you insist on pestering me with your lousy advertising layouts. Please don't bother me any more today. Maybe we can talk about it some other time." And he hangs up.

Here's another one: Suppose you know a Mr. James Van Dyck Randolph, who is a stuffed shirt, and you want to bewilder him. If possible, get him on the phone when he has a hangover. The conversation should go like this:

> You: Who is this?
> Mr. R: Mr. Randolph speaking.
> You: He's not here at the moment.
> Mr. R: *Who's* not there?
> You: Mr. Randolph is not here.
> Mr. R: But *I'm* Mr. Randolph.
> You: I'm sorry sir, Mr. Randolph just stepped out. Could I have him call you back?
> Mr. R: Listen, you idiot! I didn't call any Mr. Randolph! I *am* Mr. Randolph, and *you* called *me!*
> You: If you'll let me have your number, I'm sure Mr. Randolph will be back any minute. He just stepped across the street to get a drink.

There's a third shaggy telephone joke that was quite popular in 1952. Some of the boys are making a night of it in a restaurant. They pick an acquaintance named Sam for their victim. At perhaps two-thirty in the morning, one member of the party calls Sam's number and gets him out of bed.

"Is Benny there?" he asks.

"Benny who?" says a sleepy Sam.

"Benny Green. Is he there?"

"You have the wrong number."

"Oh, I'm sorry."

That's all for the moment. The boys wait fifteen or twenty minutes, long enough for Sam to get back to sleep; then another one calls, and asks for Benny Green, and Sam patiently explains that the caller has a wrong number. Another interval, and another call for Benny Green. This keeps up until Sam is beginning to lose his temper. Then the final call is made:

"Sam?"

"Yes," wearily, "this is Sam."

"This is Benny Green. Any calls for me?"

Mr. Thurber has written about practical jokers who use the telephone. He remembers the case of a man named Paul Revere who, back in 1930, lived in a Massachusetts town and who was a descendant of the horse rider. Mr. Revere had to cope with innumerable phone calls on the eighteenth of each April, especially at night after he had retired. The callers would sing out, "The British are coming!" or "Wake up and get going!" Mr. Revere finally arranged to have his phone disconnected each time the fateful anniversary rolled around.

Mr. Thurber also recalls the dreary Broadway play of some years ago, in which the third-act curtain rose on an empty stage. The telephone on stage was ringing. It continued ringing—apparently an actor had missed his cue. Finally Robert Benchley, who probably had been dozing in his aisle seat, spoke up for all to hear: "Why doesn't somebody answer that? I think it's for me." The next day, Mr. Thurber reports, one of the critics wrote, "The only amusing line in the play was spoken by Bob Benchley who, unhappily, was not in the cast."

Two different men of my acquaintance have strong feelings about people who get the wrong number when they make a telephone call. I'm glad I don't share their attitudes, that I can manage to be patient with such callers; otherwise I might be in trouble. My phone is one digit removed from the phone in a local clergyman's home and careless dialers, usually seeking conversation with the Reverend Mr. Mason often disturb me. I'll confess I've been tempted at times when the callers ask, "This Reverend Mason?" or "Is Reverend Mason there?" I could do a real bang-up job of shocking them, but I haven't yet, and I won't. That is, I hope I won't.

When Hugh Troy lived in Greenwich Village he frequently got calls intended for a bookmaker. Hugh never told the callers they had the wrong number.

"Who win the fifth at Belmont?" a caller would ask.

"Belt Buckle," Hugh would say.

"Who?"

"Belt Buckle win it."

"I don't get it. Sounds like you said Belt Buckle."

"I did say Belt Buckle. Belt Buckle win the fifth at Belmont. Fat Cricket run second."

Then Hugh would hang up.

We come now to Elmer Roessner. Mr. Roessner, a veteran newspaperman, now operates a prosperous agency which gives advice to the advertising-lorn, and writes sparkling short stories and articles for the magazines.

Mr. Roessner believes that people who call wrong numbers are fair game. He has, in fact, developed this belief into a minor philosophy. Let's permit him to expound it:

> In the early years of the telephone, wrong numbers were excusable. Telephone mechanism was imperfect. The public and the operators were untrained and the latter were often grossly overworked. But by this time the public knows that the telephone exists and the public has had a fair opportunity to use it.
>
> In days past, the responsibility for error was uncertain. It might have been one of several operators. But with the coming of the dial telephone, the responsibility rests with the caller. If you are in a dial area and you are summoned to the phone by an incorrect

call, the chances are overwhelmingly that the caller remembered his number incorrectly, looked it up carelessly or dialed it faultily. He is clearly invading your privacy. If someone forces his way into your home with an uninvited telephone call, robbing you of peace of mind, robbing you of relaxation, robbing you of sleep, he should, by the same process of reasoning, be mowed down.

When the telephone rings and an unfamiliar voice asks, "Is Gracie there?" I apply the same formula. Sometimes the call is for Lulu, or for Joe, or for Mack's Meat Market. Whenever it is apparent that a wrong number is called, I laugh, as hollowly and as mockingly as I am able and then, without a word, I hang up. Never a cuss word, never an explosion. Just a laugh—and then a dead line.

I am beginning to think this treatment is not drastic enough. I would like to propose certain formulae for handling wrong-number calls of varied character. A woman's voice asks, "Joe's Pork Store? I want to order a pound of sausage meat and . . ." You say, "Hold on there. We're not going to sell you another ounce of meat until you shed some of that fat. After all, we've got some pride in this neighborhood. Besides, pigs like you give this store a bad name. Why don't you go on a lettuce diet?"

More drastic is this formula: A voice asks for Mike, who has a different number from yours. Feign excitement and say, "Something terrible is happening. Don't tie up the wire. Wait right there and we'll call you back."

The calls for the Gracies, the Lulus and the Catherines may be answered in this fashion: In a tremolo of excitement exclaim, "Gracie just broke her leg! Find a doctor somewhere and come right over!"

If you are a man, you can be a little more brutal. Say, "Gracie is through with you. I've moved in and we don't want you calling any more."

A woman, however, can still top this. She may say, "Gracie is up in her room with a customer. Call back in half an hour."

Don't cuss them out. That's a waste of time. Hurt 'em. Lash 'em. Nail 'em to the cross. Above all, don't feel sorry for them. People who dial wrong numbers are drunks, fumblers or boobs. They're got it coming to them. Lay on!

Take courage from my Aunt Fanny. Although past sixty she has a girlish voice and a giggle to go with it. When her number is called in error, she says gently, "Gracie isn't here. My name is Fanny. Won't I do?"

If the caller shows interest, Aunt Fanny trills along, remarking on how romantic wrong numbers can be. Coyly she lets the caller draw out a description of herself, and she's got the voice to say she's nineteen, a blonde, good-looking and a good dancer. Yes, she likes a drink once in a while. A date? Well—yes. If her caller will be at Mulberry and Bingo Streets in an hour, she'll drive up in her car.

She takes great pleasure in thinking about the insufferable bum standing for hours at the corner of Mulberry and Bingo.

Elmer Roessner is the only man I know about who has made a profound study of the art of double talk. This is an art which falls definitely within the category of practical joking. It has been brought to a high degree of perfection by certain practitioners on Broadway and in Hollywood, but it is not a new thing. Mark Twain, in 1870, wrote a report of his first interview with Artemus Ward, and Ward's conversation at that meeting was pure double talk without recourse to invented words. It is a delightful essay.

Mr. Roessner, however, has concerned himself with the new and improved double talk, in which meaningless words are employed. He has put his findings into an essay, first published in *Esquire* in 1940. This is the last word on double talk and with Mr. Roessner's permission, and for the reason that it is basic to our subject, I set it down in toto:

A careless person, listening to double talk at the movies or on the radio, may conclude that it is a simple matter of giving utterance to jumbled syllables.

Such a conclusion is erroneous.

Double talking is a minor art. It is qualitative, not quantitative. To think that the greater volume makes the better double talk is to think that the bigger canvas makes the better picture; to believe that the most confused sounds make the best double talk is to believe that the greatest number of pigments makes the most beautiful painting. Double talk, to be successful, must be rhematic and have a volitation of its own.

Furthermore, double talk must not be confused with the mumbles. The mumbles is an almost entirely different art. Its methods are different, its uses are different. In fact, the mumbles and double talk are fitted to two entirely unlike classes of personalities. The successful mumbler may be an indifferent double talker; a good double talker will not bother with the mumbles.

It is true, as Stephen Leacock will point out, that both arts are best practiced by persons of a puckish disposition. The mumbler, however, is usually a physical type; often an Aries or Taurus. A double talker is likely to be more intellectual; he may be under the sign of Sagittarius or Capricornus. See George Bernard Shaw's *Admirable Bashville*.

The mumbler, having a victim's ear, utters a series of unintelligible, or almost unintelligible sounds. But, and this is important, the successful mumbler lightly peppers these sounds with occasional words. These words are clear and sharp and—note this carefully—stir definite mental reactions in the hearer.

Let us have an example. An artful mumbler approached a man named Jones whose hobby is tuna fishing. After Jones greeted him, the mumbler said, "Nice day. Reminds me uh umble umble ah awa acka umble acka umble tuna fish. Acka awa ah umble aw umble ah awa uh umble four hundred pounds."

The last three words were emphasized. Jones, aroused, asked, "What did you say?"

The mumbler replied in an annoyed tone, "I said, 'Reminds awa acka umble uh umble tuna fish. Umble awa uh awa uh umble um um umble four hundred pounds.'" He enunciated the last words as if he were speaking to an idiot child.

Jones fairly screamed, "What did you say about tuna fish?"

The mumbler looked hurt. He said, "I don't know what has become of you lately, Jones. You used to be interested enough in fish stories to listen." With that he turned on his heel and left. Jones consulted his doctor.

Another example: One Smith was in love with a girl named Jennifer. A mumbler telephoned him and, imitating a radio in an electric storm, said, "Say, awa ackle ah awa ackle ackle aw hackle hw Jennifer acka awa other man hackle aw ah aw."

Smith cried, "What's that?"

The mumbler said, with elaborate patience, "I said, 'Hacka awa ha ackle awa ha awa ha hacka ha Jennifer last night ho haw beer garden. Hacka awa ah ah awa acka ha drunk and thrown out!'"

Smith's voice trembled as he pleaded, "What did you say about Jennifer, old man?"

The mumbler answered, now speaking clearly, "Jennifer? Who said anything about Jennifer? What are you trying to do, drag me into one of your private quarrels?" and hung up.

The double talker scorns such simple devices. A true double talker will never use a telephone when he can approach his victim directly. He makes no attempt to conceal his utensils. The words he speaks are enunciated clearly; he will spell them if called upon. At times, he will not hesitate to put double talk in writing. See James Joyce's *Finnegans Wake*.

As suggested before, double talk does not consist in firing disjointed syllables at a listener. The double talker carefully selects the syllables he uses. He knows the value of good ammunition and he uses it sparingly.

If you would be a double talker, first select a number of syllables or "word parts," as they might better be called. A novice should never attempt double talk in company without full command of at least twenty of these word parts; he cannot be an expert until he is master of a hundred.

These word parts should not be simply barbarian sounds; they should not be onomatopoetic syllables; they should avoid the effect of babbling. Avoid, therefore, word parts like the following:

umble	uggle	ibble	ski	itch
arrah	ootle	oddle	affle	upple

These words parts may be suited to some kinds of mumbling, but not for double talk. The double talker avoids bubbling and repetitious sounds, preferring sounds that resemble accepted words. The more closely his sounds resemble accepted words and the more they suggest that there should be words like them, the greater are their effectiveness.

These are sound, proved, double-talk word parts:

urment	istan	antive	ative	ently
incan	apid	avid	istesse	ome
artage	namic	erot	irgan	uctor
onter	vendir	islong	ackid	onate
eton	asia	ogion	izans	orial

The double talker, once he has learned these word parts, need add only a letter or a short syllable here and there to have a brand new vocabulary, sure to puzzle, harass or dement his victim. But the double talker does not let go a broadside. If he sidled up to somebody and said, "Ristan surmentate, huh? Brackid moistesse zincan lapid," it would neither be double talk nor the mumbles. The hearer would simply laugh.

Instead, the double talker primes his shots with good, hardy words, especially prepositions, articles and adverbs. See how much better it would be to approach a stranger and say, "Napid day, isn't it? There's quite a ristan in the surmentate, don't you think? It was brackid this morning, but it became moistesse later. Do you think the zincan flavid days are here?"

If the stranger is not honest, he will pretend to have understood and remark that he wouldn't be surprised if they were. Once a victim makes a bluff like that, he's fair game. He's on the rise and he can be plinked. The double talker may go on, "I was at a political meeting last night and we discussed Roosevelt's muctor namic. I got so mad I hit a stranger. What do you think of his vendir? I say he has no gonter and that he fomently lacks all trace of lartage. What do you think?" And if the stranger meekly says, "Well, I say yes and no," the double talker comes back with, "Oh, you're one of those pirot Fislong citizens, huh? Well, do you know what I think of your kind? You're just garavids."

Perchance the stranger is honest and says, in the first place, that he doesn't understand. In this event, the double talker simply says, "Oh, a gonate, huh? You don't durnamic in a walage, do you?" and looks for another victim.

Double talk should not be considered simply as a means of puzzling the simple folk or of unmasking fools. It has its practical applications. I recall the episode of a double talker who attended an art exhibition. Interest centered on a painting that looked like the small of the back of a mulatto who had two skin diseases. Experts gathered around and remarked on the dynamic qualities of the painting, its torque and its vibratory incidence. They bandied about a lot of words they had borrowed from civil engineering, electronics and psychiatry. At length the double talker was asked his opinion. Every eye turned upon him. He drew himself up and said with utter finality, "Matisse has no garbistan. He simply hasn't got garbistan. I say to hell with him."

The experts nodded sagely and the picture was withdrawn the next day.

Double talk has other practical uses. It may be used to thwart an annoying salesman; it may be used to cover up an embarrassing moment; it may be used to impress one's wife. The double talker is never at a loss to utilize his talents. He may go into the movies, he may write a book, he may become a military expert. His art is a hacqueton to soften the world's blows; hyratory though his phonate onslaught be, it is no whigmaleerie. It may become a logion that the violescence of his wit is no outgrowth of hypoplasia. It seldom vesicates. Nor is his a cancrizans humor. It is mature, straightforward and risorial.

14

Ribber's Paradise

Most people who have given the matter any thought say that Hollywood is the world capital for practical jokers. Yet Abel Green, editor of *Variety*, once told me that midtown Manhattan is actually the ribber's paradise. Show biz calls a practical joker a ribber. Mr. Green says there are more talented ribbers operating in New York than in Hollywood and that most of the prime ribs executed in Hollywood were invented on Broadway.

The fact remains that people in show biz play more practical jokes than the people of any other group. There's an absence of formality in their business and not much in the way of a restraining hand to interfere with their horseplay. Then, too, a talent for mimicry has always been an important feature of practical joking. An actor knows how to keep a straight face while taking his victim over the jumps, and he is able to assume different voices on the telephone.

There used to be a horrifying joke played by theatrical people on a man with a furious hangover. The victim has been spotted the night before in a cabaret, drunker than Jim Moran's hoot owl. The following morning the ribber telephones him at his home, knowing he is suffering the tortures of the damned and knowing, too, that the poor fellow isn't quite certain about what happened the night before. The ribber employs a most convincing foreign dialect, usually Italian, and pitches his voice to a tone of excited anger. He shrieks that the hangover insulted his wife in such-and-such a club last night. Terrible and unforgivable behavior! Used bad language to her! The hangover begins to sweat, and perhaps tremble a little more than is normal. The caller's anger grows with each passing sentence. He begins to use a few bad words himself. He announces that he is coming over and beat the skunk half to death. He says he is going to bring along his knife. Nobody can insult his wife—like that and get away with it. The victim usually tries to explain that he remembers nothing, that he had been drinking too much, that he's not normally the kind of guy who misbehaves and insults ladies, that he's truly sorry, that he's willing to apologize and make things right. But the hot Latin is not to be mollified—these expressions of repentance only serve to aggravate his rage. And he finally shouts, "You are as good as a dead man!" And hangs up.

The legitimate theater has always had its tradition of practical jokes. Quite often when an actor or actress blows up on stage, a prank is behind it, though the audience seldom knows about it.

One fairly common trick is used when two characters are required to meet and shake hands on the stage. The joker has an oyster—unshucked, cold and slimy—or a ball of cold cream concealed in his hand—most discommoding to his victim.

The arrival of telegrams or telephone calls during the action of a play often provides backstage amusement for the cutups. A telegram arrives, say, for Claypool Pennyfeather. It is supposed to inform him that he has just inherited half a million dollars, but it really doesn't say that. It says, "For God's sake, your shirttail is hanging out behind!" Or it contains some other message calculated to upset him and, perhaps, cause him to garble his lines.

Sometimes the telephone on stage is secretly hooked up to another instrument. The bell rings and Claypool Pennyfeather answers. It is a call of warning—the mob is on its way over to eliminate him. Yet as he protests and emotes, alien words pour from the receiver at his ear. Someone backstage is yammering obscenities, calling him names, trying to throw him off stride in his big dramatic scene.

There is a story about Eve Arden and a stage telephone. She was playing in a summer theater and was in the midst of a long and important speech when the telephone rang. It wasn't supposed to. She stopped and glanced at the actor who was on stage with her. There was just enough of a smirk on his face to tell her that he had arranged the rib. She stepped quickly to the telephone, answered the call, then turned to the actor and said, "It's for you." His efforts to ad lib a telephone conversation were quite unconvincing and when he finished his poor performance, Miss Arden resumed her speech as if nothing had happened.

Stage situations in which food or drink is served have long attracted the talents of the practical joker. More than once a dignified performer has bitten into a cheese sandwich made not of cheese but of cold cream. Even more effective is the trick of putting alum in the actor's drink. Alum puckers the mouth and sometimes fetches ludicrous results in the most gripping dramatic scenes.

The chief aim of the stage joker, of course, is to confuse and embarrass his victim in full sight of the audience. An actor with his back to the audience, or with only his profile in view, can often do it by looking cross-eyed at the person to whom he is talking. Or he can achieve his result by out-of-character comments and asides. A Broadway star was once driven frantic by a fellow actor who, throughout one important scene, kept telling him in undertones that there was a horrible bug on his coat collar.

"It's almost on your neck now," the joker would whisper, causing his victim to cringe and squirm, to the complete mystification of the audience.

The practice of veering from the script and inserting ad lib remarks, thus messing up cue lines, also has a long history in the theater. Playing King Lear, the great Edwin Booth addressed Edgar: "What is your study?" Edgar replied, quite properly, "How to prevent the fiend, and to kill vermin."

Booth then dead-panned a line that Shakespeare forgot to write:

"Skeeters and sitch?"

It took Edgar quite a little while to get back on the track.

There has always been a spate of practical joking around the radio and television studios and I think the business probably reached its peak in the early 1930s at the Columbia Broadcasting System's headquarters on Madison Avenue. This great flowering of the practical joke was due, in large measure, to the presence of one man, Morton Downey, and one group of men—the actors who performed on the *March of Time,* which was then one of the top programs in the country. The *March of Time* actors broadcast only once a week, but their presence was required for rehearsal almost every day. They had to be immediately available for script changes, and there were long hours in which they had nothing to do. They kept the place in an uproar. There was a lounge in the building where there were usually a few outsiders, people waiting to keep appointments. These people were given some frightful shocks. The *March of Time* actors staged half a dozen different murders in that lounge and then one day worked up a magnificent pay-roll robbery with much firing of blank shots in which even the receptionist shrieked and clutched her breast and fell dead across her desk.

Morton Downey was a one-man riot. There were a good many people at CBS who, though they loved him, would have nothing to do with him. Tumult and confusion followed wherever he went. One day, walking down a corridor, he glanced into a small studio and saw Ted Husing just beginning a fifteen-minute sports broadcast. Mr. Husing was sitting at a table and reading from a script. Mr. Downey walked in. He took off Mr. Husing's coat, and Mr. Husing kept on talking into the mike. He took off Mr. Husing's necktie, and then his shirt, and the broadcast went on. He got down and removed Mr. Husing's shoes and socks. Mr. Husing tried to kick him in the face, but Mr. Downey had his way, and Mr. Husing still was talking. The show must go on! Now Mr. Downey jerked Mr. Husing to his feet and Mr. Husing had to bend forward in order to continue talking into the mike. Off came the pants and off came the underwear, and out of the studio went Mr. Downey. Mr. Husing finished his sportscast as naked as a jay bird.

In those days Morton Downey's own program was broadcast from a small studio in the building, with an orchestra conducted by Jacques Renard. The day of the big studio audience had not yet arrived, although chairs were set up for a dozen or so members of the public who wanted to witness a real-for-sure radio show.

Mr. Renard was a man of great physical bulk, and played upon the violin, sometimes performing a solo bit in the midst of a selection. His fiddle was a Stradivarius and he played it well.

Mr. Downey, somewhere along his exciting life's road, had picked up a remarkable technique. He could stroll casually in front of a man and with a single flip of his wrist, open every button on that man's fly. He made life miserable for Mr. Renard with this little trick. He would wait until Mr. Renard started his violin solo. Mr. Renard would be facing the small studio audience, composed mostly of women. Mr. Downey would walk past him and Mr. Renard's fly would come open. Mr. Renard, out of modesty, would sometimes turn around and face the wall while he finished his solo, or he would bend forward, as far as he could, and play it from that grotesque stance, shielding his embarrassment with his fiddle.

The coming of the zipper put a severe crimp in Mr. Downey's activities and may have discouraged him so completely that he gave up most of his playful pursuits and consecrated his life to bottled pop.

This same program was in rehearsal one day when Mr. Downey got into an argument with one of the musicians. As I remember it was an argument about politics and the musician was strong in his opinion and Mr. Downey equally stubborn for the opposite view. The quarrel grew loud and heated and Mr. Downey got his Irish up, and began to threaten the musician, and the musician called him an indelicate name. Mr. Downey now let out a shriek of anger, looked wildly about the room and his eye fell upon Mr. Renard's violin case. He yanked it open, seized the Stradivarius, rushed over to the musician, raised the instrument in the air and brought it down with a splintering crash on the man's head. Jacques Renard witnessed the whole affair, unable to stop Mr. Downey, unable to move, and as his precious violin crashed into shreds, he gave forth a howl of pain and staggered to a chair in a fainting condition. It took several minutes to restore order and to reveal the true state of affairs. Mr. Downey had deliberately provoked the fight with the musician. Earlier in the day he had been making a movie short over in Brooklyn and had come upon a handsome breakaway violin—an instrument designed for shattering over a man's head without harming him. He had bought this violin, crept into the studio and substituted it for the Strad.

More than fifteen years after these incidents, Mr. Downey went to Boston to do a show and it was a sentimental occasion for it meant a reunion with Jacques Renard. Mr. Renard, however, sent word to Mr. Downey that he would not appear unless Mr. Downey promised that there would be no horseplay. Mr. Downey assured Mr. Renard that he was a changed man, mature in his outlook, no longer addicted to the foolishness that characterized his younger days. So they met and had their program and a joyful reunion and when it was over Mr. Renard found his coat pockets loaded with live bullfrogs.

Almost every leading radio performer has been afflicted, at one time or another, with the clock gag. Unknown to him, the studio clock is set ahead ten or fifteen minutes. The whole company then pretends to go on the air. One character faces the mike and begins a speech and gets his tongue twisted. He tries valiantly, but his sentences become more garbled than ever and then, in a wild fit of anger and disgust, he lets go with a sizzling volley of profanity, horrifying the victim, who is usually the star of the show.

Arthur Godfrey, who is incidentally a close friend of Morton Downey, is a man well able to unhinge the people around him if he's in the mood. Once I flew with him in his plane from New Jersey to Florida. Mrs. Godfrey and I were playing gin rummy in the cabin while Arthur was flying the plane with his co-pilot, Frank Lavigne, sitting beside him. Somewhere over Georgia, Arthur came back and asked me if I'd like to fly the ship. I didn't realize he meant it, and went forward with him and took his seat (Frank was now doing the piloting). Arthur showed me the principal dials to watch—it was important to keep the ship level and to watch the altitude and two or three other things I've forgotten about. He showed me how to work the controls.

"Got it straight?" he yelled above the noise.

"I think so," I yelled back.

"Let him have it, Frank!"

Frank let me have it. Almost before I knew it, I was piloting that thing. I had trouble for a while, being accustomed to driving a car, feeling that I had to keep looking through the windshield, and this made it difficult for me to continue watching those dials. But I caught on fast and for a little while I felt like the Lone Eagle. Frank Lavigne seemed to have the utmost confidence in me, for he lounged back and lit a cigarette and took it easy, just glancing at the instrument panel now and then to make sure we weren't upside down. Arthur, meanwhile, went back to the cabin.

Then came trouble. I figured it was the wind. The plane would take a notion to start pointing itself upward, and I grew taut as a drumhead, struggling with those controls to level it off, and then the nose would go down and we'd begin to lose altitude fast, and another struggle to correct this condition. After that we'd begin to tilt, first to one side, then to the other, and this slow rolling back and forth became so disconcerting that I concluded we had flown into a hurricane, or that one side of the plane had fallen off; I got a little panicky and yelled at Frank to take over, and he did. Arthur came forward and resumed his seat, laughing at the sweat standing out on my forehead, and I returned to the cabin. Mary Godfrey was grinning, and she told me. Back in the cabin, while I was piloting an airplane for the first and probably the last time in my life, Arthur had been responsible for all my difficulties. He'd walk to the rear of the cabin and stand there a few moments, then walk quickly forward to the front, and stand there. After that he'd move from side to side. These movements were sufficient to cause the eccentric tilting of the ship.

In his day as the most original of all early-morning disk jockeys, Arthur sometimes gave his associates some uneasy moments. One morning he sat in his little studio, earphones clamped to his head. Back in the glassed-in control room sat his engineer. A record was playing. When it was finished, Arthur began talking into his microphone. That is, he pretended to talk, but no words came out of his mouth. He made like he was talking, laughing, gesturing. In the control room the engineer, sitting half awake, suddenly saw Arthur. Arthur was talking, but there were no words. The engineer sprang from his chair and began madly fussing with switches, trying to locate the trouble and correct it. Arthur let him go for almost half a minute, then began talking—in the middle of a story.

In Washington one of Arthur's friends and associates was

Arch MacDonald, who had his own program. One day Arthur hung around the studio until the MacDonald show went on the air. Arthur got the engineers to rig a microphone in another studio so that he would be hooked in to the MacDonald program. He wore earphones so he could hear MacDonald talking. Then he began to interpolate bits of business into MacDonald's monologues. At the conclusion of one of MacDonald's sentences, Arthur would go "Sssssssssssssssss" into his mike. Then after another sentence, he'd deliver a gentle hiccup. He kept this up all through the program, and the station switchboard began to catch fire. People from all over Washington were calling in. "Hey, if you don't know it," some of them said, "your man MacDonald's drunk as a goat!" Some were indignant, demanding that the station yank MacDonald off the air.

Arch MacDonald was a trifle sore about it. But he got back at Arthur. He took one of Arthur's recordings of a popular song. He bored a hole in it, just slightly off center. Then he began playing that record every day on his program. He'd begin by praising Arthur's marvelous baritone voice, and its exceptional quality in this particular recording. He'd tell how thousands of listeners were requesting that he play the record, and then he'd slip it on the turntable and let it go. The fact of its off-center position on the turntable produced an almost spectacular effect. Arthur's voice rose and fell, so that the thing didn't sound so much like a song as it sounded like an elderly hog engaged in a death struggle with a wildcat. Each day MacDonald played it through and when the horrible noises were over, he'd say sweetly, "Isn't that a lovely ballad? Have you *ever* heard my good friend Arthur in better form? I tell you, he has the *grandest* style!" Before it was over, he had Arthur begging for mercy.

Over the years the vice-presidents of the networks have taken a lot of abuse, but usually it has been vocal. There is one vice-president at Columbia who recently got a more worrisome treatment. One day he received a telegram from Denver, saying, "Your sand is on the way." It was signed, "Ajax Freight Corp." A day or so later another wire came, this time from Kansas City, saying, "Sand will arrive on schedule." There were follow-up wires from Indianapolis, and Pittsburgh. He could depend on the sand. For a while he was disturbed, but then he concluded it was just some-one's idea of a joke, and put it out of his mind. Then one afternoon he went home to Westchester to find a mountain of sand beside his house. A whole carload of it had been delivered during the day. He was never able to find out who sent it.

Not long ago the staff of a Chicago radio station was being bothered by the constant presence of an insurance sales-man. This man not only pestered the staff members, trying to sell them insurance, but he used the station telephones to call other clients. One of the station engineers finally figured out a scheme for getting rid of him.

The insurance salesman was usurping a desk in one of the offices. The engineer called him from the phone in a studio. He spoke with a German accent, identifying himself as the president of a prosperous manufacturing company. He said that he was actually, at that moment, telephoning from his new Cadillac, which was equipped with a radiophone. He had just bought the car and he wanted full and complete insurance coverage at once. The happy insurance man told him that, as of that moment, he could consider himself protected from fishtail to front bumper.

In the control room the engineer now turned on a sound-effects recording of a scream and a splintering, ear-splitting crash. Then silence.

The insurance man frantically began calling police sta-tions, hospitals and morgues, trying to find out what had happened. He had a most uncomfortable hour or so, be-fore it dawned on him that he had been duped. He departed the station and came there no more—he would not, as a gentleman, ever again associate with such crude people.

Maurice Carruthers was a New York radio actor who needed work badly. He heard about a part that was available in a soap opera, and he thought he was perfect for it. He called on Joe Rogers, producer of the show, but Rogers turned him down. Mr. Carruthers was understandly nettled. He decided to get even with Joe Rogers. He began dropping into several restaurants and bars frequented by other radio actors, including many who were out of work. He'd sit down with a group of these people, a sad look on his face, and say, "Lord, I sure wish I had paid attention in school and learned Etruscan."

"What's Etruscan?" someone asked.

"Don't be stupid," said Carruthers. "Etruscan's a language. Joe Rogers is desperate for someone who knows Etruscan. He doesn't want someone to *speak* Etruscan. He wants someone who can speak English with an Etruscan dialect. I can do a little bit of it, but not the way he wants it. He doesn't want the ordinary Etruscan. He wants the Middle-West type Etruscan, the businessman type."

Apparently there are few actors, anywhere, who would ever admit to not knowing Etruscan. Joe Rogers' phone began ringing and it rang for days, as the word went round. "Maybe you didn't know it," his callers would say, "but I happen to do a very good Etruscan. Fact of the matter is, Tony Miner once said I do the best Etruscan of any actor he ever knew."

Joe Rogers, of course, had never heard of Etruscan.

People in the radio and television business, I am reliably informed, take themselves quite seriously. Whenever a mistake is made, even a small mistake, the repercussions are heard all over town. Thus the joke played on NBC a couple of years back was no laughing matter.

It was during the first days of the Dave Garroway *Today* show. As you probably know, this morning television program is staged in full view of sidewalk crowds on New York's West Forty-ninth Street. And at occasional moments during the two-hour proceedings, the camera turns on the clot of people standing before the plate-glass windows.

One morning, during the first week of the widely advertised show, the camera turned to the crowd on the sidewalk. Suddenly two men held up a large sign, which read, "Listen to Herb Sheldon Mornings on WJZ Radio, 6:30 to 8:15 A.M." The cameraman didn't realize what was happening and stayed on the sign long enough for viewers throughout the Eastern half of the United States to read it. The people at NBC were not amused, not in the slightest; I understand, however, that the people at WJZ and the rival network broke right down and laughed about it.

One evening I was a guest performer on a certain television panel show. One of the regular members of the panel was a newspaperman of my acquaintance. The interlocutor was a man notorious for his fussiness, and for his nervous fear that something was sure to go wrong. When the panel was seated at the long table, just before air time, the newspaperman unbuttoned his coat and exposed his necktie. It was a hand-painted job, showing the full length naked figure of a beautiful girl, front view. The master of ceremonies clapped his hand to his forehead, then demanded that the tie be taken off. It was too late. "Hide it!" he yelled, and the show was on the air. The master of ceremonies never gave a more jittery, squirmy performance. All through the half-hour program the newspaperman continued to toy with the top button on his jacket, sometimes unbuttoning it absent-mindedly and then fastening it again. The thing was so upsetting that the m.c. got the man fired from the show the following day.

15

Times Square Local

If there are still people in the audience who stand by their opinion that all practical jokes are bad practical jokes, let us summon a gentle and civilized human being to the witness chair—Miss Helen Hayes. Miss Hayes has been married for many years to Charlie MacArthur, who has a reputation for being a genius in the art of rigging thimbles against pomposity. Miss Hayes testifies that if Mr. MacArthur "had had a hot-foot sense of humor I wouldn't have stayed married to him a month."

"But actually," she wrote a few years ago in the *Reader's Digest*, "he is not at all the irresponsible, irrepressible, middle-aged pixie. He hates gags as such, and never perpetrates a prank without a good reason for it. The reason may be his distrust of ungoverned authority, or his desire to deflate pretense or pomposity; or his unerring sense of what is the right thing in the particular circumstances and for the particular people; sometimes it is anger, for he never blows off steam the way other people do, but prefers to ease his feelings by doing something out of the ordinary."

Miss Hayes, it would seem, gives a man plenty of leeway, for she is speaking of a man who, on at least one occasion, gave her a sort of non-inflammable hot-foot before the world. Mr. MacArthur wrote a radio script for Miss Hayes.

He pretended that he was having some difficulty getting it finished, and delayed handing it to her until a few moments before air time. She stepped to the microphone and began reading it . . . and it was "a sardonically witty attack" on the drama critics who had been most lavish in their praise of her.

It must be remembered, however, that Miss Hayes is not bereft of a sense of humor. One New Year's Eve she was playing in *Victoria Regina,* at a Philadelphia theater. In the final scene of the play, as the aged Victoria, she delivered a long and tremendously effective speech about her dead consort, Albert. Outside in the street the New Year's Eve crowds were whooping and blowing horns, and Miss Hayes had to almost shout this final speech. Keep in mind that the role of Victoria was easily one of her greatest; she not only convinced her audiences that she *was* Queen Victoria—the other members of the cast also fell under her spell. So on this night in Philadelphia the final curtain came down, and then rose again on the entire cast. Queen Victoria stood at the footlights. Suddenly she reached into the voluminous folds of her skirts and withdrew a big tin horn, and placing it to her mouth, blew a blast at the audience. She turned and faced the other performers who had been lined up behind her. They were standing jaws agape, staring at her incredulously. And she gave *them* a blast on the horn. It took a few moments, but in the end the whole house was roaring its approval.

As for Mr. MacArthur, I have read that in his younger days he had a novel method for winning arguments with Broadway producers who tried to make alterations in his scripts. Mr. MacArthur would step to a window of the producer's office, climb out, and hang by one hand from the sill, threatening to let go unless his script was left unmolested.

During one of his Hollywood engagements he was assigned to complete a screenplay. The studio was anxious to get the script but Mr. MacArthur was in no hurry. It was several weeks overdue when the Head of Production—always a frightening creature to most men—walked into the MacArthur office, determined to get some action.

"Well, what about it?" he said gruffly. Nobody should ever speak gruffly to Charlie MacArthur.

Mr. MacArthur picked up a fat script off his desk and smiled. The producer beamed, and reached for it, but Mr. MacArthur jerked it back.

"No," he said, "I'm not going to give you this. It's good, all right, but it isn't my best. I want you to have my best."

Whereupon he began slowly tearing the script to shreds and dropping the pieces in a wastepaper basket.

"Come back in a week," he said to the producer, "and I'll have something worthy of my genius."

Up to that moment he hadn't written a line—he had torn up an old script that belonged to somebody else. But he knew what he was going to do, and in a week's time had it done.

Mr. MacArthur always enjoyed flummoxing Alexander Woollcott and Mr. Woollcott tried to stay as far away from the playwright as possible. Once at a Hollywood hotel Mr. Woollcott entertained at a small dinner party and Mr. Mac-Arthur, though uninvited, showed up for it. Mr. Woollcott, as was his style, loudly and sternly requested Mr. Mac-Arthur to leave. Mr. MacArthur went out and borrowed a waiter's costume, and disguised his features a bit, and returned to the party unrecognized. He stayed pretty much off to one side until he heard Mr. Woollcott ask for water. He picked up a pitcher, walked over to the host, dumped it over his head and said, "Is this what you wanted, sir?"

One of the most famous practical jokes of our time was played on Mr. Woollcott during the period when he was doing his Town Crier program on the radio. It began when Mr. Woollcott received a heart-wrenching letter from "Minnie and Susan"—two elderly sisters living in poverty in a single room of a tenement somewhere in the vicinity of Troy, New York. Both Minnie and Susan were ill, crippled with rheumatism, and oh, so devoted to Mr. Woollcott's inspiring broadcasts! They begged that, just for them, Mr. Woollcott read the Twenty-third Psalm, and Mr. Woollcott did it, in a volcanic eruption of sentiment. His story of the two sisters, and his reading of the Psalm, brought a tremendous response from the public—everyone wanted to help those two sweet and forlorn old women.

A month passed and a second letter came from "Susan Lovice Staples" containing the news that Minnie had died of weakness and privation, but not before she had heard that wonderful broadcast. Susan wrote something of the history of herself and Minnie, all quite touching, and Mr. Woollcott carried her letter next to his heart and insisted on reading it to everyone who would listen, and later read it over the air. Now he sent investigators to upstate New York to search for the surviving sister, but she could not be found. He appealed to her on the air to come forward, but there was no further word from her. Finally a letter came from a "Nurse Obrien" telling of Susan's death at the conclusion of a Woollcott broadcast. "She stretched out both her arms," said the letter, "like she was taking hold of your hands. . . . Once she called your name and blessed you and once she said something about some still water. She died at just eleven o'clock."

Mr. Woollcott employed every trick of the detective's trade in trying to locate the home and the graves of the two sisters, but in spite of all the clues in the letters, nothing was found. For a long time he refused to believe that he had been hoaxed; but the day came when he had to face the facts. He accused a number of people—including Charlie MacArthur. I have been told by several individuals who knew both men that it was definitely a MacArthur joke. But Mr. MacArthur assures me it was not. "If I had done it," he said, "I'd admit it happily. But I didn't."

During World War II, Mr. MacArthur was needed for a special assignment by the Pentagon. He was notified that his job was such that he would need to have a commission,

and he was asked to name what rank he would like to have.
"I would like to be a fort," he responded.

During one of the periods in which he was living in
Hollywood, Mr. MacArthur spent many afternoons, at the
West Side Tennis Club. He has, for a long time, fancied
himself as a pretty expert chess player and he went to the
club to play chess. Sometimes he would get his friends to
bring in an unsuspecting victim, telling him the great José
Capablanca was visiting the club. Mr. MacArthur would
assume what he thought to be an excellent Spanish accent
whenever he was introduced to a victim, and then he'd
agree to a game of chess. Mr. MacArthur was good, all
right, and usually defeated these fellow amateurs, enjoying
himself throughout the games by using the Spanish accent.

One afternoon the MacArthur cronies arrived with a fresh
sucker, Mr. Coatesworth. Mr. MacArthur was introduced
as the great Capablanca. "We play a game or two, eh?" he
suggested. The newcomer agreed. Gladly. For, of course, he
was the real José Capablanca. He had Mr. MacArthur
against the wall within six moves. And he exasperated Mr.
MacArthur still further by making each move quickly,
apparently without giving more than a moment's study to
it, then dashing out to the pool for a plunge, leaving the
phony Capablanca puzzled and fuming. When, at last,
Mr. MacArthur had decided on his move, his opponent
would return from the pool, casually and quickly make his
own move, and dash off again.

When it was all over, and truth stood revealed, Mr. Mac-
Arthur said he knew all along that he was playing the real
Capablanca. That's what he said.

I asked Charlie MacArthur what he considers to have
been the best all-around practical joke he ever heard about.
He spoke of several, but he seemed to favor the story of
Waldo Peirce and the turtle.

Peirce, an artist and poet and fabulous character, was
living in Paris and the concierge at his hotel became quite

fond of him and went out of her way to do special things for him to make him happy and comfortable. He felt the need to repay her for these kindnesses. He knew the lady was fond of pets so one day he brought home a present for her, a tiny turtle. She was overjoyed, and spent many happy hours coddling and nursing the creature, and worrying about its diet. Peirce, at the beginning, had no idea of carrying the transaction any further but, as so often happened, his imagination took over. Within a few days after the original gift, he substituted a turtle a size larger. The next day the turtle had grown another two inches in length. Madame was ecstatic. Her pet was flourishing wonderfully under her tender care. She talked about it constantly to everyone who would listen. Day by day the turtle grew bigger until Madame found herself in possession of an enormous and cumbersome creature, almost as big as a baby grand. She still loved the beast, and exclaimed over it and the way it had prospered under her care. But her American lodger could not let matters stand as they were. Now he began *reducing* the size of the huge turtle, day by day. The lady became frantic with worry, staying up nights, scarcely leaving her pet long enough to permit Peirce to substitute a smaller turtle. She was on the verge of losing her senses when the artist decided matters had gone far enough, and told her the truth.

Dick Maney, the theatrical press agent, has an off-beat sense of humor that sometimes leads him into strange adventures. Walking on Broadway one evening his eye fell on the Paramount Theater's doorman—a fellow close to seven feet tall. Mr. Maney walked over and tried to climb him to find out if he was snow-capped.

When he was working for Jed Harris, the producer, Mr. Maney lost his patience several times. Mr. Harris introduced a system of interoffice memos, which Mr. Maney thought was silly. He began sending memos to Mr. Harris. Such as the following:

To: Mr. Harris.
FROM: Mr. Maney.
RE: What time is it?

And another:

To: Mr. Harris.
FROM: Mr. Maney.
RE: What ever happened to Dorothy Arnold?

Before long the memo system was discontinued. The same thing happened on a somewhat bigger scale at the Twentieth Century-Fox studio in Beverly Hills, with Nunnally Johnson and Harry Brand conspiring to bring it to an end by making a joke of it.

Monty Woolley, the actor, has been described as "an untidy sleeper." This presumably means that he creates snarls when he sleeps—snarls in the bedclothing, snarls in his hair, snarls in his beard—and that perhaps he gets himself into grotesque postures. At any rate, his close friend Cole Porter has made a hobby of taking photographs of Mr. Woolley in the act of sleeping. Mr. Porter, it is said, has several dozen different shots and enjoys, at polite gatherings where Mr. Woolley is himself present and awake, bringing them out and showing them off.

Several years ago during a period when Mr. Woolley was not working and not much interested in working, Mr. Porter telephoned him from Boston. The songwriter seemed unusually excited. He said that some of Mr. Woolley's friends had decided the actor ought to be starred in a musical comedy. Would he be interested?

"Certainly I'm interested," said Mr. Woolley, "but would I have to sing?"

"Yes," said Mr. Porter, "you'd have to sing, but not much. The important thing would be your dancing. You'd have to waltz quite a bit. Can you waltz?"

"I think I could," said Mr. Woolley. "But just what kind of a role is it you have me playing?"

"A whoremonger," said Mr. Porter, which somehow concluded the conversation.

Of newspapermen as pranksters, A. J. Liebling has written:

"Newspapering, despite urgent prodding from schools of journalism, has always lagged behind the learned professions on the march to seemliness. Lawyers wrestled and played practical jokes on each other in Lincoln's time, but newspapermen continued to rough each other up for many decades thereafter."

William Harlan Hale was working on the staff of the Washington *Star* when his editor decided he should go to New York and write some stories about the World Series. One noontime he was in Bleeck's restaurant with several members of the *Herald Tribune* staff. The company was excellent, the stories were good and the drinks seemed exactly right; but Mr. Hale was not going to fall into that age-old trap that often overpowers the best of newspapermen. He had a job to do—he had to go uptown and cover the World Series. He complained about it to his friends, and remarked how much more fun it would be to just sit around Bleeck's all afternoon. The boys were at a table in a backroom of the establishment, and the time had just about come for Mr. Hale to hop into a cab and head for the ball game. Then someone glanced at the single window in the room. Drops of rain were beginning to patter against the glass and in another half minute a real gully-washer was descending on the city. Mr. Hale was pleased and so were his companions, who assured him there could be no ball game in this kind of a downpour. So they all relaxed, and settled down for a long and pleasant afternoon. Three hours later the party broke up and Mr. Hale with his friends emerged into Fortieth Street to find the sun shining brightly and the pavement dry. Mr. Hale had been city slickered. His friends had enlisted a waiter, who stood behind the building with a garden hose and played a heavy spray against that single window all afternoon.

A dozen years ago the most famous juvenile creature in all Christendom was Charlie McCarthy. And on a Friday night, in the Waldorf-Astoria Hotel, Edgar Bergen's celebrated dummy was kidnaped.

The whole nefarious operation was engineered by Frank Farrell, who was then drama editor of the New York *World-Telegram*. There are some who think that Mr. Bergen was in on the play—that the kidnaping was a pure publicity stunt. I'm quite sure that wasn't so. There are others who think Mr. Farrell's motive was simply to create a good lively story for the front page of his newspaper. I doubt that, too. Mr. Farrell is a ribber. He is never happier than when he has a gag going. He knew that Mr. Bergen was in New York with Charlie and he knew they were staying at the Waldorf-Astoria. He found out that on this particular Friday night Mr. Bergen was going to a dinner party where he would not be expected to entertain. Mr. Farrell reasoned that the dummy would be left behind in the Bergen room.

Mr. Farrell went to the Belmont Plaza and took a room for himself, using the name of E. Bergen. Then he telephoned the floor clerk at the Waldorf-Astoria.

"This," he said, "is Mr. Bergen. I wonder if you would be so kind as to go into my suite and get Charlie for me. He's in a bag and you can have one of the bellboys bring him over to this party at the Belmont Plaza."

Before long the bellboy arrived, carrying the bag, and handed it over to Mr. Farrell. Mr. Farrell sat around and admired his achievement for a while, then got another daring idea. He checked out of the hotel and went to the Stork Club, where he placed the bag in the checkroom. He strolled on into the club and was startled to find Mr. Bergen sitting at one of the tables. He didn't stay long in the club, for he began to get nervous, fearing Mr. Bergen might somehow catch a glimpse of that bag. So Mr. Farrell left with it and took it down to the neighborhood of the

Battery, where he found a place to hide it.

A few hours later the abduction of Charlie was discovered. Mr. Bergen had a sort of Scandinavian tantrum over it, and his floor at the Waldorf-Astoria was soon swarming with police detectives.

Early on Saturday morning Mr. Farrell arrived at his newspaper to find the place in a mild uproar over the kidnaping. At the city desk he was told that no trace of the dummy had been found, that Mr. Bergen was genuinely upset, that Charlie McCarthy was insured for $2,500, and that whoever had done the job was in trouble.

Mr. Farrell finally walked over to Lee Wood, the executive editor, and said: "Lee, I've got a hot dummy on my hands."

Mr. Wood and B. O. McAnney, the managing editor, told Mr. Farrell there was only one course open to him—he must go up and face Mr. Bergen and all those cops and confess. He did it, and was promptly placed under arrest. The photographer who went with him was arrested. He phoned Mr. McAnney, pleading urgently for help, and Mr. McAnney sent Alton Cook, a close friend of Mr. Bergen, to intercede. Mr. Cook was arrested. In the end the newspaper had to appeal to Thomas E. Dewey, then the New York District Attorney. Mr. Dewey felt that Mr. Farrell should be sent to Sing Sing, but finally agreed to let him off.

"It was fun while it lasted," Mr. Farrell said later, "but I don't think I'll ever again kidnap a dummy as long as I live. From now on I kidnap nothing but live people."

Oscar Levant, the lugubrious pianist and actor, was divorced by his first wife, who then married Arthur Loew, of the theater family. The Loews made their home on Long Island. One morning, around four o'clock, Mr. Levant telephoned his former wife and got her out of bed.

"Hello," he said, "this is Oscar."

Mrs. Loew was understandably irritated.

"What do you mean by waking me up in the middle of the night?" she demanded.

"Well, I just wanted to ask you a question."

"Yes?"

"What's playing at Loew's 86th Street tomorrow?"

The story of the Newfoundland dogs is supposed to have originated in a New York advertising agency. One of the executives lived in an uptown apartment where he kept his two big dogs. His wife went away to visit relatives for a week, and made her husband promise that he would leave his office twice a day, at 11 A.M. and 4 P.M., and exercise the dogs. If they didn't have their romp twice a day, they would get sick, and he said he'd do it.

Then he made a discovery. He found that whenever the telephone rang in the apartment, the two dogs would begin racing up and down the rooms, and get plenty of exercise. All he had to do, then, was phone his apartment at eleven and again at four, let the bell ring fifteen times, then hang up. He told his associates about it, to show them how smart he was.

One day, one of these associates managed to get the key to the apartment. He left the office quietly and went up there and let himself in, just before four o'clock. He waited till the phone started ringing. He let it ring a dozen times, then lifted it off the hook, placed his face close to the mouthpiece, and began panting heavily—in the manner of a big dog. Then he hung up.

Ben Serkowich, who has been in the motion picture business for many years, was sitting one day in his Broadway office talking with an old friend, a Lieutenant in the Air Force. In an adjoining office was a Miss Carson, a girl who knew all the answers but had three fourths of them wrong. Mr. Serkowich got a phone call from a man in a Brooklyn theater, who remarked that it had just started to rain furiously in his neighborhood. Mr. Serkowich glanced out his window and noted that the sun was shining and the pavements were dry on Broadway. Finishing the phone call, he told the Lieutenant about the rainstorm in Brooklyn. The Lieutenant looked at a flag on top of a building across the street, then calculated the approximate distance of the Brooklyn theater, and said, "It'll hit here in twelve to fifteen minutes."

About this time in walked Miss Carson and Mr. Serkowich introduced her to the Lieutenant.

"This young man," he said, "is just back from overseas. He was shot down and taken prisoner by the Grand Lama of Eyesore, who taught him a lot of oriental mysticism. He learned quite a good deal, for example, about weather control. Ask him to do something about the weather."

Miss Carson appeared skeptical, but she was interested in the Lieutenant for he was young and handsome and dashing. She hemmed and hawed a bit and then Mr. Serkowich quickly scribbled something on a piece of paper and handed it to her. It said, "Ask him to make it rain in ten minutes."

"Let's see you make it rain in ten minutes," she said, looking out at the Broadway sunshine. "I know, of course, that you can't do it, but go ahead and try."

"I'll try it," said the Lieutenant, "if you'll keep absolutely quiet." He turned his two fists upside down and placed the knuckles together in front of his chest. Then he began to chant, using long strange-sounding words which he remembered from government directives. He rolled his eyes around and then lowered his head and appeared to be in deep meditation. He stretched it out as long as he could and then told Miss Carson, "That's the best I can do. It ought to rain now in a couple of minutes."

It did—a deluge came out of nowhere (Brooklyn)—and Miss Carson is talking about it to this day.

Estelle Winwood, the actress, has great commiseration for all people who are in trouble. Once she was on a ship, traveling from England to South Africa with a company of friends. She became interested in a woebegone young man who seemed to do nothing all day but scrub decks and polish brass. She felt sorry for him, because he had such a dull and backbreaking job. Then one day he disappeared and Miss Winwood's friends told her that he had been loaded with chains and iron balls and thrown into the hold, simply because he had violated the regulations by talking to her. She brooded over the thing for a while and then marched into the Captain's quarters and told him off, demanding that the poor young man be released immediately and restored to his rightful place in God's fresh air. The Captain heard her out and then said he would reduce the punishment; he'd put the boy to work in the galley. Miss Winwood felt real good about her achievement until her friends told her that the young man had never been in the hold—that he had simply been transferred to the galley.

On this same voyage Miss Winwood recalls that she saw the Equator plain. As the ship approached the line she was told that under certain favorable atmospheric conditions, it was possible to *see* it. She was provided with a pair of binoculars and stationed at the rail with instructions to place the glasses to her eyes when she heard a gong sound. She followed these instructions, pointing the binoculars at the water, and there it was—a distinct dark line running through the sea. She didn't learn, till later, that a black thread had been fastened across the lenses of the binoculars—one of the most ancient of all seafaring jokes.

The late Frank Tinney employed a gag to startle his acquaintances along Broadway. He would engage an open, horse-drawn cab, and get into the seat with a live pony. The cab would move down Broadway until Mr. Tinney spotted one of his friends on the sidewalk. He would then yell out, "Hey Bill!" at the same time dropping out of sight on the floor and grasping his companion's halter. Bill would look up to see a pony sitting in a cab and bowing in his direction.

16

Hollywood

In one of the canyons around Hollywood stands a fantastic house, a sprawling, arabesque castle with Moorish towers, sunken gardens and secret patios. The grounds are honeycombed with hidden tunnels and almost every room in the house has a sliding panel. A good part of the castle was constructed of materials left over from the sets of old Douglas Fairbanks pictures. Mr. Fairbanks himself was a frequent visitor at the castle, as was John Barrymore.

Today the property belongs to Mac Brainerd, a genius in the field of electronics. He walks into a room, waves his hand to the right, and all the lights go on. He waves it to the left and the logs begin burning in the fireplace. Whenever his telephone rings, a machine answers, and records the name and number of the caller, and talks to him in a familiar but courteous manner. When Mr. Brainerd is in his car, half a mile away, he can turn on the furnace, open the garage, light the entire house, light the yard and turn on the television simply by pressing buttons on a special instrument panel in his automobile. There's a huge swimming pool on the premises, equipped with a bewildering sound system. A swimmer can hear music whenever he is underwater; he can't hear it after he comes to the surface.

This house formerly belonged to Jack McDermott, a writer and director for the movies. Mr. McDermott had no talent for electronics but he would go out of his way for a joke. Guests in his home never lacked for excitement, especially with all those sliding panels and secret tunnels. Unfortunately none of those guests has ever given the world a record of the range of jokes in Mr. McDermott's repertoire. Those who have been asked to recall some of them have responded by passing a hand across their foreheads, getting a wild look in their eyes, and saying, "Please! Talk about something else! I'd rather not even think about it."

It is known that in the time of Mr. McDermott there was much drinking in the castle. It is known, too, that whenever a guest passed out, he would be placed in bed in his comfortable room, and then Mr. McDermott would release two dozen pigeons, some dyed green and some red, in the room. He apparently had a theory that when the victim woke up, he'd be soothed by red and green pigeons.

He kept a hopped-up Model-T Ford on his premises and sometimes he'd insist that his guests go for a ride with him. They'd set off with Mr. McDermott at the wheel, careening at a dangerous speed through the mountains. When the guests complained about his recklessness, as they usually did, he'd wrench the steering wheel off its post and hurl it over the nearest cliff. This was most unsettling to his passengers, who didn't know he had installed foot controls for steering.

The big swimming pool existed in Mr. McDermott's time, without the underwater music. He had his fun by providing his guests, especially the ladies, with swimming suits that dissolved when they got wet.

It is my understanding that Mr. McDermott's house was the true locale of the famous Upside-down Room. This is a room in which all the furnishings, drapes, pictures, fireplace, are upside down. The rugs and furniture are fastened to the ceiling while the floor contains a single object—an elaborate chandelier thrust upward from the center.

A guest at a party in the house takes too much to drink and passes out. He is carried into the Upside-down Room and placed on the floor (ceiling) midway between the wall and the chandelier. When he awakens, he has a bad time of it.

Ten years ago I wrote a description of the Upside-down Room and said it was in a mansion on the outskirts of Lima, Peru. That's what I had been told. Since then I have read that it is in a big house on Long Island, and Lucius Beebe has written that it was contrived by "a rich Englishman with an appalling sense of humor." Now I am told by Fred Beck, a wise and knowledgeable man, that it was in Mr. McDermott's castle. I'm inclined to believe it, for it would almost have to be in Hollywood. The people of the motion picture industry and allied businesses pause in the day's occupation to play practical jokes on one another. Pause often. There have been so many Hollywood jokes that I can only furnish a small sampling in this monograph.

A movie studio is a walled enclosure crawling with numerous wild and unpredictable jokers. They defy any sort of classification for their exploits are of widely divergent color and range. And more often than not they involve the people in the upper salary brackets.

The late Buddy De Sylva was given many unpleasant moments by his close friend, Leo McCarey, especially during the filming of the picture *Going My Way*. Mr. McCarey was directing the picture and Mr. De Sylva, as head of the studio, had the job of looking at the rushes each morning. *Going My Way* was a picture about the priesthood and the studio was exercising extraordinary care in handling a touchy subject. Mr. McCarey and Bing Crosby, however, decided to have some fun with the boss. At the conclusion of the regular shooting schedule each day, they'd improvise an additional scene and shoot it. Nothing too shocking, but definitely a scene that would cause trouble. For example, they had one scene in which a boy's choir was singing. The sweet-faced lads in their cassocks sang a hymn slowly and impressively, until they arrived at a line which went, ". . . and when I die . . ." at which point the rhythm changed and the word "die" became "Dinah!" as they went into a real steaming herky-jerk version of that popular song. It was reported that Mr. De Sylva, viewing the rushes the next morning, fell out of his chair.

One day a gooney-looking young man showed up on the set and spent the entire day just staring at Mr. McCarey. Finally Mr. McCarey demanded the meaning of this behavior. The young man said he had applied for a job as a director and had talked to Mr. De Sylva. The head of production had sent him out to the sound stage with instructions to study Mr. McCarey's every movement and thereby learn how a truly great director operates. The following morning Mr. De Sylva arrived at his office to find an unshaven, ragged bum waiting for him. The bum said: "Mr. McCarey told me to study you, so I can learn to be a big executive. Mr. McCarey said it'll only take part of one day."

At another studio there was a screenwriter who was under contract at a thousand dollars a week. He got in trouble with the front office and a bitter feud developed. He made himself so unpleasant to the studio heads that they decided they wouldn't simply buy up his contract and get rid of him. They'd make him suffer. So they assigned him to finish out his contract as a messenger and guide around the studio. Some days later a group of the company's stockholders arrived from the east and after business conferences, decided to take a tour of the sound stages. By chance the unhappy screenwriter was given the job of escorting them over the lot. He did a fine, courteous job and when the tour was over, the stockholders offered him a nice tip.

"No, thanks," he said. "It's nice of you, but I'm really very well paid. I get a thousand dollars a week."

"Don't be ridiculous!" said the stockholders.

"I'm not being ridiculous. Look, here's my latest pay check."

There was hell to pay in the front office after that, and

the writer's contract was paid off and he was allowed to go in peace.

Actors, as we have noted, are great practical jokers. There was one fairly prominent actor at a big studio who often talked to his associates about his wife in England, and how their first child was expected. Everyone expressed polite interest, of course, and then one day the actor showed up jubilant, exhibiting a cablegram announcing the birth of a son. Hearty congratulations all around. Three or four weeks later he arrived at the studio with the first photograph of his new son, eagerly showing it around. The child in the picture was pretty close to being a monstrosity, somewhat on the order of that famous picture that was supposed to be Hitler as a baby. The poor people who had to look at it, and then at the beaming face of the father, needed all their theatrical training to carry through, and exclaim, "Oh, he's *cute!*" The actor, of course, had no child.

If the actors all reformed, the screenwriters would still keep things humming. Not long ago two writers were having lunch together at one of the studios, and made the interesting discovery that they were patients of the same psychoanalyst. They retired to an office and between them cooked up a fantastic and complicated dream. Then each man, on his day to visit the analyst, told him he had had that dream. The analyst is said to have thought for a while of going to an analyst.

Two other writers leased a big house for a year. Their landlord promised to redecorate the place, but they could get no action out of him. Finally they went to a lawyer and had a paper drawn, in which the landlord gave them permission to paint the interior at their own expense. They waited until two days before their lease expired, then had everything in the house—walls, floors, ceilings and even the plumbing fixtures in both the kitchen and bathrooms—painted solidly black.

* * *

The Walt Disney studio has always been a hive of busy practical jokers. There was one artist who had a hobby of acquiring unusual automobiles, and who talked incessantly about them. One day he arrived at the studio with his latest —a custom-built job. He insisted on dragging everyone outdoors to inspect it. Then, while he worked at his drawing board, his pals decided to have some fun. They found a metal wheelbarrow of the type used to transport concrete. They managed to get this thing wedged into the back seat of the car. Then they filled it with water. The car's owner spent two hours dipping the water out with a pan, trying to avoid spilling it on his fine upholstery, and then found he had to dismantle the wheelbarrow in order to get it out. He wasn't speaking to people for quite a spell.

A certain technician at the Disney studio handled film all day long and his friends convinced him that, as a consequence of this work, his body was storing up an enormous charge of electricity. If he didn't do something about it, he might some day soon disintegrate in a bolt of lightning. He became deeply worried about the amount of electricity running through his body and sought advice, so one afternoon he was called into one of the offices. A consultation was held with sound men and electricians, and these experts solemnly told him there was only one way to clear out his system. They had him sit in a chair with his pants leg rolled up. Copper wire was wound around his leg, then threaded up through his trousers and out at the zipper. From that point the wire led to the office window and then dropped to the ground, where it was attached to a large can of water. The electricians called this the "run-off wire" and explained that all the juice would flow out of his body in about an hour. The human storage battery was sitting there quietly discharging power. In a circle around him were the technicians, jotting down notes, inspecting a meter, glancing at stop watches. Then in walked Walt Disney himself. He took pity on the victim and broke up the party.

An extremely serious young Englishman came to work at

the Disney studio. The jokers in the shop looked upon him as something sent by Providence and they began scouting for opportunities. The Englishman made a habit of bringing his own lunch to the studio and each noontime he'd go to a nearby grocery store and buy a bottle of milk and a can of fruit. The conspirators went to the grocer and made a deal with him. They bought some canned fruit plus some canned vegetables. They took the labels off the fruit cans and put them on the vegetable cans, and they bribed the grocer to use this disguised stock whenever their victim made a purchase.

So it came about that the Englishman would return to his desk from the grocer's with, say, a can of peaches. He'd open it and find it contained string beans, or creamed corn, or peas. Then he began finding, instead of fruit, such things as hash and spaghetti. Being a man with little humor, he was not amused; he was filled with wonder. He began telling his associates about it, and asking what he ought to do. They said it was truly a phenomenon, and that he ought to write to Ripley about it. So he sat down and composed a long letter, explaining the matter in great detail. He mailed the letter and then, noting that it was lunch time, walked to the grocery store to have another try. He bought his bottle of milk and a can of pears. He returned to his office and got out his can opener, wondering what surprise he might find this time. He opened the can. There were no vegetables in it, and no fruit. Inside the can was a small test tube, tightly corked. And inside the test tube was a piece of paper. The Englishman pulled the cork and fished out the paper. It said:

> *Dear sir:*
> I don't believe a damned word of it.
> *Robert Ripley*

This within an hour of the time he had mailed the letter to Ripley! The perpetrators of the deed say that he talked for days about the "miracle" and never did get wise to the fact that he had been had.

Alfred Hitchcock has become world-famous for his methods of dealing with suspenseful situations, so it cannot come as a shock that he also has a reputation as a practical joker. His gags are known on both sides of the Atlantic. He used to enjoy handcuffing people to things and leaving them there. He once had an old horse delivered to Sir Gerald du Maurier's dressing room at St. James's Theatre. On another occasion he amused himself by sending four hundred smoked herring to a friend as a birthday gift.

A young actor once told me how he called on Mr. Hitchcock in his room at the St. Regis Hotel in New York. They left the room and got into the elevator. At one of the middle floors two old ladies stepped into the car and stood with their backs to the two men. Mr. Hitchcock and the actor had been talking about a motion picture but now the Hitchcock voice changed. A melodramatic tremor came into it, and he said:

"You know very well I *had* to shoot him. Had no choice. Don't really think I killed him. Aimed four shots at his leg. Left him there in a pool of blood. Lying on the floor. Suppose anybody heard the shots? You've got to stand by me in this. Have the taxi pick me up around the corner."

The moment this little monologue started the two old ladies began to stiffen. By the time the car reached the ground floor they were clearly in a state of horror. They were practically running when they left the car and zipped out of the hotel, heading for the street and safety, not even pausing to notify the management that foul murder had been committed on the premises, and the murderer was making his getaway.

One of Mr. Hitchcock's victims in London tried to get back at him. He prepared a filthy concoction and poured it into a rare brandy bottle, replaced the seals, and presented the bottle to the director. Days passed, and not a word from Mr. Hitchcock. Finally the man could stand the suspense no longer.

"That brandy I gave you," he said. "Did you get a chance to sample it?"

"No," said Mr. Hitchcock, "I'm sorry to say I didn't. Didn't want to mention this to you, but my mother took sick. Doctor prescribed regular doses of brandy. We fed yours to her. I'm afraid it didn't help. Afraid she's going to die."

Darryl Zanuck, one of the most important men in Hollywood, began as a writer and in his early days lived in a club inhabited by writers. He remembers coming home and finding his jackets and shirts padlocked together at the buttonholes. Usually, however, Mr. Zanuck is the prankster, and even today retains employees whose jobs include participation in Zanuck-devised jokes.

He once chartered a yacht for a trip to Mexico. Mexican reporters boarded the vessel to interview Mr. Zanuck but he wasn't present. Instead they found a character wearing a monocle who was introduced as "Ambassador Gerard, goodwill plenipotentiary from the British Empire to Mexico." The Ambassador was attended by an efficient secretary. The secretary was Darryl Zanuck and the Ambassador was an actor named Doug Gerard. The Ambassador was acclaimed in Mexico City, where he spent money lavishly. The Mexicans were quite amused by the fact that he drank large quantities of liquor and on one occasion, in a fashionable night club, danced a solo tango in his bare feet.

At the studio Mr. Zanuck has on his payroll a man named Sam Silver who is a barber as well as a physical trainer. One day Mr. Zanuck walked into Sam's barbering hut flashing a large emerald. Sam was impressed—it was the biggest emerald he had ever seen. Where did Mr. Zanuck get it?"

"There's a maharajah from India visiting the studio," said Mr. Zanuck. "He asked for my autograph and when I gave it to him, he presented me with this rock. They say he gives emeralds to everyone who does him a favor."

A gleam came in Sam's eyes. Couldn't Mr. Zanuck arrange to have Sam shave the maharajah? Mr. Zanuck said the potentate was coming back to the studio the next day, and if he got a chance he'd suggest it.

A dark-skinned actor was engaged, and arrayed in oriental costume, and the next day Mr. Zanuck brought him to the barber.

"Would your highness do me the honor of leaving me shave you?" suggested Sam.

"Impossible!" said the maharajah. "No one but a Mohammedan is allowed to touch my skin." He started to walk out, then turned back. "However," he said, "I do need a shave. If you were willing to become a Mohammedan, then . . ."

With visions of emeralds dancing in his brain, Sam consented. He was told to kneel, and beat his head against the floor while the maharajah uttered the proper words. After that Sam shaved him, and performed as neat and gentle an operation as was within his power. Then he stood by, waiting for his emerald. The maharajah merely nodded to him and started to walk out. Sam was panicky. He urged his highness to submit himself to a first-rate massage. Again his highness was horrified. The body was even more sacred than the face. But if Sam would agree to a further sacred ceremony, perhaps it would be all right. There was more kneeling, more head beating, more mysterious words, and then Sam gave the maharajah a rubdown. At the conclusion of this operation, the maharajah expressed deep satisfaction, and handed Sam an emerald that even dwarfed Mr. Zanuck's stone.

Sam rushed off to a jeweler's to get an appraisal.

"What's this worth?" he asked excitedly. The jeweler didn't even bother to use his glass.

"If," he said, "you had a carload of these, the whole thing would be worth about thirty cents."

The late Douglas Fairbanks had two pronounced weaknesses: he worshiped royalty, and he couldn't resist playing practical jokes. Sometimes the two passions impinged. No titled person could visit Hollywood without being entertained by Mr. Fairbanks. And once he had royalty or nobility in his house, Mr. Fairbanks might very well turn loose a ribber on the victim—a clumsy butler, or a waiter who spilled soup on the guest.

Mr. Fairbanks is said to have invented the joke in which a swimming pool is made virtually unswimmable. Someone would be giving an elaborate outdoor party with the swimming pool as the center of activities. During the night before the party, Mr. Fairbanks would arrange to have a truckload of ice, in hundred-pound slabs, delivered and dumped in the pool. By party time the water would repel a walrus.

And Mr. Fairbanks is reputed to have been a victim of a major joke predicated on his love of royalty. He maintained a huge cellar stocked with rare wines, but his friends found he was inclined to be stingy about opening the good stuff whenever they were around. So they launched a conspiracy. They let word get to Mr. Fairbanks that the King of Sweden was coming to Hollywood, traveling incognito, and that the King had expressed the wish to visit Mr. Fairbanks at Pickfair. Mr. Fairbanks, of course, was overjoyed. He was advised by telegram to have three cars at the airport at a given hour. He was there. Off the plane came an actor playing the King and doing it well. With him were a dozen secretaries and advisors. The party was driven to Pickfair and almost at once the King suggested that he'd like nothing better, at the moment, than a fine glass of wine.

The wine-drinking started on a respectable scale, but before long the King and all his entourage were in the cellar, yanking out corks, tilting the bottles, spilling more than they drank. Mr. Fairbanks was alarmed, and even shocked.

He tried to get the party back upstairs, but the King would embrace him and call him friend and Mr. Fairbanks would weaken. Before they were finished, Mr. Fairbanks was down to one or two bottles of domestic claret, and the King and all his courtiers were drunker than seven thousand dollars.

Mr. Fairbanks carried his practical joking beyond the grave. He had four close friends and each of these had been given to understand that he would be remembered in the Fairbanks will. So Mr. Fairbanks died, and the will was opened, and there was no mention of these friends. They were understandably upset, and may have said some harsh things about the departed.

Sixty days passed, and then the four men were assembled by Mr. Fairbanks' actor son. He said that his father had given him an envelope with instructions that it was not to be opened until sixty days after his death. Now it was opened. It provided that each of the four should receive sixty thousand dollars.

The late Sid Grauman, theater owner, was sometimes called the king of practical jokers in Hollywood. He was full of tricks. He walked into a meeting of Paramount's board of directors one day wearing overalls and carrying tools. He began tapping with a hammer on a radiator and before long the chairman, Adolph Zukor, was frowning. The tapping grew louder and pretty soon the plumber was whaling away with the hammer, defying Mr. Zukor's orders to leave, even threatening to give Mr. Zukor a couple of clouts on the skull.

The other directors were about ready to gang him when he revealed his identity.

At the time Queen Marie of Rumania visited America and included Hollywood on her itinerary, almost every big star and producer in town was a-quiver at the mere thought of getting to meet a real monarch. There was to be a single reception for her, and a select list of guests was invited.

Mr. Grauman was not on the list.

At great expense he hired a ballroom in one of the biggest hotels in Los Angeles. He engaged actors and actresses and had them properly costumed. He sent engraved invitations to many movie people who, like himself, had not been invited to the other affair. The invitations stated that the bearer would be permitted a rare privilege—seeing the Royal Court of Queen Marie in actual operation. The Queen had found it necessary, while in Los Angeles, to hold a sort of emergency meeting of the Court, and she was willing that certain selected citizens be permitted to look at it from afar.

The guests were not permitted to enter the actual room, but were escorted to a balcony, or allowed to peer in through the several doors. There sat the Queen on a gilded throne, surrounded by beautiful ladies-in-waiting and surrounded, too, by her various Ministers. Her Royal Highness pretended that no one was looking and carried on affairs of state, consulting with each of her Ministers in turn after they had bowed and scraped and kissed her hand. Mr. Grauman sat through the whole affair in a corner of the balcony, enjoying himself immensely.

Came the day when Mr. Grauman decided to try his hand with Douglas Fairbanks. Mr. Fairbanks and his wife, Mary Pickford, were leaving by train for New York, then sailing for Europe. Mr. Grauman got in touch with a man who furnished animals and birds to the movie studios. He hired a trained duck—a duck that could be depended on to kick and flap his wings and quack loudly. He had the duck trussed up and elaborately packaged, in the style of those firms which cater to gourmets. Just before the train departed, the package was delivered to Mr. Fairbanks. When he opened it, he found himself in possession of the noisiest going-away gift in history.

But Mr. Fairbanks recognized that duck. He knew that the duck was worth several thousand dollars. He knew that it was costing Sid Grauman fifty dollars a day to hire the noisy bird. So, on the following day he sent a telegram to Mr. Grauman, saying:

"God bless you! Food on this train horrible. We ate the duck."

Mr. Grauman's victims, at one time or another, included almost everyone of any importance in Hollywood. The time came when a group of his friends organized a gigantic testimonial dinner for him. It was a splendid affair, held in one of the big hotels, and the banquet room was packed. When dinner was over, the toastmaster arose and began his glowing tribute.

"We are assembled," he said, "to do honor to the greatest showman of our time—a man we all love—that grand old white-haired master of the theater . . . Frank Whitbeck!"

Mr. Whitbeck, a prominent casting director, rose from his chair in the middle of the room and bowed gravely, and sat down. Then, one by one, some of the most celebrated people in Hollywood got up and spoke, praising Frank Whitbeck, and there was never once a mention of Sid Grauman. His victims had turned the worm.

If the business of confusing strangers may be called practical joking, Groucho Marx certainly belongs in this compendium. He can achieve, with a random remark, the results that other jokers may strive for with days of planning. One day he and Goodman Ace were walking on Fifth Avenue. They came to St. Patrick's Cathedral just as a wedding party was entering. The bride got out of a car and started across the sidewalk. She had reached the first step when she felt a hand on her shoulder. It was Mr. Marx. In a sad, fatherly tone he said, "Don't do it. I tried it twice— it's no good." That girl went on into the church but she was not moving as fast as she had been before, and there was a wild and wondering look in her eyes.

Mr. Marx gives people fits in department stores. He was in one of the nobbiest of New York's stores when he spied a barrel-shaped woman, obviously a wealthy customer with a zimmeleen waiting at the curb. She had a small dog in her arms. Mr. Marx stepped up to her.

"How much for the dog, miss?" he asked politely.

The woman eyed him as if he were offal. She sputtered. She informed him haughtily that the dog was not for sale.

"I'm sorry," said Mr. Marx. "I thought you were a sales-girl."

That was all—just enough to ruin the proud one's whole week.

Mr. Marx also confuses people who attend meetings of various kinds. He may go to a forum where some burning political issue is being discussed. When the argument reaches its most violent point, he will suddenly stand up, raise both hands to command silence, then say, "Gentlemen! They have just fired on Fort Sumter!"

One evening a friend in Hollywood took him to a séance. The medium brought in a spirit from Out Yonder, a gabby character who had all the answers. People asked questions about their loved ones, and the spirit responded with messages from them. This went on for quite a time, until almost everyone present had communicated with the departed. Then came a pause.

"Are there any more questions?" asked the spirit voice.

"I have one," spoke up Mr. Marx, who had said not a word up to that point.

"Please ask it," said the spirit.

"What's the capital of South Dakota?" said Mr. Marx.

He once applied for membership for his children in a swimming club. The application was denied with the frank explanation that the club did not admit Jews. Mr. Marx telephoned the club president and explained to him that his children were only half Jewish.

"It seems to me," he said, "that you should issue special memberships, permitting them to go into the water up to their navels."

*　*　*

Zero Mostel, who can sometimes give people the impression that he is criminally insane by just sitting still, went to Hollywood in quest of fame and fortune. He was accompanied by Ivan Black, who had him buy a new suit for $125, and then told him he ought to appear in the nicer restaurants, where he would be seen by important people, and that his job at the beginning was to make a good impression on those people. As a starter, Mr. Black took him to the Mocambo.

They sat down at a table and Mr. Mostel picked up a knife and a piece of bread. He began buttering the bread. Then, at a faster pace, he began buttering his coat sleeve, moving the knife like a man stropping a razor, covering the sleeve with butter clear up to the elbow. Finishing that, he held up his left thumb and began buttering it as if it were a small ear of corn. Then he stuck the thumb in his mouth and licked it off. At this point he noticed that a waiter was staring at him.

"Whatta you starin' at?" demanded Mr. Mostel.

"Nothing," said the waiter apologetically.

"Anything unusual about what I'm doin'?" asked Mr. Mostel.

"No, sir. Not a thing, sir."

"Well, then, step lively and bring more butter for my thumb."

There is an artist living in Hollywood who has a glass eye. That is, he has a couple of dozen glass eyes. Some of them are bloodshot, in varying degrees, to match up with the rest of his hangovers. The others have little paintings on them. On patriotic occasions he sometimes appears with an eye on which is painted an American flag. It is most disconcerting to people who find themselves in conversation with him. This man has a little joke he sometimes pulls in restaurants. Get a hold of yourself now. He'll sit studying the menu, with a waiter standing by. Absently he'll pick up a fork, raise his head, and begin scratching his eyeball with the fork. I don't want to see him do it. I'm even a little sorry I mentioned it.

Dave Epstein is a successful public relations man in Hollywood with his own organization which is devoted, in large part, to publicizing producers and directors. A dozen years ago Mr. Epstein hit upon a little device by which he could get the names of his clients in the Hollywood columns during those periods when the clients weren't actually making any news. He invented a character named Ned Farrington, "prominent producer in Broadway's legitimate theatre." Mr. Epstein would send items to the columnists, such as, "Ned Farrington, the prominent New York producer, spent $286 in long-distance tolls last week talking to Clarence Brown at Metro. Big deal cooking?" Or, perhaps, "Jack Furrow planes out tomorrow for Gotham and important conferences with Ned Farrington, the Broadway production genius." This sort of thing went on for a couple of years and then Jim Henaghan, who was writing a column for the Hollywood *Reporter*, got wise to the little deception. One morning Mr. Henaghan's column contained the following note: "The many Hollywood friends of Ned Farrington, Broadway producer, were inexpressibly shocked to learn that he died in his sleep last night." Killed him off, just like that, and Mr. Epstein didn't like it.

A decorative feature of the CBS executive offices in Hollywood is the ivy planter. Each office has one or more of these fancy pots. One night, not long ago, someone made the rounds of all the offices, removing the ivy and replacing it with vines of the Italian vegetable, zucchini.

Eddie Sutherland, the veteran director, learned the art of the super-pratfall when he worked years ago as one of the Keystone Cops. Long after his performing days were over, Mr. Sutherland could startle people with it. Standing perfectly erect, he could suddenly throw his feet into the air and land on the floor with a crash without doing himself any physical harm.

After he had become a prominent director, he was a guest one night at a dignified party where the discussion turned on great dramatic situations. Mr. Sutherland suggested that, to his way of thinking, one of the most dramatic scenes in all literature was that described in Browning's *Incident of the French Camp*, which closes with the line, "Smiling, the boy fell dead." Mr. Sutherland said he'd like to demonstrate his thesis, and enlisted the aid of an actor to play the part of Napoleon at Ratisbon.

The actor stood with hand in vest and Mr. Sutherland recited the last few lines of the poem. At the proper moment the actor spoke his single line, "You're wounded." Sutherland said, "Nay, I'm killed, sire." Then he smiled, rather wistfully, as a deep hush lay over the room, and suddenly he went into the air, his body twisted, and down to the floor with a crash. It was, truly, a classic exposition of the dramatic art.

John Barrymore always loved a good jest. Even on his deathbed he couldn't resist having a moment's fun with his closest friend, Gene Fowler. Mr. Fowler was almost in a daze from the knowledge that his friend was dying. At the hospital the great actor continually asked to see Mr. Fowler and finally Mr. Fowler walked in.

"Come closer, Gene," whispered Mr. Barrymore, "and hold my hand." Mr. Fowler moved up beside the bed. "Lean over closer, Gene," whispered the dying man, "I want to ask you something very important." Mr. Fowler leaned down, tears in his eyes, and Mr. Barrymore said, "Tell me, Gene, is it true that you are an illegitimate son of Buffalo Bill?"

Al Horwits, a talented studio publicity man, got his training as a baseball writer in Philadelphia back in the days when both local teams customarily occupied eighth place in the standings. Alton Cook says Mr. Horwits turned to practical joking as a release from cellar-depression. Mr. Horwits is a master of the phony message. He is believed to have invented the telegram which is sent to a hopeful actor in Hollywood, saying:

DISREGARD MY PREVIOUS WIRE
ZANUCK

Soon after he became a star Van Heflin was sent out on a personal appearance tour under the guidance of Mr. Horwits. When the tour was completed Mr. Horwits suggested that Mr. Heflin write letters of appreciation to all the people who had co-operated. Mr. Horwits made up the list of names and included on it J. Oliver Prickett, whom he described as the Universal studio executive responsible for all such tours. Mr. Heflin wrote Mr. Prickett a nice letter.

Mr. Horwits then wrote a letter under Mr. Prickett's name, to Mr. Heflin, saying, "I never have heard of you, don't know who you are, but I do know the measures that people in your profession will use to catch attention and ingratiate themselves and get publicity. If you send me any more such letters, I will turn them over to the F. B. I."

When he got back to Hollywood, Mr. Heflin, his brow creased with worry, went to the studio to talk with Mr. Prickett. He soon found out that he was only one of many victims of Mr. Horwits. At that time Mr. Horwits was in the company's New York office but before long he was transferred to Hollywood. He and Mr. Heflin became warm friends and the day arrived when Mrs. Horwits was arriving from the East to join her husband. While Mr. Horwits was meeting her at the airport, Mr. Heflin and his wife invaded the Horwits hotel room downtown and left it decorated with items of female underwear, lipstick smears and hairpins.

But these things never seem to end. The two couples were having dinner together that evening. They met in the hotel dining room and Mrs. Horwits handed Mrs. Heflin an overnight bag containing the underwear and hairpins. "Here are some things you forgot," she said, "the last time you were up in Al's room."

Mr. Horwits was dining at the Stork Club one night with George Frazier, the writer. They were speculating about who might get the big public relations job that had just been vacated at Twentieth Century-Fox. Mr. Frazier remarked that in his opinion, Drew Berkowitz was the man.

Thus began the Drew Berkowitz myth, which Earl Wilson has cited as evidence that Broadwayites are bigger hayseeds than the hayseeds of the Paw Paw Belt.

Mr. Frazier and Mr. Horwits talked on about Drew Berkowitz, discussing his qualifications, his character, his popularity. Various Broadway characters stopped by the table and joined in the talk. Most of them said they knew Berkowitz but they were divided in their opinions of the man. "Good old Drew Berkowitz!" one would exclaim. "Good frienda mine. Comes from St. Louis, my home town." And someone else would say, "I knew him in Hollywood. Big fella. Great golfer. Used to play with him at Lakeside. A prince, if he likes ya, but if he don't—watch out!" Finally Mr. Horwits faked a phone call to Joseph Schenck and came up with the information that Drew Berkowitz was in. He had the big job.

The news spread all over town. Some of the Broadway columnists printed it. Word got around that Drew Berkowitz was holed in at the Sherry-Netherland Hotel and the phone calls began pouring in there. People wanting to congratulate him, get on the good side of him, get jobs for themselves or for unemployed pals. He was paged in the leading restaurants, where people sat around and talked about him familiarly, telling how close they were to him, how Drew Berkowitz would give them the shirt off his back. His name was, in fact, such a big subject around town that another film company took steps to try to get him away from Twentieth Century-Fox.

Mr. Horwits and Mr. Frazier enjoyed the whole thing immensely, for the reason that nobody on Broadway would admit that he didn't know Drew Berkowitz.

Another mythical character of the motion picture industry is Sam Mitnik. He was born in 1947 in a small town in Maine when Warner Brothers was holding the premiere of the film *Life With Father*. Art Moger of Boston was in charge of the press and was irritated by the behavior of a small-town Maine reporter who put on a cynical air and demanded, "Who you got? What big names you got coming? Where are all the big shots? Who you got coming?"

"Sam Mitnik, for one," said Mr. Moger. "That satisfy you?"

"Sam Mitnik himself?" said the reporter. "Hey, that's worth a story."

But Sam Mitnik didn't show up. Mr. Moger faked a telegram from him saying he couldn't make it—he was called to London, something about a merger of two of the biggest film companies.

Thereafter the name of Sam Mitnik became important at many major film-industry meetings and banquets. Speakers quoted him as the wisest man in the business. Chairs were sometimes reserved for him at the head tables. But always the telegram would come—Sam Mitnik, the colossus of the cinema, had been called away to handle some tremendously important deal.

There is an important movie actor who has great fun with his friends on the sound stages. He dips his fingers in water, comes up behind his victim, delivers himself of a vigorous sneeze and, at the same instant, flips the water onto the back of the victim's neck. It has been predicted, several times, that he will die with his boots on.

The late John P. Medbury, newspaper humorist who lived in Hollywood, spent a good part of his time rigging practical jokes. He was a great one to throw parties, but none of his parties was ever ordinary. Once he invited all his friends to come to his house and meet his beautiful new wife. He hired a two-toothed hag from Central Casting and introduced her as his beloved Gladys. Actually Gladys was a stunning beauty and later on took an active part in her husband's conspiracies.

The Medburys planned a spaghetti dinner. They drew up a list of guests, in two groupings. One group was composed of people they knew who had a passion for formal dress. They sent invitations to this group, telling them to wear the most informal of sports clothes—slacks for the women, no neckties for the men. The second group was made up of men and women who abhorred dressing for dinner. They notified these people that, owing to special circumstances, the affair would be strictly formal.

And so they came. The guests were horribly upset, and the Medburys dashed around with worried looks, apologizing, saying they simply couldn't understand how on earth the mix-up ever happened. The unhappy guests were trying to tell them that it was all right, and then the fight started. Mr. Medbury had hired a special spaghetti cook—a fat lady. The butler had gone into the kitchen and told this fat lady that she was putting too much basil in the spaghetti sauce. The fat lady ordered him out of the place and when he refused to leave, hit him with a skillet. The two of them, shrieking and howling, deployed into the living room, each carrying a cauldron of spaghetti. They were throwing this pasta wildly at each other and in a few minutes there was spaghetti all over the house. It was an excitingly delightful party and, as Fred Beck says, quite typical of a Medbury dinner.

Mr. Beck tells me that Mr. Medbury was riding the Super Chief from Hollywood to Chicago when he met a screenwriter acquaintance in the lounge car. They shook hands and Mr. Medbury said, "On your way back to the studio, I see. Been in New York?"

The screenwriter looked startled for a moment, then said he was on his way to New York. Mr. Medbury started laughing.

"You're on the wrong train," he said. "I know exactly what happened to you. You got on the wrong train when we stopped at Albuquerque. *This* train is going to Hollywood."

According to Mr. Beck, who is normally an honorable man, the screenwriter got off at the next stop with the intention of catching another train going in the opposite direction. I'm inclined to doubt it, except that I knew Mr. Medbury, and he was a sharp one.

Al Pearce had his old radio gang on the road for personal appearances in the Pacific Northwest. During their engagement in Spokane, a United States Senator invited Mr. Pearce to a poker party at his fishing lodge. Mr. Pearce left the theater still wearing his tuxedo, drove to the Senator's lodge and joined the poker game. After a while he asked for the location of the bathroom. "Right through that door," said the Senator, "and straight ahead, down the hall." Mr. Pearce opened the door, took three steps into the darkness and plunged fifty feet into the ice-cold water of the lake.

A hammy bit player was causing trouble on the set of a movie being directed by Leo McCarey. This fellow insisted, the moment the camera was turning, on edging himself forward into a better position. Mr. McCarey warned him again and again to stay in his proper spot, but the actor, on the next retake, would move forward. At last Mr. McCarey summoned a studio carpenter and had him nail the ham's shoes to the floor.

Buster Keaton was once one of the film colony's champion jokers and is reputed to have invented the collapsing cabana. This was a small structure, set up on a privately owned beach for the use of females in changing their clothes. Mr. Keaton, always good at timing, would throw a lever and the walls of the little building would fall away, usually revealing a great deal.

17

Statesmen at Play

People who argue that practical joking is The Sport of Creeps, belonging to infants and imbeciles, appear in court without having studied the evidence. It is possible to demonstrate that the practical joke is an intellectual pursuit. Imaginative professors and scientists, professional philosophers and statesmen, all of these have contributed to the picture.

A President of the United States, if he has any humor at all, is almost certain to indulge in small pranks now and then. His activities are so vast and varied and he is surrounded by so many solemn institutions, that the opportunity to shock people is almost always before him. A President with a lively sense of humor must be under constant temptation to startle his associates, in the same way that Helen Hayes startled her fellow performers in *Victoria Regina.*

It is unlikely that George Washington ever indulged in practical jokes; his biographers seem to be agreed on one thing—he was a humorless man. Yet most of our presidents have had their gay moments. The record is slim, for the reason that a presidential joke is usually confined to a small group and that group is made up of individuals pledged to secrecy. The public has somehow never relished a sense of humor in its Chief Executive. Abe Lincoln was criticized more for cracking jokes than he was for staying away from church. And Adlai Stevenson found out that the frown is mightier than the smile in politics.

Dwight D. Eisenhower seems to me to be a somber sort of man, not altogether humorless, but inclined to disapprove of anything resembling a practical joke. I wouldn't want to be the one who filled his bathtub with lemon Jello. Yet his Vice-President, Richard Nixon, figured in a gag that had some of the political bigwigs trembling in their boots soon after the Eisenhower administration took office.

Mr. Nixon attended the annual ribbing dinner of the Gridiron Club in Washington. In a sense, this affair is a succession of practical jokes. At the 1953 dinner the club members staged a skit dealing with the financial troubles of Mr. Nixon which were a prominent feature of the campaign. The skit was quite cruel in its handling of Mr. Nixon's family affairs, including the Nixon cocker spaniel, and when it was over, the new Vice-President stood up, anger showing in his face.

He began speaking, and a horrified silence fell over the room. Mr. Nixon was going to answer insult with insult. His associates in the new government turned white. They were all so anxious for the administration to get off on the right foot, and this display of poor sportsmanship on the part of the Vice-President could have grave consequences. But Mr. Nixon went right on. He defended his honesty with the same jut-jawed fervor he had employed in his famous television broadcast. He said that he, personally, could put up with a good deal of libelous attack, such as he had just witnessed, but that the club members had done one unforgivable thing—they had attacked a fine and noble lady. Very well, he said, thrusting his jaw forward—these unprincipled attackers would now have an opportunity to meet that lady face to face and repeat their scurrilous charges.

The curtain on the stage drew back and revealed the Nixon spaniel, Checkers, seated on a platform. The roar of laughter that followed almost blew out the walls.

Calvin Coolidge was reputedly a man without humor. He sometimes attended these same Gridiron dinners, sitting through them without cracking a smile. On his way home from one of them, he remarked, "All that tom-foolery's a waste of money."

Yet Mr. Coolidge had his moments. Louis Sobol once told a story about a dinner at which President Coolidge was given a handsome cane. The man who made the speech of presentation said: "The mahogany from which this cane is fashioned is as solid as the rock-bound coast of Maine, as beautiful as the sun-kissed shores of California!" Mr. Coolidge got up and accepted the cane, and looked at it a few moments. The audience sat hushed. The President raised his eyes, said, "Birch," and sat down.

Hanging in the White House was the Stuart portrait of John Adams, and Mr. Coolidge could see it from his chair in the State dining room. One evening he called in a servant and said, "I'm tired of looking at that old bald head. Have some hair put on it." According to White House legend, the portrait actually was touched up a bit.

There is a story, too, about an evening in the press room at the White House. Several of the correspondents were having a game of poker. Suddenly the door opened and Mr. Coolidge, who had been having a late stroll around the grounds, walked in. He said nothing. He walked to the window, jerked down the shade, and then walked out.

His practical jokes were certainly not elaborate. He loved to alarm people by ringing bells. Sometimes he'd press down all the buttons on his desk and bring people on the run from every direction. On other occasions he'd simply press the button which meant he was in danger, fetching the secret service men with pistols drawn. Sometimes in the evenings he'd sneak out to the main gate and ring the bell, and then hide in the shrubbery to watch the sentries arrive on the double.

The one Coolidge joke that has considerable merit was simple enough. He sent a servant to notify Secretary of State Charles Evans Hughes that "the barber is waiting for you at the White House and is ready to shave off your whiskers."

Abraham Lincoln was primarily a storyteller, as we all know, and in his later years, at least, had no inclination toward practical joking—except that many of his stories were concerned with pranking. When he was a boy and a young man, however, he indulged in all manner of practical jokes. Perhaps his most famous was the incident of the footprints on the ceiling. He had a smaller lad walk through a mud puddle. Then Abe picked the boy up, carried him into the house and held him upside down to make the prints on the ceiling. It is said that his stepmother wanted to lick him for it, but "laughed away all her strength."

Grover Cleveland's youth also was spangled with practical jokes. After he became President, he went on a fishing trip to the Saranac region of New York State, accompanied by Dr. S. B. Ward. The two men, in rough clothes, were resting on a log near Lake Placid when a party of fourteen hunters came along. They said they were on their way to Prospect House to have a look at the President. Mr. Cleveland asked them why they wanted to see him. The ensuing remarks were far from complimentary. They wanted to see if he looked as much an idiot as he really was. They said even worse than that. Through it all Mr. Cleveland kept a straight face and in the end told them he was in full agreement with their estimate of the President. They resumed their journey never suspecting his identity.

Franklin D. Roosevelt never backed away from a good practical joke and, in fact, thought up quite a few himself. Once he read that people at social functions pay no attention whatever to the murmured words that are required under given circumstances. A famous hostess, for example, bidding her guests good-by after a party, had said to each of them, with a smile on her face, "It was a terrible thing for you to have come. I do hope you never come again." And the departing guests, each busy framing his own proper retort, had not even noticed what she was saying. Mr. Roosevelt decided to test the thing. He chose a big White House party, where the reception line was half a mile long. As each guest came up and took his hand, the President flashed his celebrated smile and murmured, "I murdered my grandmother this morning." According to the popular story, not a single guest was conscious of what he said. One former associate of Mr. Roosevelt, however, denies it. He said a certain Wall Street banker was in that reception line, arrived before the President, and heard the words, "I murdered my grandmother this morning." The Wall Street man then said, "She certainly had it coming," and passed on.

Mr. Roosevelt was a prankster in his correspondence with some of his warm friends. In 1928, for example, he wrote to Josephus Daniels, a man of high moral principles: "The next time you come to New York I insist on your bringing Mrs. D. with you. It will not do to have a repetition of the scandal of your last visit when you disappeared entirely for most of one day and all of one night. It was all I could do to keep it out of the metropolitan press."

One of Mr. Roosevelt's most famous jokes was played on his Attorney General, Francis Biddle. The story is told by Judge Samuel Rosenman in his book, *Working with Roosevelt.*

The President and several of his assistants, including Judge Rosenman, were working in the Cabinet Room one afternoon early in the war, when Mr. Biddle was announced. Mr. Roosevelt quickly instructed his associates to keep their faces solemn. Mr. Biddle entered the room.

"Francis," the President began sternly, "I'm glad you came. All of us have just been discussing the question of civil liberties in the war, and I have come to a decision to issue a proclamation—which I am going to ask you to draft —abrogating so far as possible all freedom of discussion and information during the war. It's a tough thing to do, but I'm convinced that it's absolutely necessary and I want to announce it in the speech we are working on now."

Mr. Biddle, then as now, was one of the nation's foremost champions of civil liberties. Says Judge Rosenman:

"Biddle looked at us all, quite thunderstruck. Seeing that we all seemed to be in dead earnest, he immediately launched into a fervent argument against it. It was unprepared, but it was certainly vehement and, I must say, very persuasive. He stood up for greater emphasis and, pacing up and down, declaimed and declaimed against the idea. It went on for fully five minutes before the President and all of us burst out laughing."

There is reason to suspect that Harry S. Truman was the most active practical joker ever to occupy the White House. (Cries of "And how!" and "You said it!" and "He pulled the chair out from under the hull country!") Even though he put many jokes into actual operation, it would appear that he thought of even more which, for one reason or another, he didn't perpetrate. Two of his chief assistants were once on a trip to Cuba and Mr. Truman, in the White House, decided it would be fun to have them seized and imprisoned as smugglers when they returned to the mainland. In the end he abandoned the idea, remarking, "What's the use? They've got White House pull."

On another occasion his daughter Margaret brought two schoolmates home with her and the three girls decided to sleep in the Lincoln Room. Mr. Truman told them of the legend that the ghost of Abe Lincoln sometimes walks at night in the Lincoln Room. The girls went to bed and Mr. Truman sat with his wife for a while. Suddenly he had an idea. He'd arrange to have Lincoln's ghost appear that very night. He was real hot for the scheme, but somebody vetoed it.

In 1947 President Truman was preparing for his trip to

South America. He was to be accompanied by correspondents for the wire services, including Tony Vaccaro of the Associated Press. Mr. Vaccaro was first notified that he wouldn't have to take yellow fever shots if he didn't want to. He didn't want to. Mr. Vaccaro had a lively horror of the hypodermic needle and everyone knew it. Then quite suddenly the order was changed and Mr. Vaccaro was escorted, almost by force, to the White House clinic. "I don't believe in shots!" he protested loudly, but the doctor told him to lower his trousers and lie down on a couch, facing the wall—the President himself had decided that everyone on the trip had to take the shots.

Mr. Vaccaro was lying there, facing the wall, hull exposed, when he heard the door open. Footsteps across the room. Cold metal against his hide. Then a voice, "This won't hurt you a bit, Tony." He recognized the voice and turned and found the President of the United States bending over him. In the President's hands was a huge hypodermic device ordinarily used by veterinarians, its cylinder loaded with a red fluid. Mr. Vaccaro took one look at this weapon and started to shriek; then he saw the big grin on Mr. Truman's face, and sighed with relief as he realized it was all a joke. He did manage to say, "Mr. President, I don't ordinarily greet the President of the United States from this position."

Benjamin Franklin, traveling through New England, arrived one evening at a wayside tavern, hungry, cold and tired. He had his horse stabled and then walked into the tavern's public room to find every seat near the fire occupied by neighborhood loafers. He stood about for a while, shivering, but no one offered to move.

"Landlord," he finally called out, "have you any oysters?"

The landlord had oysters.

"I want you to give my horse a half bushel of them," ordered Dr. Franklin.

The fireside loafers perked up their ears. The landlord gave Dr. Franklin an argument, but Dr. Franklin insisted he wanted the oysters fed to his horse. The landlord started out with them, and every one of the loafers trooped after him, anxious to see a horse eat oysters. They returned shortly to find Dr. Franklin sitting before the fire.

"Your horse won't eat the oysters," said the landlord.

"Well, then," said Dr. Franklin, "bring them here to the fire and roast them—they'll do very well for my supper."

Whenever men who worked with Thomas A. Edison get to reminiscing about him, they usually talk about the amount of time and energy the great inventor put into practical jokes. On one occasion Mr. Edison found out that the night watchman at his laboratory was inclined to sleep on the job. Mr. Edison knew about a strange substance called vermiculite which, when lighted, instead of burning increases tremendously in volume. The inventor quietly acquired a large supply of vermiculite and placed it in a box with one end open. The box was set in the office where the watchman usually did his napping, and a time fuse was attached to it. During the night roars of fright came from the office. The watchman had awakened to find himself engulfed by the billowing, foaming stuff, which continued to expand at a rapid rate until he was all but buried alive. Mr. Edison and an assistant dug him out and had no more trouble with him sleeping on the job.

Mr. Edison's laboratory aides, often victims of his pranking, sometimes got back at the boss. There was one night when the inventor and his assistants labored until 3 A.M. Then the work was interrupted while a breakfast of ham and eggs was served. As the food was being brought in, Mr. Edison fell asleep at the table. The others quickly removed his plate of ham and eggs from in front of him and substituted a plate with a few crumbs and scraps of food on it. In a few moments Mr. Edison awoke. He glanced down at the empty plate, patted his stomach with satisfaction, burped lightly, and said, "Well, let's go, boys!"

* * *

There are no class distinctions in the world of practical jokers. I once knew a radical newspaperman who hated big corporations, and who was always mulling over schemes calculated to destroy them. During one period he wandered around Manhattan hanging "Out of Order" signs on public telephones—signs he had printed at his own expense. Another time he got mad at the subway. He'd go into one of the busy stations at the rush hour and drop nickels into all the turnstiles (this, of course, in days of yore). When the coin is in the slot, the turnstile is locked from the inside, so that people on the inside can't get out. He succeeded in creating some majestic confusions.

On the other hand, Wall Street is a hive of practical jokers. I've been told that the governing board of the New York Stock Exchange is kept busy dealing with them.

The famous hat joke had its origin in Wall Street. A certain broker, unpopular with his fellows, had an expensive Homburg which he got at Lock's in London. The conspirators sent to Lock's for four hats exactly like it, even to the initials, but with the sizes graduating upward. Then, day by day, they began substituting hats. On the first day, their victim didn't give it much thought—his hat was just a trifle loose on his head. But the next day it was looser. Each time he'd put on one of the substituted hats he'd immediately take it off and examine it carefully; no question about it; it was his hat. And then he began feeling of his head, for it appeared to him that his head was shrinking. He was in a bad state of nerves by the time he found out the truth.

A variation of the hat joke involves the victim who carries a cane. Each day the jokers saw off an eighth of an inch at the bottom, until the man begins to believe that he is growing taller.

Newcomers to the stock exchange are sometimes given a cruel kind of hazing. The plot is rigged for them to suddenly get a large order for certain stocks and then, through devious paper manipulations, he is made to believe that, in his very first operation, he has bungled the job and wiped out his customer.

The boys in Wall Street used to spend money like water in perpetrating their jokes. There was once a stock broker who owned a fabulous antique clock which he had bought in Germany. He talked about this clock more than most brokers talk about their golf scores. It was three years older than Stonehenge and something was always going wrong with it. Its owner had an arrangement with a clockmaker in the financial district who did all the repair work on the antique. It was his custom, when it stopped running, to pack it in a box and fetch it with him to his office, where he kept it under his chair all during the day. Then, when the market closed, he'd carry it over to the clockmaker. His friends decided to have some fun with him. They had their agents in Europe search for a duplicate of the clock. It took quite a while but finally the duplicate was found, and it cost them *fifteen thousand dollars*. It was shipped to New York, and the boys waited for the next time their friend brought his clock downtown. Meanwhile they took a hammer and smashed their substitute clock, their fifteen-thousand-dollar antique, into bits, and put the wreckage into a duplicate box. They had no trouble making the substitution and that day, when the broker reached the clockmaker's shop and opened his package, smelling salts had to be used to restore him.

In the 1860s a man named Horace Norton, founder of Norton College, was introduced to Ulysses S. Grant, and the General handed Dr. Norton a cigar. He didn't smoke it, but cherished and preserved it as a memento of the meeting. In 1932 a Norton College reunion was held in Chicago and Dr. Norton's grandson, Winstead Norton, brought out the cigar, now aged seventy-five. Winstead Norton stood up before the assemblage and delivered a sentimental oration. During his speech he lit the cigar and declaimed between puffs:

"And as I light this cigar with trembling hand it is not alone a tribute to him whom you call founder, but also to that Titan among statesmen who was never too exalted to be a friend, who was . . ."

BANG!

After seventy-five years a Ulysses S. Grant joke paid off.

As everyone knows, the novelty joke business has prospered enormously in the United States during the last few decades. Maurice Zolotow did some research on the subject and found that there are 3,800 store outlets for devilish gadgetry and that the overall take is approximately four million dollars a year. What seems more important, he established the fact that children are not the chief customers—the overwhelming majority of buyers are men past thirty.

The late Henry Ford used some of these gadgets, including the hand buzzer—a small device which he concealed in his palm, and which went off with a sharp buzz whenever he shook hands with someone, at the same time stabbing the victim's hand with a metal point, giving the effect of an electric shock. T. Coleman duPont, probably the most colorful member of the Delaware clan, was a steady customer of the joke stores. So was Alexander Woollcott, and the lardy King Farouk of Egypt.

Not long ago Jimmy Cannon, the columnist, wrote, "It's a knock against civilization that the novelty stores featuring devices for practical jokes are multiplying on Broadway." Yet the scourge is not confined to this country. The English also enjoy mechanical jokes. The gadget stores in London do a brisk business, and part of it is export trade. In 1951 it was revealed that large stocks of novelty jokes were being shipped to darkest Africa, where the native witch doctors are finding them most useful in impressing their congregations. Items most popular with the Africans included a cushion that uttered a vulgar noise when sat upon, the exploding cigar, and the ornamental ring that squirts water in the beholder's eye.

In addition to the retail outlets, several large mail order houses in this country deal in novelty jokes. Their customers order by catalog and I have the latest issue of one such booklet. Among the items in it are:

Stinking cigarettes—"a good joke on moochers."
Lifelike coiled snakes.
Electric shocking books.
Fake blood.
Squirting cigars.
Plate tilters.
Dirty soap—"the more you wash, the dirtier you get."
Trick tea bags—when dunked, produce a "hideous green" color.
Auto bombs, smoke bombs and stink bombs.
Disappearing ink—looks like ink when spilled on tablecloth or clothing, but disappears as it dries.
Chewing gum—turns teeth black.
Fake spiders, and fake flies (to be dropped in victim's drink).
Hot toothpicks—"spoil their big meal—almost burns their mouth out."
Squirting peanut.
Collapsing knife and fork.
Rubber candy, and pepper candy.
Dummy nail—for sticking on victim's auto tire.
Imitation bed bugs.
Dog floor mess.
Go-out matches.
Dribble glass.
Mangled finger—"horrible, ugly, bloody."

18

Professional Ribbers

One of the most adroit creators of pandemonium in all history was Luke Barnett, king of the professional ribbers. His reign was between the two World Wars and many of the nation's most celebrated citizens had nightmares because of his activities. Testimonial dinners, labor union conventions, private gatherings of wealthy Americans, annual meetings of boards of directors—all were put into an uproar with the appearance of Mr. Barnett. The late Raymond Hitchcock called him "the greatest impromptu actor in the world."

Mr. Barnett began his career by playing the clumsy waiter, but he was too good to remain in that role. During the twenties and early thirties he was in constant demand and he always gave satisfaction. He had a whole series of imitators and some of them were quite good; but none could touch him for versatility.

The business of engaging professional ribbers is almost nonexistent today. Social historians might say that we have become a more sober and serious people or, at least, that our leading citizens are more sober and serious. I prefer to think that the business of the professional ribber declined from being overworked—there was a time when a banquet wasn't a proper banquet unless there was a ribber loose in the room, spilling soup on the guests and otherwise insulting them. The pattern grew too familiar and it became almost impossible to fool the customers any longer.

Luke Barnett was a favorite among the leading American men of wealth and many of them were his victims. He was engaged once by Alfred A. Corey, industrialist, to appear at Corey's fishing lodge at the upper end of the Michigan peninsula. Mr. Corey was entertaining a dozen of the richest men in the country and he introduced Luke Barnett as Blib—a man who had been in the Corey family's employ for years. Mr. Corey told his friends that Blib was a trifle eccentric, but was a hard worker and had a good heart and that they should overlook his deficiencies. Blib himself, a big, lubberly, unshaven and dirty man who spoke with an accent, hovered about the premises, glaring at the rich guests as if he had murder in his heart. Soon he began muttering, always within hearing of the guests. "Rich pipples!" he'd say with great disgust. "Someday I blow them all up!"

Mr. Corey's brother, W. E. Corey, then president of the United States Steel Corporation, was present and was a party to the gag. The rich guests assembled one evening for cocktails. Before going in to dinner the Coreys summoned Blib. They told him they wanted him to bring in some logs for the living-room fire, and that he could take one drink for each log he fetched. Then the company went into the dining room. All during the dinner there were loud thumps and horrendous crashes from the living room, and the guests raised their eyebrows, but the Coreys just smiled. Then with the completion of the dinner, the company filed back into the living room. The fire was roaring, there were logs all over the floor, in the chairs, on the tables, and stretched out drunk on a sofa was Blib, muttering over and over, "Dirty rich bastards!" The Coreys led him away and once again assured their guests that there was no harm in good old Blib. He just needed humoring.

The following day Blib was assigned to take John D.

Ryan, the copper king, out fishing. They were in a rowboat and Blib began by splashing Mr. Ryan with the oars. He talked loud, and insisted on singing arias in some foreign tongue, much to the distress of Mr. Ryan. In spite of Blib's unseemly behavior, Mr. Ryan succeeded in hooking fifteen bass, but Blib managed to let all of them get away. At last Mr. Ryan lost his temper and began abusing Blib, and Blib made a short but loud speech denouncing rich pipples, and then told Mr. Ryan that *he* could row the boat back to camp. Mr. Ryan complained to the Coreys the moment they landed, but Blib put up a stout defense. "He tell lies, Mr. Corey," said Blib. "He say he catch fish. He no able catch fish, so he put blame on poor old Blib." Mr. Ryan was outraged and retired to his personal quarters to nurse his indignation. Almost at once Blib appeared under his window, talking about the bomb he was making to blow up the damn rich pipples. The copper king packed his bags and fled to his private railway car in the Escanaba yards.

The following day Blib was turned loose on Colonel William B. Thompson, another copper magnate. Colonel Thompson wanted to go hunting and Blib accompanied him, both men on horseback. Blib succeeded in scaring off any game the Colonel might have got; he criticized the Colonel's shooting; he let the horses get away and then he pretended to hurt his own leg, so that the Colonel had to support him all the way back to camp. Colonel Thompson was packing *his* bags when the Coreys decided it was time to reveal all.

As a phony waiter Barnett went to work one evening on Charles M. Schwab at a dinner in the Hotel Plaza, New York. He hovered over the steel man, criticizing his table manners. As Mr. Schwab would start to pick up a certain fork, the waiter would step forward and slap his hand, and silently indicate another fork. Once he cuffed Mr. Schwab quite forcefully and said, "Plizz put the elbows down. You think you still in Spigelmier's?" Barnett was referring to the grocery store in Pennsylvania where Mr. Schwab had clerked thirty-five years earlier (Barnett himself came from the same town).

Few major celebrities of the period escaped Barnett's ribbing. His victims included Earl Carroll, Sam Harris, and Count Felix von Luckner. Julian Eltinge, the famous female impersonator, was thrown into such a rage that he chased Barnett out a window and down a fire escape. Eddie Guest, the Michigan versifier renowned for his benign nature, got so mad he said bad words. Lillian Russell openly boasted that anyone who fell for a Barnett rib was too gullible to let live. A few days later a distrait foreigner rushed up to her on the street, wild with excitement, demanding the use of her automobile to rush him to the hospital to see his dying wife. She let him take the car and, of course, Barnett had scored again.

He played the waiter one evening at a dinner attended by Gentleman Jim Corbett and Frank Tinney. He went to work first on the former heavyweight champion, who always prided himself on his social graces. "Lowlifer!" the waiter would growl at Corbett and when Corbett frowned, he'd add, "Get smart aleck with me and I slap you dirty face!" Corbett retained his poise and remained the gentleman, so Barnett turned his attentions to Frank Tinney. The celebrated comedian couldn't take it and rushed the insulting waiter and in a moment they were rolling over and over on the floor. A squad of policemen, in on the joke, arrived in the banquet room and seized the two brawlers. They were hauled to a stationhouse and Tinney was yanked around quite roughly before the gag was finally revealed.

Some of Barnett's finest performances were staged in his home city, Pittsburgh, during the 1930s when the Congress of Industrial Organizations was in process of getting started.

In 1932 Heywood Broun went to Pittsburgh to speak at a dinner where labor union matters were to be discussed. Luke Barnett attended in the role of a small-calibre political leader from a Polish district. There were to be three speakers representing three partisan viewpoints. Senator Pat Harrison spoke as a Democrat and then Elihu Root, Jr., as a Republican. Broun was to uphold the Socialist point of view but before he could get started, the Polish ward leader got up and began talking. He said he was thoroughly satisfied with matters as they stood, that he had heard a radical was to speak, that he didn't want to hear no goddamn radicals, that if any radical got up to speak he for one would leave the room.

People began to shush Barnett, then to yell at him, telling him to sit down, that he was insulting Mr. Broun. But now Heywood Broun arose and urged that the gentleman be allowed to continue, reminding the gathering of the sanctity of free speech. This action by Broun seemed to enrage the Polish gentleman. He began yelling at the bulky columnist from New York. He screamed that Broun had insulted Al Smith and Jimmy Walker, and that both Smith and Walker were friends of the Polish people. At this point the toastmaster ran over and began slugging Barnett—faked blows that looked real enough—and Broun started bellowing for order and peace. A semblance of quiet was restored and then Barnett, with tears streaming down his face, approached Broun and offered to apologize. "Oh, to hell with apologies!" said Broun, who by this time was considerably upset. "So that's the way you feeling!" shrieked Barnett, off on another outburst. He put up his dukes and began winding up to deliver a haymaker. A cop rushed into the room and grabbed him and the uproar was on again, with Broun now defending Barnett against the law. Somewhere along about this point the Chair decided the joke had gone far enough.

A few years later a convention of the Congress of Industrial Organizations was in session at Pittsburgh. At that moment the Wagner act was sacred to the organization. A delegate arose in the midst of the proceedings and, in Polish dialect, began an impassioned demand for drastic revision of the Wagner act. The meeting was stunned and John L. Lewis came slowly to his feet, silencing the renegade by sheer force of majesty.

"What's your name?" roared Lewis at the delegate.

"What's *yours?*" Barnett bellowed back at him, and a roar of laughter went up, bringing an end to the episode.

Barnett is a master of several dialects, including the German, and in more recent years he has enjoyed himself playing a visiting Austrian dignitary. With some pleasure I must report that he gave Jim Moran an uncomfortable half hour during the period when Moran was working for Fred Waring. The boys in the Waring organization got together and brought Barnett in as the editor of a famous Austrian magazine devoted to classical music. The Professor, as he was called, was in New York and wanted to get some information about the Waring style of music, and Jim Moran was assigned the job of talking to him. The Professor walked into Moran's office and began things by announcing that he was somewhat deaf, but that he could "hear tings goodt" by pressing his thumb and forefinger against the throat of a person. He apologized profusely for his failing and asked permission to hold Mr. Morandt's throat during the talk. Mr. Morandt was quite agreeable. They sat, then, for a half hour with the Professor squeezing Mr. Morandt's larynx while he asked questions, occasionally applying such pressure that tears came to Jim Moran's eyes. Jim says it was one of the greatest performances he has ever witnessed, even though he was a nervous wreck by the time it was over, and couldn't swallow for half a day.

Luke Barnett's son Vince, the movie actor, carried on in his father's tradition for quite a while, until his somewhat distinctive features became so familiar that his victims were likely to recognize him. He conducted his operations mainly in Hollywood and his best performances were his impersonations of German secret agents. Once he appeared at a party given for a British army officer who was in California to buy warplanes. Vince Barnett attended

Carnegie Tech and was at one time a pilot, and knows planes. At the party he approached the Britisher and began asking searching questions of a technical nature. After a while he pretended to get drunk and fumbling, letting little remarks slip out to indicate that he might be a German agent, then clumsily trying to cover up his slip. The Englishman got so alarmed that he slipped away and telephoned an executive of Lockheed Aircraft, who hurried over to the party to find that the Nazi agent was his old friend, Barnett.

In Washington, General Hap Arnold introduced Vince Barnett to General Malin Craig at the time Craig was chief-of-staff. Vince told General Craig, using a heavy accent, that he represented a group of Slovak citizens of Long Beach, California, and that these citizens wanted some military planes so they could practice flying. General Craig said such a request was not proper, whereupon his visitor began yelling about red tape and politics.

"My dear sir," said General Craig, "there are no politics in the Army."

"Then how did you get your job?" howled Barnett.

Suddenly the visitor from Long Beach grew calm, and a sly expression came into his face. Backing away from the General's desk, he took a roll of ten hundred-dollar bills from his pocket, and one by one began dropping them on the floor, grinning suggestively at General Craig.

"Maybe," he said slowly as he continued dropping the bills, "maybe when I get home I will maybe find waiting for me a commission in the great army air corps."

General Craig had a telephone in his hand, ready to call the FBI, when the ruse was exposed.

One of the most successful of the professional ribbers, in the manner of Luke Barnett, is William Stanley Sims, whose specialty is appearing in the role of technical expert at various conventions.

Sims was introduced once at a convention of neurologists as Dr. Worthington Smythe, of Oxford. Impressive with waxed mustache and monocle, he mounted the platform. Looking out over his audience, he noted that several of the doctors were whispering among themselves.

"Come, come!" he objected. "If you American doctors will pay a bit more attention, perhaps your undertakers won't be so busy!"

The audience accepted the reprimand and quiet fell over the hall. Dr. Worthington Smythe asked for a volunteer from the audience, and a noted American neurologist stepped to the platform. Dr. Smythe had him strip to the waist, then began poking at him, inspecting his chest, peering at his navel. Suddenly he turned and picked up a paint brush and swiftly painted a battleship on the man's back.

Even more startling was his appearance at a meeting of the American College of Surgeons. The chairman had just announced that "Dr. Eric von Austerlitz, the noted Viennese surgeon, would not be able to appear as scheduled because he had been called into an emergency consultation and . . ."

At this point the door was flung open and in came Dr. von Austerlitz, wearing his operating-room costume, instruments in his hands, and followed by a nurse carrying a tray of other instruments. Quite obviously the doctor had rushed straight from the operating room to the convention platform. He began a lengthy technical description of the surgery just concluded.

"In short," he wound it up, "I removed the patient's entire alimentary canal, turned it upside down and stitched it back in that position."

The assembled surgeons sat as though stupefied; then one man spoke up.

"What," he asked, "was the patient's trouble?"

"Hiccups," said Dr. Eric von Austerlitz.

Frank Libuse has, for years, made a profession of playing the clumsy insulting waiter in night clubs. He learned long ago that the simplest devices are often the most effective. He can infuriate customers by simply bringing the check with the first course. He has spoiled the whole evening for a party of diners by hovering around the table, pretending to look for something that had been lost—peering under the table and under the chairs, lifting plates, and so on. If such simple matters fail to have the desired effect, he is likely to whip out a large fish and start beating another waiter over the head with it—a sure-fire method for livening up the evening.

As a matter of historical interest, let us go back to 1916 and a Navy League Dinner held in Boston. Attending were several hundred veteran naval officers. When the provisioning was completed, the chairman arose and announced that the main speaker, Secretary of the Navy Josephus Daniels, had been unable to come to Boston but instead had sent one of his assistants. The young assistant got to his feet, cleared his throat several times, clawed at his collar and otherwise displayed his acute discomfort, for he was Robert Charles Benchley, making one of his first public appearances.

Mr. Benchley announced with some hesitation that the theme of his speech was "Prohibition and the Navy"—a subject most dear to the heart of his chief, Secretary Daniels. An undercurrent of growls was heard from the audience, but Mr. Benchley pressed on.

"We are making great changes of diet in our Navy," he said. "Above everything else, we are respecting a recent vote taken among all the officers and men of the service. Complete prohibition is being set up. Grape juice is only our opening gun. Before we are through, we shall have driven even the memory of vile spirits from our jolly jack-tars!"

There was a stir and a buzz from the audience—the Daniels philosophy as to grog was not very popular. For a few moments it was feared the hard-bitten officers would begin shelling the speaker with crockery, but he pitched his voice a little higher and continued:

"We are already making plans to have tea, choice of milk or lemon, and cakes, choice of cookies or ladyfingers, served on the mizzen hatch at ten bells P.M. Perhaps I should explain that in navy parlance this means twenty minutes past four."

Now the audience began to catch on that it was being hoodwinked, and Mr. Benchley continued for quite a while, getting funnier as he went along, and everyone had a fine time.

This must have been one of the earliest of the phony-speaker ribs. Most certainly it was one of the earliest artistic expressions of a delightful American, Bob Benchley. There is one earlier that we know about. At Harvard, Benchley was studying diplomacy and in the course of the course, he was assigned to write a term thesis on the famous Newfoundland Fisheries case. He turned in his thesis and was promptly talked out of a career in diplomacy, for he had written of the Newfoundland Fisheries case from the viewpoint of a fish.

19

Four Rare Specimens

When Eugene Field died, nearly sixty years ago, he was one of the most popular writing men in the United States. He is still talked about and written about today, but not so much because of the things he wrote. He is remembered mainly for his practical jokes.

His biographers trace his career as a prankster back to his childhood. Before he was ten years old he went to work on his grandma. She had a custom of eating peppermint lozenges while in church, believing that they kept her stomach from growling. Little Eugene spent days searching for flat pebbles shaped exactly like the lozenges. Early on a Sunday morning he substituted the pebbles for the candies in Grandma's purse. His whole plot was predicated on his observation that Grandma seldom glanced at the peppermints before popping them into her mouth; but, alas, on this morning she chose to look, and discovered the deception. We might be tempted to grieve for the little boy whose scheme failed in spite of all the work he had put into it. I prefer to think that he had at least a small reward for his efforts—that Grandma's stomach growled like a Great Dane all through church services.

Eugene lived with his grandmother, and an occasional visitor to the house was a Mrs. Ramsey, a stiffish and prim

wife of a leading deacon of the church. Eugene always noticed one major fact about this Mrs. Ramsey—she bore a
striking resemblance, facially, to Grandma's little brown
cow, Molly. One Sunday afternoon, Mrs. Ramsey arrived
for tea. Eugene pilfered her bonnet and shawl and fixed
them carefully on the little brown cow. Then he led Molly
up to the sitting-room window, guiding her into a position
where she seemed to be looking in, and then tapped on the
glass. The effect, apparently, was startling, for Grandma
was unable to restrain herself and went into a hysterical fit
of laughter. She was in trouble at church after that, but
apparently she didn't mind too much.

Eugene's legal guardian was a respectable citizen named
Melvin L. Gray. After the boy went away to attend Knox
College, he sometimes telegraphed his guardian for money.
If the money was not forthcoming within a reasonable pe-
riod of time, he'd send another message, saying that if he
had to exist one more day without funds, he would be
forced to go on the stage, billing himself as "Melvin L.
Gray, Banjo and Specialty Artist."

He continued his whimsical exploits at the University of
Missouri where, for one thing, he painted President Read's
big chestnut horse white and shaved all the hair off his tail.

In time he became editor of the Denver *Tribune*. In his
office he had an extra chair, for visitors. There was a hole
in the seat of this chair of a size to permit visitors to jack-
knife into it, and the hole was kept covered with a sheet of
cretonne. Dozens of visitors, including many prominent citizens of Denver, went through it, and some grew quite
indignant. Editor Field, however, mollified most of them
by explaining that he could usually judge a man's character
from the manner in which he extricated himself from the
trap.

Field's most celebrated Denver joke was occasioned by
Oscar Wilde's visit to the Rocky Mountain city in the 1880s.
Wilde's journey through America was one of the great sen-
sations of the period, attended by much advance publicity

and by considerable sputtering on the part of American moralists, of whom there were even some in the West. Wilde was to lecture in Denver and was scheduled to arrive on an afternoon train. Crowds gathered in the downtown streets, hoping for a glimpse of the "monster" as he was called by the wowsers. About an hour before the train came in, an open landau moved through those streets. In it was Eugene Field, magnificently decked out as Wilde. He wore knee-length velvet britches, silk stockings and slippers with jewel-studded buckles. Golden curls cascaded over his shoulders and he wore a monocle. In his hand he held a long-stemmed sunflower. He paid no heed whatever to the sidewalk crowds, lolling back against the cushions, stirring himself occasionally to sniff effeminately at the sunflower. The crowd hooted, and bombarded him with eggs and vegetables, but he pretended to ignore even direct hits. This preliminary performance, of course, took all the steam out of Wilde's actual arrival as well as his entire stay in Denver.

From Denver, Field moved on to Chicago, where he achieved his greatest celebrity and became, according to some historians, the first American columnist. He worked for Melville Stone on the Chicago *Daily News* and Mr. Stone suffered quite a few indignities at the hands of his star writer. The paper's staff never knew what next to expect from Field. Sometimes, in the bitterest sub-zero weather, he would arrive at the office wearing a linen duster, an old straw hat, and fanning himself with a palm leaf fan. During one period he was trying, without success, to get a salary increase. He arrived in Mr. Stone's office with his four small children. Field was wearing ragged overalls and a disreputable hat and hadn't shaved. The children were in tatters, their hair uncombed and streaks of dirt on their faces. The five of them marched in, lined up before Mr. Stone's desk, and the children began chanting, "Please, sir, won't you raise our father's wages?"

At Thanksgiving time it was Mr. Stone's custom to give each member of the staff a turkey. Field wrote him a note, asking if he might have a suit of clothes instead of the turkey. Mr. Stone accommodated him by presenting him with a suit of convict stripes. For weeks afterward Field wore the convict suit whenever distinguished visitors arrived and were being shown over the premises by the publisher. He'd appear in the stripes, a sorrowful, beaten look on his face, and begin sweeping out the offices. Later he added a ball-and-chain shackled to his leg, and kept a set of burglar tools spread out on his desk.

Much of Field's writing satirized the upper-crust Chicagoan's search for culture, and some of his jokes were aimed in the same direction. At that period an English poetess, Mrs. Felicia Dorothea Hemans, was the rage in America; she was author of *Casabianca,* which concerned the boy standing on the burning deck, and *The Landing of the Pilgrim Fathers,* among other things. She ranks high among the versifiers dealing in sweetness and light. Field once called on a prominent Chicago bookseller and, speaking in a whisper behind his hand, said he wanted to get hold of an unexpurgated edition of Mrs. Hemans. He convinced the bookseller that Mrs. Hemans was, in actuality, a pornographic writer—that her works had been cleaned up for the American market. The bookseller made an effort to order an unexpurgated edition of her poems, and Field continued pestering him about it. When he finally caught on, the bookseller, in league with a few of Field's newspaper colleagues, went to some expense to have an "unexpurgated" edition printed, with the Hemans poems rewritten and loaded with obscenities.

Where Eugene Field is called America's first columnist, Fred C. Kelly is called the originator of the Washington column. Mr. Kelly is the official biographer of the Wright Brothers; he is the author of *George Ade—Warmhearted Satirist* and editor of a collection of Ade's best work; more recently he has written the life of Kin Hubbard. Booth Tarkington once wrote a salute to Mr. Kelly, calling him "one of the most interesting men in the country."

Mr. Kelly, who lives now in Maryland, has furnished me with some of the better practical jokes recorded in this volume. He has, for many years, enjoyed a close acquaintanceship with leading American literary figures, and he says almost all of them were pranksters in one way or another.

If Mr. Kelly has a single identifying trait today, it is probably his use of confusing stationery. Some people seem to think that Ernie Pyle originated the custom of collecting letterheads and envelopes from a wide assortment of hotels and resorts, and using this stationery in his correspondence. Mr. Pyle's letters from Albuquerque, for example, might be written on stationery of the Palace Hotel in San Francisco, and when he was writing from San Francisco, he might use stationery of the Clark Hotel in Jeffersonville, Indiana. Mr. Kelly, with a strong assist from Homer Croy, really began this sort of business years ago. In his travels Mr. Kelly is always on the lookout for organizations and enterprises with peculiar names, and he acquires a dozen or so letterheads and envelopes from these people, and uses them later in his correspondence, mixing them up, of course. I have before me a recent letter from Mr. Kelly. The envelope bears the return address of the Missouri State Penitentiary; the letterhead is printed in large red letters, advertising the 29th Annual Nebraska Rodeo at Burwell.

(I have heard about a musician, member of a dance band that is often on tour, who amuses himself by manipulating hotel stationery. He'll pick up a supply of letterheads and envelopes from, say, the Brown Hotel in Louisville, and later, in Roanoke, Virginia, sneak them into the writing desks at the Hotel Roanoke.)

Mr. Kelly says that many years ago, during a journalistic trip around the East, he happened to stay in two different George Washington Hotels—one in Virginia and another in Pennsylvania. Arriving at the George Washington Hotel in Pennsylvania, he happened to notice that he had picked up a couple of sheets of the other hotel's stationery. So he wrote one of his friends a letter on the Virginia hotel's letterhead, and enclosed it in an envelope of the Pennsylvania George Washington. The friend didn't even notice the discrepancy, but the idea for mixing up stationery was born. And out of it came a simple but maddening joke involving Christmas cards.

Let us say that in 1953, at Christmastime, Mr. Kelly receives a card from one of his neighbors signed, perhaps, "Paula and Bill and Little Towser." Mr. Kelly saves that card until Christmastime the following year. He gets an envelope of the proper size, puts the card into it, addresses the envelope to someone he knows and then has a friend in New York or Toledo or Kansas City mail it. Let us suppose it is addressed to Mr. and Mrs. Schuyler Kudner of North Salem, N.Y. Mr. and Mrs. Kudner find it among all their other Christmas cards.

"Who on earth's this one from?" asks Mrs. Kudner. Mr. Kudner examines it, repeating the names, "Paula and Bill and Little Towser." The Kudners will, quite probably, worry about the thing for weeks. They'll awake in the middle of the night, thinking about it. "Maybe," says Mr. Kudner, "it's those people we met on the ship . . . no, *his* name was Ken. Let me see now . . ." And it goes on and on.

One of Mr. Kelly's closest friends is Dr. Clyde R. Miller, for many years a leading figure in American education and a professor at Columbia University. Years ago Dr. Miller was associated with the Cleveland school system. He began receiving those maddening Christmas cards. Dr. Miller is himself a prankster of extraordinary attainments, and it didn't take him long to catch on. There was a certain executive in the Cleveland school administration who was in disfavor with Dr. Miller, and Dr. Miller finally concluded that this man was the culprit—deliberately trying to drive him crazy with those Christmas cards. "I'll fix him," said Dr. Miller, and began waiting for an inspiration to strike.

It came in a dentist's office as Dr. Miller was having a tooth extracted. He asked the dentist what he did with extracted teeth, and found out that there was a whole drawer full of them. The dentist didn't want them, so Dr. Miller took them. He now began his campaign against the peace and dignity of the man he believed had been sending those Christmas cards. One morning this man arrived at his desk and, opening the middle drawer, saw a human tooth in it. He gave some thought to it, couldn't figure it, and finally threw the tooth away and forgot about it. The next morning there was another tooth in the same drawer. And the morning after that, and so on for a week, and then the man appeared before an important gathering to deliver a speech. He stepped to the podium and pulled his manuscript out of his pocket. A dozen human teeth fell out of it, spilling all over the stage. The man was so unnerved that he was barely able to struggle through his address. It was several years later that Dr. Miller, to his great embarrassment, found out that Fred C. Kelly had sent those phony Christmas cards.

Dr. Miller is a man who enjoys manipulating teeth to startle people. There was a time when he would get on a subway train and take a seat and ride along for a while. Then suddenly he'd begin twisting his features in pain, and clapping a hand to his jaw, and finally he'd reach into the back of his mouth with thumb and forefinger, and give a tremendous yank, and out would come a large molar, which he'd hold up and examine carefully . . . while the other passengers stared incredulously.

Dr. Miller has been credited with an impressive gag which does not belong to him, but was the invention of Roy Taylor, of Columbus, Ohio, a relative of James Thurber. Dr. Miller says that he was merely an innocent bystander on several occasions when Mr. Taylor chose to drive people frantic. Accompanied by Dr. Miller, he would wall into, say, a large barbershop. Ignoring the barbers and the proprietor, Mr. Taylor would whip out a tape measure, a notebook and a pencil. He would begin measuring off the whole front section of the shop, jotting down figures, murmuring to himself or addressing his remarks to Dr. Miller.

"We'll put the brick partition right through here," he'd say. "By the way, when they deliver the brick, have 'em back the truck across the sidewalk, take out this plate-glass window, and dump the stuff right in here. Make it easier. Now, let me see."

By this time the proprietor of the shop would be moving in, wide-eyed and wondering. "Right across this section," Mr. Taylor would say, "will be the wall closing off the women's toilets."

"Just a minute," says the proprietor. "What the hell's going on here?"

"Don't bother me now," Mr. Taylor would say irritably.

"Don't bother you!" the proprietor would yell. "I'm the proprietor of this place—what the hell you think you're doing, anyhow?"

"I'm simply working from the blueprints," Mr. Taylor would say, "getting the measurements for the alterations."

"*What* alterations?" from the excited proprietor.

"How do I know what alterations?" Mr. Taylor would say. "I'm only an engineer, working from the blueprints, taking the measurements. Now, let's see. I think the wash bowls ought to go right about here and . . ."

"What about my lease?" the proprietor would roar.

"I wouldn't know nothin' about your lease. I just follow orders and go according to the blueprints. Well, I think that does it. Remember about the bricks—dump 'em right through this window."

And then Mr. Taylor and Dr. Miller would walk briskly out of the place.

Fred Kelly has told me about the lecture tour once undertaken by two famous writing men, Bill Nye and James Whitcomb Riley. They were traveling in the Middle West and boarded a train in an Ohio city. Nye was supposed to take care of the train tickets but after they were in their seats, he suddenly discovered that he had only one ticket. The conductor was approaching with his punch. Nye suddenly said to his companion, "Look, the only way to work this is for you to get down on the floor. Drop down there and I'll lay this suitcase across you and he won't even notice you. Hurry! Get down, quick!"

Riley dropped to the floor, crouching as low as he could get, and Nye placed the heavy suitcase across his back, just as the conductor arrived at their seat. Nye handed the conductor two tickets.

"Who's the other one for?" asked the conductor.

"It's for my friend down there," said Nye, indicating the poet crouched beneath the suitcase.

"What's he doin' down there?" demanded the conductor.

"Oh," said Nye, "he always travels that way."

Mr. Kelly attended Purdue University with the class of 1904. One day a friend told him it was a lot of fun to correspond with classmates and find out what had happened to them. Mr. Kelly found out that the class secretary was a Chicago businessman and so he wrote a letter to him, asking if he might have a list of the names and addresses. In reply he received a very stuffy letter; among other things the class secretary demanded to know why Mr. Kelly wanted the list. Mr. Kelly was understandably aggravated. He wrote back and said that he had been taken by a swindler, who had sold him a stack of Peruvian bonds which had turned out to be worthless. He said that he thought he might be able to foist these worthless bonds off on his old classmates. He heard no more, of course, from the Chicago businessman, but he wasn't finished. He began writing a whole series of letters to the man, having them posted from a small town in Ohio. They were supposedly from a distant relative of the man and were all signed "George." Each letter reported on the failing health of "Aunt Hattie," and spoke of how Aunt Hattie often talked sentimentally of her cousin in

Chicago, and prayed that she'd be able to see him before she passed on. This campaign continued to the point where "George" finally announced, in a jubilant letter, that he was bringing Aunt Hattie to Chicago to have her teeth extracted, and that while they didn't want to get in the way, they'd just love to see their relative's lovely house, and they'd stay in a hotel if necessary, even though it would be very expensive, and they needed every cent they had for the dentist. Before he had finished Mr. Kelly felt that he had amply repaid the Chicago man for his overbearing manner.

Wilson Mizner has been brought back to public attention in recent years by Alva Johnston's writings. Mizner apparently never played practical jokes just for the fun of it; his chief weapon against people who had offended him was a searing wit, although a few of his exploits come fairly close to being practical jokes.

Back in 1904 his brother Addison was hobnobbing with the gentry in New York and had become a favorite of the top ladies of the Social Register. The presence of the raffish Wilson in New York was sometimes an embarrassment to Addison, who begged his brother to stay away from any and all social events. One night Addison Mizner attended the New York Horse Show in the company of three warhorsesses of Society—Mrs. Stuyvesant Fish, Mrs. Hermann Oelrichs and Mrs. O. H. P. Belmont. Addison distributed bribes among the attendants, urging them to forbid admission to Wilson in case he showed up. He did show up, and distributed bribes of his own. He walked up to the box where Addison sat with the three society leaders and launched into a lecture on the kind of company Addison was keeping. He concluded this lecture by saying, "You've killed yourself in this town by appearing in public with a lot of madams."

Wilson Mizner was often the victim of practical jokers. Once he was invited to speak at a dinner following a heavyweight fight. The dinner was for Paulino Uzcudun and was attended by other Basques resident in the United States. These people brought along their wineskins, and when Wilson arose to speak he was in trouble. Each time he opened his mouth one of the Basques would send a jet of wine into it, or into his face and, as a climax to the proceedings, Uzcudun himself crawled beneath the table and gave Wilson a hot-foot.

One of the best jokes ever played on Wilson was aimed at his loud pretensions to being a gourmet. He was financially interested in the Brown Derby restaurant in Hollywood and ate there regularly although he always complained about the food, setting himself up as an authority on the higher cuisine. Bob Cobb, who ran the Brown Derby, and the restaurant's chef, grew weary of his complaints after a while. One day Cobb was in a Turkish bath when he noticed a flat sponge being used by one of the attendants. He remembered that Wilson was forever talking about the glories of a dish of tripe prepared with a certain sauce. Cobb took the sponge back to the restaurant and turned it over to the chef. When Wilson came in, Cobb told him that the restaurant had just engaged a new chef, who had once cooked for the King of Spain, and who was a wizard with tripe. After a while the sponge, which had been parboiled, was brought out, covered with a special tomato sauce. Wilson inhaled the aroma of the sauce, exclaimed over it, and fell to. He ate every shred of the sponge, pausing only to announce that Cobb had finally come to his senses and hired a chef who knew how to cook.

Brian G. Hughes was a paper-box manufacturer in Manhattan and died in 1924 at the age of seventy-five. He was a wealthy man and enjoyed spending his money on practical jokes. He was a plump little fellow with a ruddy countenance, sharp eyes and a walrus mustache. His wealth permitted him access to many institutions where an ordinary practical joker would be stymied. In fact the entire Board of Aldermen once fell victim to his whimsy.

He appeared unheralded before the board one day and announced that he had a piece of property in Brooklyn that he desired to give to the city for a park. While the deed was being transferred to the city, various aldermen rose to pay tribute to Hughes for his magnificent public spirit. Then a delegation of aldermen was named to set out forthwith for the purpose of inspecting the new park property. They found it to be an immense tract measuring two feet by eight feet on Sixth Avenue in Brooklyn—a parcel of land that cost Hughes just thirty-five dollars.

On another occasion the box manufacturer approached various historical societies, offering to give them the "Lafayette Mansion." He explained that the house had been used by the Marquis de Lafayette during much of the time he was in this country helping fight the Revolution. Several societies in turn accepted the gift with copious thanks, only to find that the "mansion" was a dilapidated shack, used by hobos. One society struck back at Hughes after discovering the deception.

"We accept your gift," the society wrote to him, "but in turn we beg to present you with a piece of property which would be ideal as a residential place for your distinguished self for the remainder of your days on earth."

The address of this ideal residential place was that of an insane asylum in Connecticut.

Hughes was once having his mustache trimmed in a barbershop near his factory when a boy walked in with a handsome alley cat. The boy wanted to sell the cat for the price of a drink. Hughes gave him ten cents and took the cat.

Some time later the animal was entered in the city's annual cat show. The entry was described as the last of the famous Dublin Brindle breed and bore the name Nicodemus, by Broomstick out of Dustpan by Sweeper. Nicodemus won first prize and was competing in the same show a year later when the secret got out.

The cat joke was widely publicized, yet the management of the horse show at Madison Square Garden fell for another Hughes joke a few years later. He turned up with a horse called Puldeka Orphan, by Metropolitan out of Electricity. Puldeka Orphan was on his way to the grand prize and was quite the sensation of the show. The judges were particularly impressed by the horse's intelligence—the manner in which he responded to the ringing of bells. Then Hughes made the mistake of whispering the truth to a steward, and the jig was up. Puldeka Orphan was a plug, a veteran of the Metropolitan Street Railway Company carbarns. For years Puldeka Orphan had pulled the cars often over Manhattan streets and Brian G. Hughes had bought him for eleven dollars and fifty cents.

A popular actress, Lavina Queen, never forgave Brian Hughes for the joke he played on her. The actress received word that a coveted decoration was to be bestowed upon her by the Prince of Amsdam, Cyprus and Aragon. She was to be made a Princess of the Order of St. Catherine of Mount Sinai. A large drawing room in the old Waldorf-Astoria was the scene of the ceremony. Accompanied by a number of her friends, the actress arrived and took her place on an improvised throne. The incense was so thick that everything in the room looked like a painting by Monet.

Then came the Prince of Amsdam, Cyprus and Aragon— a bearded, dark-skinned person lavishly robed and jeweled. He carried a velvet pillow on which reposed a parchment and a glittering golden star. The prince, followed by a train of attendants, approached the actress, jabbering a language never heard before by mortal ear. He read from the parchment and then pinned the star on the honored one's breast.

Only after Lavina, and the public, learned that it was all a joke and that the Prince was actually Brian G. Hughes, did she examine her golden star more carefully. With the gilt scraped away, the insignia of the Order of St. Catherine of Mount Sinai proved to be an old Jersey City police badge.

By all accounts Hughes' skulduggery occupied more of his time than business matters. He would turn up, for example, in a barroom on a rainy day, have a drink or two, and leave his handsome umbrella hanging on the bar. Then he'd retire to a corner and watch the eventual, inevitable theft. It delighted him to follow the culprit to the street where, on being opened, the umbrella discharged posters and banners proclaiming: "This Umbrella Stolen from Brian G. Hughes."

He distributed banquet tickets for banquets that were never held. One night he left a kit of burglar tools and a half dozen empty picture frames lying on the steps of the Metropolitan Museum of Art. The next morning the museum was in tumult as guards and directors alike raced up and down the corridors, trying to determine which masterpieces had been stolen.

Hughes may have invented a type of joke practiced later by certain Broadway characters—the creation of a traffic snarl. Hughes was a master at it. During the rush hour he'd board a streetcar, making certain that he was in the front of the crowd trying to get on. Then he'd pretend to be a deaf mute. Slowly he'd write a note for the conductor, saying, "Does this car go to Yonkers?"

The line back of Hughes would begin clamoring, but he'd continue to block the door while the conductor wrote on the paper that this car did not go to Yonkers. Hughes would then write, "Where can I get a car that goes to Yonkers?" By this time the traffic would be backing up behind the car and the honking of horns would add to the general din. The conductor, grown frantic over all the noise and confusion, nevertheless would be compelled to treat this handicapped man in a kindly manner. He would carefully write out directions for getting a car that goes to Yonkers. Hughes would then take the paper and slowly put on his glasses and read it over several times. Then he would take off the glasses, put them in their case, put the case in his pocket, look the conductor squarely in the face and say in a normal tone of voice, "That's funny. A fellow on the street told me that *this* car goes to Yonkers."

One of the most celebrated gags to spring from Hughes' mind was the great South American Reetsa Expedition. He announced to the press that he had financed the expedition with the aim of acquiring that rare tropical creature, the Reetsa. For almost a year the New York newspapers carried extensive accounts of the expedition's progress—reports provided, of course, by Hughes. Finally came word that a Reetsa had been captured. All of New York talked about it and thousands gathered at the pier when the ship came in bearing the first Reetsa ever seen this side of the Equator. Hughes himself proudly led the beast down the gangway. It was nothing more than a mangy old steer.

Spell Reetsa backwards.

20

Assault on the Ghosts

There is a long and interesting literature concerned with hoaxing in the literary and art worlds. It is too extensive for the purposes of this book, even though some of the hoaxes bear a striking resemblance to the practical joke. We may concern ourselves, however, with two recent projects aimed largely at the great American institution known as ghosting. It happens that both of them were executed in 1952.

The whole world is familiar with the fact that statesmen, including Presidents of the United States, maintain staffs of writers for the production of speeches as well as books and magazine articles. It may not be so generally known that other people pay money to have books and articles written under their names; there have even been daily columnists who maintained staffs of researchers and writers to produce their ignoble effusions. The public doesn't seem to mind it, but there is one group that does. A person who has spent many years training himself in the writing trade is almost certain to be irritated by someone who comes along and, without a shred of talent, begins making a big name for himself as a writer through the medium of hired talent, or ghosts.

One man who considers the ghost-writing industry to be

disgraceful is our old friend Hugh Troy. Early in 1952 he
was going about his normal business in Washington when
two facts came to his attention. He read about how the
president of a leading Eastern university had delivered a
speech, part of which was taken word-for-word from an
article by another college president. The implication was
quite clear—the offending educator's speech had been ghost-
written, and the ghost had copied from the article. At about
the same time it was announced that a course in ghost-
writing was being inaugurated at the American University
in Washington.

The facile mind of Hugh Troy went to work. He inserted an advertisement in the Washington *Post* as follows:

Too Busy to Paint?   Call on
               THE GHOST ARTISTS
1426 33rd St., N.W.   Phone MI. 2574
          WE PAINT IT—YOU SIGN IT!
Primitive (Grandma Moses Type), Impressionist,
Modern, Cubist, Abstract, Sculpture . . . also
                 WHY NOT GIVE
                 AN EXHIBITION?

It was a Hugh Troy joke, but it brought him an enormous headache. The mail poured into his home, and the
telephone rang constantly for days on end. An astonishing
number of Washingtonians wanted to have pictures painted,
and pass those pictures off as their own work. The newspaper reporters called on Mr. Troy, and gleefully wrote
stories about his stunt, and then the editorial writers
took up the cudgels. Newspapers from coast to coast edi-
torialized about the blight of the ghosting business; the
London *Times* devoted half a page to the matter, joshing
the American people for their gullibility. And *The New
Yorker* commented at some length, saying among other
things:

It turned out that the man behind this enterprise

was Hugh Troy, veteran of many a satirical mission. But let no one be fooled. Mr. Troy's jokes go to the heart of the matter; the sober carry on in earnest what he indicates in fun.

But where Mr. Troy was having his little joke on the business of ghosting, his "satirical mission" was by no means successful. He made no dent in the business. In fact, a day or two after his ad was published in the *Post*, other ads began appearing—ghost artists who would paint for their clients, and who meant it.

Morton Sontheimer, former newspaperman turned successful magazine writer, was author of the second adventure and in the process wrote a short masterpiece. Mr. Sontheimer's guns were not trained exclusively on ghost writers; he was concerned about all the vast and varied Learn-to-Write-by-Mail rackets that are advertised extensively in various journals. These included, of course, the ghost-writing agencies which advertise.

Mr. Sontheimer sat himself down and composed a "short story" called *Taken for a Hamburger*. It bore the name of "Joseph Staff." This Joseph Staff wanted to be a writer and so he had written this thing, and now he was sending it around to all the assorted racketeers who advertised that they would criticize, revise, rewrite and instruct, for a fee. I consider Mr. Sontheimer's phony composition to be of such high merit that I am reprinting it, with his permission, in its entirety. Here then is *Taken for a Hamburger*, by Joseph Staff:

> Manys the time I have taken a girl for a hamburger after the movies or similar evenings but how manys the fellow who himself was nearly taken for a hamburger on the very first date in his life?
>
> It happened to me and I shall never forget it as long as I live. Gather around and I will unfold the details of this amusing happenstance in the life of a

boy who up to that time, had never had a date before
in his life. I was a boyscout and I was away for the
first time in my days at camp. Our camp was situated
in the beautiful Delaware Water Gap country in Pennsylvania far from home and parents with beautiful
pines and firs all around and the smooth rolling river
only a stones throw or two from the camp for swimming, bathing, washing, and everything but drinking
which we were not supposed to do from it.

As boys will away from home I got an overpowering
desire to have a date like the older boys were always
talking about (and in not very scout like language
sometimes too). Amongst those they were talking
about were the butchers two daughters in town which
was a good piece away from the camp and you had to
drive it. My big opportunity came one morning when
I heard a couple of the older boys talking about going
into town for the mess hall meat which was always an
enviable job to get. So after much bickering and
dickering I got them to agree to take me along.

At the German butchers in town I helped them
load into the back of the car three huge wooden tubs
filled with I know not what on account of the paper
over top of them. While this was going on the girls
were also helping and I heard them whisper they
would meet the boys around the corner after and go
for a ride with us.

This they did.

At first everybody laughed about me being along
because I was extremely younger than the rest but
finally Sam Gershuny my older friend said, "Go ahead.
Make time, kid."

I didn't need a second urging as one of the girls was
younger than the other and a lovely bucksome Tu-
tonic type with flaxen hair and flashing blue eyes who
appealed to me. The heighth of my ambition at the
moment was to osculate this merry miss and I thought,

to paraphrase an old proverb, osculate than never so I pulled her over to me and tried to plant a kiss on her delicious lips.

Shrieking and laughing she gave me a shove and I landed smack in one of the tubs sitting down. I was so chagrined I stayed there for the rest of my trip which was directly back to camp where they wanted to drop me before continuing their ride.

But when I got out, viewing me from the back, you couldn't tell me from a hamburger for that was what I had sat in and the paper broke and I had it all over the seat of my trousers. I thought the cook, a grown man would raise all Harry but he did not. He laughed too and said, "We only lost half a pound or so and when its cooked it wont make any difference. Only you better get out of here when I start cooking this stuff or I am liable to take you for a hamburger."

FINIS

That was the little gem which Mr. Sontheimer sent around to the advertisers. Mr. Sontheimer (as Joseph Staff) got answers from them all. Most of them praised him as a man with a definite talent, which needed a little expert guidance. They would furnish this guidance, at prices ranging from $15 to $240. Some offered to rewrite it, others to instruct him by mail in the proper methods for telling such a fine story, and so on. The point is, they *all* assured Joseph Staff that he had the spark, that he was potentially a big money-maker in the writing game.

21

Larking with the Literati

The late Stephen Leacock, one of the great humorists of
the present century, once wrote that "there are certain
forms of so-called humor, or, at least, fun, which I am quite
unable to appreciate. Chief among these is that ancient
thing called the practical joke."

Mr. Leacock then proceeded to describe a practical joker
as a man who puts a tack on a chair, who stretches a cord
across a passageway and then rings the dinner bell so someone will trip and break his leg, who puts thistles in beds
and who puts tar in tomato soup. Mr. Leacock was sincere,
no doubt, in his distaste for jokes of this kind, although I
can't imagine where he ever encountered anyone who would
put tar in tomato soup. I don't think tar would dissolve in
tomato soup and, therefore, that joke wouldn't be very
effective; there are so many other and better things that
could be used if a person simply *had* to put something in
tomato soup.

Having read a good deal of Mr. Leacock's writings and
knowing something of his sense of humor, I venture to
suggest that the Canadian got as much fun out of a good
practical joke as the next man. We know that, among other
things, he was an ardent fisherman and that he sometimes
went off on fishing expeditions with other men. It seems

likely that he was exposed to practical joking on such occasions and it is my guess that he participated in the sport. We know, too, that he had great admiration for some of the people who belonged to the old Algonquin Round Table, and there were not any members of that crowd who scorned the practical joke. Judging from the written record, the Algonquin coterie spent almost as much time at pranking as they did at writing.

John Peter Toohey, one of the original members of the group, was abnormally sensitive about the prices on the Algonquin menu. One day the other boys had a special menu printed with, for those times, fantastic prices: a dollar for a piece of apple pie, ninety cents for coffee, and so on. Mr. Toohey looked at these prices, flung the menu to the floor, and stormed out of the place vowing never to return. He did come back only after he found out he had been gulled.

The chief victim of the Algonquin jokers was Alexander Woollcott and one of the chief jokers was Harold Ross. Mr. Ross and several of his friends once spent an entire afternoon making telephone calls to a prominent Long Island society woman, offering her five thousand dollars to endorse a certain brand of yeast. The discussion hinged on just what the society woman should say regarding her use of the yeast and finally Mr. Ross notified her that a single sentence would be sufficient: "Before I used this yeast my face was always a mess of pimples and blotches."

Mr. Woollcott lived, for a time, in an apartment also occupied by Mr. Ross and his wife. Hanging on the wall of this apartment was a portrait of Mr. Woollcott by C. L. Baldridge. The painting showed Mr. Woollcott wearing a private's uniform and holding a book, and he was inordinately proud of it. During a period while Mr. Woollcott was away on a trip, Mr. and Mrs. Ross persuaded the artist to paint a second portrait—almost exactly like the first, but not quite. The second portrait had Mr. Woollcott's impressive figure just slightly off balance, almost imperceptibly cockeyed. When Mr. Woollcott finally came home he began studying the substituted picture with a look of perplexity on his face and the Rosses did little to ease his mind. They would say, "What's happening to it? It's *moving* or something." Mr. Woollcott also knew something was happening to it, but he couldn't make out what, and he'd spend hours staring at it from various angles, sometimes stretching himself on the floor and squinting at it. When at last he found he had been bamboozled, he was furious, for he did not take a joke well.

Once he let word get around among his friends that he wanted the twelve-volume Oxford Dictionary for Christmas. The friends got together and on the happy holiday each one of them presented him with Volume I.

Mr. Woollcott's friends learned, in time, never to give his name as a reference. Beatrice Kaufman wanted to put her daughter in a fashionable school and gave Mr. Woollcott as a reference. He wrote to the head of the school: "I implore you to accept this unfortunate child and remove her from her shocking environment." On another occasion S. N. Behrman, the playwright, gave Mr. Woollcott's name as a reference when he was seeking to lease an apartment in a fancy neighborhood. Mr. Woollcott wrote that he was astonished to learn that the real estate company was considering accepting, as a tenant, "such a notorious drunkard, bankrupt, and all-around moral leper."

Mr. Woollcott's jokes usually had a substantial point to them. He once asked Moss Hart to drive him to Newark, where he had to fulfill a lecture engagement. Mr. Hart agreed, with the condition that he be permitted to sit on the platform and that Mr. Woollcott make some mention of him. Mr. Hart had, years before, been a clerk in a Newark bookstore and he wanted the people of Newark to see how he had risen in the world. Mr. Woollcott agreed. Mr. Moss sat on the platform and Mr. Woollcott's lecture went on and on, with never a mention of his friend. Finally Mr. Woollcott concluded his talk with: "Tonight I'll dispense with my usual question period, because I know there is a single question in your minds. I'm sure you all want to know the same thing: Who is this foolish-looking young man here on the platform?" With that Mr. Woollcott walked off the stage, leaving Moss Hart in torture.

During a period when Mr. Hart was spending a couple of weeks in Mr. Woollcott's home, the critic decided to cure Mr. Hart of his intense curiosity regarding other people's mail. It seems that Mr. Hart loved to snoop around alien desks, reading whatever mail or memoranda might be lying about. One day, alone in Mr. Woollcott's study, he began inspecting the correspondence littered over the desk, and came to a letter which hadn't yet been sealed up. It said, "I'll ask you up here just as soon as I can get rid of this nauseating Moss Hart, who hangs on like a leech, although he knows how I detest him."

Earlier in this book we have had occasion to meet the father of H. L. Mencken in the role of an expert rumor-starter. The elder Mencken bought a country home outside Baltimore and when his new neighbors asked him what he intended doing by way of fixing the place up, he solemnly told them that he was going to raise blooded hogs on the sweeping front lawn. The neighbors, of course, were horrified, and got up meetings, and sent a delegation to protest. When the delegation arrived, Mr. Mencken was ready with blueprints of his proposed piggery, and these plans even provided for a large sign at the main entrance, proclaiming the estate to be "Pig Hill."

An elderly German who operated a wood-working factory was another victim of Mencken, Sr. He got into a dispute with a lumber company and consulted with Mr. Mencken, expressing the fear that the affair may have damaged his rating with Bradstreet's. Mr. Mencken suggested that he would ask for a report from Bradstreet's, just to find out. Then Mr. Mencken, in the privacy of his own office, manufactured a careful report, supposedly from the commercial credit agency. It is described by H. L. Mencken:

The bogus report was typewritten on flimsy in exact imitation of a real one. It started off by saying that the old man was a once prosperous and respected *entrepreneur*, but that his gross neglect of his business had brought it down to the edge of bankruptcy. He left his office every day, it said, at 2 p.m., drove out to a notorious resort in the country (described so as to identify his own home), and there wasted what remained of his substance gambling with a gang of police characters. It added that he drank vast amounts of beer during this play, and was already showing signs of *mania a potu*. It ended by hinting that his family was considering having him put under restraint as *non compos mentis*, and that his creditors were forming a committee to join in the action.

The old man's response to all this nonsense was almost terrifying. He leaped in the air, Goddamning horribly in English and German, and talked wildly of shaking the dust of the United States from his feet and going back to his native Bremen . . . He became so excited that my father grew alarmed, and began to confess in haste that the report was spurious.

(from *Happy Days*)

Henry Louis Mencken inherited or acquired a good deal of his father's playfulness. He has always been a great hand to use the mails in his pranking. His close friend and former associate, George Jean Nathan, has written extensively about the Mencken monkeyshines, remarking: "Never have I known a man who has had so much fun out of life as Mencken had in those years."

Among other things, Mr. Mencken invented "The American Institute of Arts and Letters (Colored), the Rev. Hannibal S. Jackson, A.B., A.M., Ph.D., LL.D., D.D., Chancellor and Financial Secretary," with offices in Washington, D.C. The Institute's stationery was on vivid yellow paper with a woodcut of "a slightly Ethiopian George

Washington." It was Mr. Mencken's pleasure to write letters on this stationery to leading Negro-hating politicians and authors in the South, informing them that they had been elected to membership and inviting them to attend the Institute's inaugural banquet, together with their wives, sisters and sweethearts.

Mr. Mencken also acquired a stack of picture postcards showing the Emperor Franz Josef's palace at Schönbrunn. He had a fresh inscription printed on these cards, saying, "Mr. H. L. Mencken's Summer Estates on the Chesapeake," and mailed them out to friends and acquaintances. He also had stationery of a fictitious legal firm, "Fishbein, Spritzwasser, Garfunkel and Fishbein," which he used to notify male friends that suit for breach of promise, in the sum of one hundred thousand dollars, had been instituted against them.

Mr. Mencken and Mr. Nathan together made various efforts to cheer up their gloomy friend, Theodore Dreiser, in the days when he was living and brooding in Greenwich Village. At night the two playful editors would creep up to the Dreiser apartment and stuff the mailbox full of strange items: Black-hand threats, letters from the President asking Mr. Dreiser to come to the White House at once, menus from Armenian restaurants autographed by Elinor Glyn and Harold Bell Wright, frankfurters tied with red, white and blue ribbons, photographs of the Czar affectionately inscribed to "Theodore, gentleman and scholar."

Paul Armstrong, the dramatist, was a good friend to Mr. Mencken and Mr. Nathan in the days when the two men were running the *Smart Set*. Early one Sunday morning Mr. Armstrong telephoned the Mencken-Nathan apartment to say that he had run into "something wonderful in the way of writing." Mr. Armstrong's excitement was high, but he insisted he couldn't describe his discovery over the phone —that he'd meet the two editors in their office right away. They fumbled into their clothes and hurried to their office and waited. Soon Mr. Armstrong came charging in, a book under his arm.

"Here," he cried, "is the goddamnedest, most beautiful stuff I've ever read! I got hold of it only yesterday and I tell you it's remarkable. You've got to read it right away and see for yourselves."

Whereupon, reports Mr. Nathan, he handed them the Bible.

It seems improbable that Eugene O'Neill would find any amusement in a practical joke. Yet Mr. Nathan reports that the only time he ever heard the celebrated playwright laugh out loud was an occasion when he was recalling a reunion of old grads at Yale University. Mr. O'Neill said he saw a group of these gentlemen, late at night, somewhat sozzled and standing on a street corner in New Haven. One of their number, on being hoisted up by the others, relieved himself in the slot of a mailbox. And Mr. O'Neill, remembering this incident, almost split his gizzard with laughter.

Allan M. Wilson of the Advertising Council in Washington tells me of a literary joke played some years ago on one of his friends, who shall be called Mr. Forwood. This Mr. Forwood was an executive with a major advertising agency in New York. The joker managed to get hold of three dozen copies of Mr. Forwood's bookplate. He then went out and bought three dozen secondhand books. He glued a bookplate into each volume, and then wrote Mr. Forwood's office address, plus the promise: "If lost, $5 reward if returned." Now he took the books out and left them on park benches, in subways and in taxicabs. Mr. Forwood's first caller was a towering hard guy, driver of one of the cabs, and when Mr. Forwood protested that he knew nothing about the book, the towering hard guy got tough, so the five dollars was handed over. Along came the next claimant, and the next, and Mr. Forwood quickly found an excuse to head for California to check up on the agency's accounts out there.

Ernie Pyle once wrote of his visit to Jack London's house in the Valley of the Moon. The author's home had been turned into a tourist home and was operated by the author's nephew. One day a party of tourists came to the place from San Francisco and in the group was an Eastern businessman. He inspected the premises pretty thoroughly and then approached the nephew.

"Say," he said, "just who *was* this Jack London, anyway? I hear everybody talking about him."

"You mean to say you don't really know?" asked the nephew.

"No, I never heard of him."

"Well, he was the greatest bricklayer in all California."

"You don't say! Well, I'll be darned!"

Oliver St. John Gogarty, the Irish author, was formerly a physician and one of his friends was George Moore. There came a time, however, when Mr. Moore did something that offended Dr. Gogarty, and Dr. Gogarty decided he would wait for an opportunity to pay off the grudge.

Mr. Moore came to Dr. Gogarty with a simple face rash, which had him disturbed. Dr. Gogarty was aware of Mr. Moore's great ambition—to be invited to Lord Invercastle's home. So now Dr. Gogarty told Mr. Moore that his face rash was quite serious, a kind of venereal disorder. He gave Mr. Moore some sugar pills and sent him home with strict orders to stay in his room for two weeks. Then Dr. Gogarty conspired with Lord Invercastle, and Lord Invercastle sent an invitation to Mr. Moore to attend a dinner party at his home. Mr. Moore appealed to Dr. Gogarty, but the doctor said no. Debt paid.

In the early days of the *Reader's Digest* one of the sub-editors was a man who cultivated a beard which gave him the look of a prophet out of Biblical times. This was in the days when the *Digest* was published out of a small establishment in Pleasantville with only a handful of editors. It was the custom then for all the editors, including Publisher DeWitt Wallace, to go out to lunch together. Pleasantville was not New York City, and Mr. Wallace was mildly embarrassed by this man with the whiskers. He wouldn't, of course, come right out and ask the man to shave them off. He chose a more indirect method. On a trip to New York City he bought a boxful of false beards. Then one day, at lunch time, Mr. Wallace and the other editors let the offending man lead the way down the street toward the restaurant, and they trooped along behind, all wearing false whiskers. The hint was quickly accepted and on the following day there were no beards in the *Digest* office.

George Horace Lorimer, the great editor of the *Saturday Evening Post*, loved a good practical joke, according to his biographer, John Tebbel. Mr. Tebbel describes some of these pranks in his book and the best of them, I think, is the one involving the red turtles. Mr. Lorimer was vacationing one summer at his brother-in-law's farm at Spring Lake, Michigan. One afternoon the famous editor found a large bucket of bright red paint in the barn. He then let word get around to all the boys of the neighborhood that he would pay cash for all turtles that were captured and fetched to him. The kids went to work with a will and soon brought a large supply of turtles to Mr. Lorimer. He put them out in the sun to dry and then spent the rest of the day painting their shells a bright red, after which he dumped them back into the lake. "For years afterward," writes Mr. Tebbel, "natives and visitors alike were bemused by the red turtles of Spring Lake."

In the 1850s the youthful James McNeill Whistler, having been bounced out of West Point, worked in the

Washington offices of the Coast and Geodetic Survey. As a fledgling artist, his job was to turn out copper-plate etchings showing sections of the American coastline. He was not content, however, to produce dull maps. He insisted upon decorating his coastline sketches with sea gulls on the wing, dragons rising out of the water, and mermaids with most of their voluptuary equipment fully exposed. When he persisted with such decorations, he was fired, and in time went on to England and fame.

Not long ago a woman in Germany went to court and asked for a divorce from the brute she had unfortunately married. She told the judge that her chief pleasure in life came from reading detective novels. Every time she brought home a new one, her husband would write the name of the murderer at the head of Chapter 1. She got the divorce.

22

Low Jinks in High Society

There may be something to the theory that men with lots of leisure have a strong tendency toward practical joking. I have recently been told about a gentleman whose name bulks large in contemporary New York society—a man who has no office to go to, doesn't like golf, refuses to get drunk, and otherwise is bereft of a normal hobby. He spends a good deal of his time at practical joking. His jokes cover a wide range and include the frequent use, in drawing rooms, of the novelty called "dog mess." One of his favorite stunts, on a somewhat higher level, takes him occasionally to the Automat. The girls in the change booths at these restaurants pride themselves on the speed and accuracy with which they slide nickels at the customers. They simply *never* make a mistake. Our man steps up to the booth and lays down a quarter. The girl slides five nickels at him. He reaches out his hand, in which he has palmed a sixth nickel, and scrapes the coins toward him. He raises his hand just long enough for the girl to see six nickels on the board, scrapes them off into his other hand, and walks quickly away.

One of the most celebrated practical jokers in the realm of Society was Harry Lehr, sometimes called "America's Court Jester." He was an intimate of leading society dames in New York and Newport and he was usually up to something comical. He once staged a dinner on behalf of a leading hostess in Newport at which the guest of honor was to be the famous Prince del Drago of Corsica. The honored guest was late in arriving. All the guests were seated when the Prince was escorted in—a monkey in full dress. He occupied the place of honor throughout the dinner. On another occasion Mr. Lehr set up a Dogs' Dinner in competition to another Newport party given by a lady for whom he had a great dislike. At least a hundred aristocratic dogs attended and dinner was served on the veranda of one of the resort's monstrous mansions. The tables were all a foot high, the crockery was expensive, and the menu included stewed liver, fricassee of bones and shredded dog biscuit.

Mr. Lehr operated in the time of huge parties. He would arrive at a New York dinner, featuring champagne and caviar and costing more than two hundred thousand dollars. He'd take his seat and say to the waiter, "Bring me a hard-boiled egg and a glass of milk."

Mr. Lehr was a real nasty man, judging from the biography written by his widow, Elizabeth Drexel Lehr. They were estranged in the later years of his life. He died in 1929 and left a small fortune to his brothers and sisters. His will included a codicil bequeathing "my houses, lands, silver plate, tapestries, pictures, carriages, yachts and motor cars" to Elizabeth Drexel Lehr. He didn't have any.

Metropolitan society editors are a tetchy, sensitive tribe and woe to the beldame who offends them. In his Philadelphia days the late Maury Paul (Cholly Knickerbocker) got into a snit about Mrs. Edward T. Stotesbury. She had paid one of Mr. Paul's bills which he had refused to honor. He sent her thirty-seven dollars' worth of potted geraniums at ten cents apiece, all delivered at once.

Max Herzberg is authority for the story of another feud between a society editor and a prominent society woman.

The editor had gone to interview this lady and she treated him with a certain haughtiness. From then on, year after year, he always described her, when she attended luncheons, teas, the opera or the races, as wearing precisely the same costume she had on the day of the fatal interview.

Maury Paul, it is said, could make or break a socialite. He actually *made* one out of thin air back in 1940, according to a story told by his secretary, Eve Brown. Mr. Paul and Mrs. William Randolph Hearst, Jr., dreamed up a mythical society beauty called Mme. Moira Vincente and published news of her arrival on our shores. In his habitually beautiful prose Mr. Paul wrote: "No visitor in recent seasons has enjoyed a wider social success than the pulchritudinous Irish-Argentine, Madame Moira Vincente. Almost since the moment she landed in the Fifth and Park Avenue sector fortified with letters to the 'right people,' this oh, so solvent and easy-to-gaze-on matron has been in a maze of entertainments . . . her gowns, jewels, coiffure and the grace with which she dances have made her outstanding, and the 5 P.M. barflies at the Racquet and Tennis Club are pulling every known wire to discover someone to present them."

Mr. Paul and Mrs. Hearst carried the ball from then on, day after day, writing additional details about the glamorous Madame Moira. "She sits," wrote Mr. Paul, "in a pitch-black room for one hour daily. During that hour, she endeavors to keep her mind completely blank and her eyes tightly closed."

Apparently Mr. Paul overplayed his hand and killed his joke. He began to write completely ridiculous things—Madame Moira could shoot a dime off the ear of a moving race horse at 750 yards. Society caught on, and the joke was finished.

Joseph Clark Baldwin, some years ago, wrote a book about his father, an aristocrat who lived in Westchester County and had personality to spare. In the old days the

Baldwins gave sumptuous dinners and Judge Baldwin usually opened the proceedings with a bit of fun. A heaping bowl of mashed potatoes was always placed to the right of his dinner plate. He would hold his hand a few inches above the potatoes for a moment, murmuring something to himself. Then he'd turn to the lady who sat on his right, and say, "My dear, you should feel the steam emanating from those potatoes. Hold your hand over them." The lady would extend her hand above the bowl, whereupon Judge Baldwin would ram it down into the potatoes.

There is a publishing executive who is prominent in New York Society and who is seen frequently in the more fashionable night clubs. He usually carries a supply of cards, specially printed. He looks around the club until he spots someone he knows. Then he bribes a waiter to walk over and place one of the cards in front of his friend. It says: "The management requests that you and your party leave quietly." This gimmick has produced some gloriously undignified scenes.

The story of Beechim and the finger bowl is recounted in Joseph G. Baldwin's book called *Flush Times of Alabama and Mississippi*, which deals with social life in the South during the 1830s. Beechim was from Tennessee and had "a great penchant for fashionable life." Visiting in New Orleans, Beechim became acquainted with a wag named Cousins and the two men went to dinner in the St. Charles Hotel. Along toward the end of the dinner Beechim had a slice of pineapple on his plate when the waiter came along and put a bowl beside each guest's plate, containing water and a small slice of lemon. Let author Baldwin, in his cryptic fashion, complete the tale:

> Beechim asked Cousins what *that* was. C. replied, "Sop for the pine-apple." B. said he thought so. "That's the way it used to be served up at the Trav-

eller's Rest in Knoxville." Beechim took the bowl and
put it in his plate, and then put the pine-apple in the
bowl, and commenced cutting up the pine-apple,
stirred it around in the fluid with his fork, and ate it,
piece after piece. B. kept his eyes on the bowl—did not
observe what was passing about him. Many persons
at table—five hundred at least—ladies, dandies, foreigners, moustached fellows; began to be an uproar on
the other side of the table; everybody got to looking
down at Beechim—eye-glasses put up . . . B. got
through with the pine-apple. Cousins had been laughing with the rest—composed himself now and asked B.
how he liked the pine-apple? B. answered in these
words: "I think the pine-apple very good, but don't
you think the sauce is rather insipid?"

When an old Englishman told B. he had been eating out of the finger-bowl Beechim got out—forgot
where his hat was—ran bare-headed to the bar—called
for his bill—never got his clothes—ran to the steamboat—shut himself up in the state room for two days;—
thing out in the *Picayune* next morning—no names
given. B. came home—saw Cousins when *he* came up—
licked him within an inch of his life with a hickory
stick.

The employment of concealed recording apparatus to
take down conversations for the later embarrassment of
those concerned has become such a common thing throughout America that we need not concern ourselves overmuch
with it here. The most common device is to hide a microphone in the powder room during a party, with the loud-
speaker in the living room. The girls go into the powder
room and sometimes talk to one another with shocking
frankness about their husbands or their dates, or perhaps
even about the host and hostess. In Pittsburgh not long ago
a teen-age boy, member of a socially prominent family,
planted a microphone in his mother's boudoir and re-

corded a long conversation between mother and daughter concerning each of the guests who had been invited to the daughter's announcement party. The two females blistered most of the invited guests. At the height of the actual party, fun-loving Tom walked in and played the whole recording for the assembled company. I don't know if society people whale hell out of their children but if they do, that boy surely got it.

Leonard Lyons has recorded the story of the time a USO company of *The Man Who Came to Dinner* played an engagement for navy personnel in Hawaii. On the first day of the engagement a young man who was an aide to the Admiral met a girl who was in the show and fell heavily for her. The following afternoon he informed the Admiral that he was feeling ill, and wouldn't be able to participate in that evening's functions. He then sneaked off to meet the beautiful young actress, having arranged to take her to dinner at one of the big hotels.

When they arrived in the dining room, the maître d'hôtel was the Admiral himself, and the waiters assigned to their table were the Admiral's other aides. The Admiral and his boys carried the farce straight through to the end.

23

Sports

Several years ago Stanley Frank, writing in the *Saturday Evening Post*, observed that clowning has almost disappeared from baseball and that there is a need for the kind of screwball behavior that characterized the playing careers of Dizzy Dean, Rabbit Maranville, Smead Jolly, Casey Stengel, Art Shires and Baron Poffenberger. The players today, said Mr. Frank, are altogether too serious.

Many of the screwball antics of past performers in baseball took the form of practical jokes. We have remarked that the business of dropping paper bags filled with water out of high hotel windows had its origins with touring ballplayers. In the beginning the bags of water were dropped on dogs, but there is sometimes a scarcity of dogs standing in front of hotels, so after a while the ballplayers started bombarding humans.

The literature of baseball, which has achieved an enormous bulk in recent years, is loaded with practical jokes. The most famous of these is the story of Wilbert Robinson and the grapefruit at Daytona Beach. The Brooklyn manager, to recount it briefly, wagered that he could catch a baseball tossed from an airplane. His players took the bet. The plane came over the beach where Mr. Robinson was waiting with a mitt. But instead of a baseball, a small grapefruit was dropped. It shot through Mr. Robinson's glove and hit him in the chest, burst and spattered juice all over his head and neck. The force of the blow knocked him down and he sat there on the sand, his eyes tightly closed. "Jesus!" he exclaimed. "I'm killed! I'm blind! It's broke open my chest and I'm covered with blood!"

The late John McGraw is said to have originated the arm hammock gag for young pitchers. Mr. McGraw had just acquired a pitcher who had never in his life been in a Pullman. The boy asked his manager to explain the mechanics of the berth to which he had been assigned. Mr. McGraw showed him the shoe hammock and told him it was for his pitching arm—that he should rest his arm in that net all night. This became a standard gag and rookie pitchers who were left-handed were instructed to get into bed upside down in order to use the arm hammock. In those days every rookie was subjected to various indignities. Many of them had come direct from the hills and would fall for anything they were told. Whenever they wanted to mail a letter their teammates would caution them to specify whether they wanted eastbound or westbound stamps. In the dressing room they'd sometimes find their shoes and socks nailed to the floor.

When Roy Cullenbine, the outfielder, first got into organized baseball, playing with a bush league team, a small-town sportswriter came to him just before game time and said, "Do your best this afternoon—there's a couple of scouts up in the stands watching you. If they like you, they'll be waiting at the gate after the game." Roy gave it his all, got four hits and made assorted circus catches. After the game he dressed quickly and hurried to the gate where he found two Boy Scouts awaiting him, eager to shake hands with him just as the man said they would.

People who wear hearing aids are sometimes subjected to a gag which makes them believe that their instrument has gone haywire, or that they have been stricken stone deaf. This operation is said to have originated a few years ago in the dugout of the New York Yankees, with Casey Stengel as chief conspirator. A visiting sportswriter, wearing a hearing aid, was seen approaching the dugout just before game time. He sat down and began a conversation with Mr. Stengel. Suddenly, in the middle of a sentence, Mr. Stengel ceased making audible sounds, though his mouth continued in operation as if he were talking. The sportswriter began fussing with his battery, while Stengel continued his silent talking, with some of his players joining in the sport. The sportswriter had a new battery and found it tuned properly and he was getting panicky when someone sneezed and brought an end to the joke.

One of the most incorrigible practical jokers in the history of baseball was Bill Phelon, a sportswriter. Some people say that Mr. Phelon's jokes, which were usually crude and sometimes vicious, furnished the inspiration for Ring Lardner's *Haircut*. Mr. Phelon's masterpiece, an inspiration of the moment, was played on his fellow baseball writer, Bill Hanna of the old New York *Herald*.

Mr. Hanna was a hypochondriac and spent much of his spare time in consultation with doctors. One doctor told him that it would be good for him to take a long walk every day. So Mr. Hanna got into the habit of walking from his office on Park Row, up Broadway to the Seventies, where he lived.

One afternoon he had just got started on his long walk home when he met Bill Phelon, who was walking downtown on Broadway. The two men stopped for a brief talk and Mr. Phelon, knowing that Mr. Hanna was a health-worrier, remarked on how poorly he was looking. Then they resumed their separate ways and an idea occurred to Mr. Phelon.

Mr. Hanna had gone about five blocks northward when, to his astonishment, he saw Bill Phelon approaching him again.

Mr. Phelon came up to Mr. Hanna, his face alight with surprise and happiness.

"Well, if it isn't old Bill Hanna!" he exclaimed, pumping the *Herald* man's hand. "Haven't seen you for months, Bill. How the hell are you? You look awful."

Mr. Hanna actually *did* look awful at that moment. "Didn't you," he began, "didn't I, that is, didn't I just meet you at the corner of Broadway and Chambers?"

"Of course not!" exclaimed Mr. Phelon. "How could you have done that—I'm walking downtown, as you see, and Broadway and Chambers is five blocks away. You'd better take care of yourself, Bill—you look horrible."

Mr. Hanna, now turned somewhat gray, proceeded on his walk uptown. Half a mile further on, a lump the size of a softball leaped into his throat, for there as plain as day, approaching him from the north, was Bill Phelon. The scene was repeated—Mr. Phelon was *so* pleased to run into his old friend, hadn't seen him in months, and my God he looked terrible.

"Bill," pleaded Mr. Hanna, "you saw me before this afternoon, didn't you? Please tell me you did!"

Mr. Phelon scoffed at the suggestion. He urged Mr. Hanna to be careful about his health, both physical and mental, and then resumed his way southward. Mr. Hanna stood there for a few moments, cold sweat on his brow, and then made a decision. He hailed a taxi and headed for the hospital.

Ira L. Smith reports that the day before the baseball season was to open in Minneapolis back in 1897, an umpire named Frank March approached the grounds keeper for the Minneapolis club. He announced that he had just received word from Ban Johnson that, for the opening game, the field was to be painted white and the foul lines black.

The grounds keeper, a conscientious man, was uncertain about how the job should be done. Umpire March proved helpful.

"Tell you what you do," he said. "Get a street-sprinkler wagon and fill it full of whitewash and use that to paint the field."

The grounds keeper made arrangements for the loan of such a wagon from the city, but before he got into the thing too deep, he anticipated trouble. The holes in the sprinkler nozzles were too small for the passage of white-wash and would clog up quickly. He asked the city's permission to enlarge the holes on this one wagon, but the city officials said no. Thoroughly perplexed, he now went to club headquarters with his problem, and someone tipped him to the truth. Baseball records, thorough as they are, contain no account of what he did to Umpire March.

A certain Western football coach has moments when he enjoys the discomfiture of his fellow man. Sometimes when he visits a race track he will walk up to one of the betting windows, assume an air of nervous apprehension, and ask the man to cash a check—a dirty, crumpled check of $3.15, written atrociously in pencil. The coach says the stunt is always productive of drama and once even included the jailing of himself before he could establish his identity.

Morris Newburger, a Wall Street man who went to Harvard, got himself all wrought up one October week end over the number of obscure colleges whose football scores appeared on Sundays in the New York newspapers. Mr. Newburger was particularly fascinated by the regular appearance in these lists of Slippery Rock.

He was having dinner on a Saturday evening when an idea came to him. He went to the telephone and called the New York *Times* sports department and, quickly inventing a couple of names, reported that Plainfield Teachers had defeated Winona, 27–3. After that he telephoned the same score to the *Herald Tribune*. He was somehow immensely gratified on Sunday morning when he found the Plainfield Teachers score faithfully recorded in both papers. As *The New Yorker* later reported the matter, "a kind of godlike feeling came over him."

On the following Saturday, Mr. Newburger was in Philadelphia, attending a real football game. When it was finished he put in calls for the *Times* and *Herald Tribune*, announcing that Plainfield Teachers had skunked Randolph Tech, 35–0. Again he made the score charts on Sunday.

Mr. Newburger now carried his whimsy a step further. He notified the newspapers that Plainfield Teachers was proud of its star back, John Chung, who was half Chinese, a triple-threat man good enough to make All-American. The sportswriters gave some space to halfback Chung and on the next Sunday reported that Plainfield Teachers beat Ingersoll, 13–0.

The Plainfield Teachers gag got out of hand; too many people knew about it, and somebody at *Time* magazine found out the truth. Mr. Newburger begged *Time* to let him have his fun until the end of the season, but the news magazine was under serious obligation to its readers and printed the truth. That, of course, ended it.

Herman Hickman, the erudite football coach turned television performer, tells about the time he broke the world's record for the shot-put at the University of Tennessee. Herman was the star shot-putter at the Southern school and one afternoon, during an important track-and-field meet, was on the line ready to let go. Suddenly the captain of the football team walked past him and surreptitiously handed him a twelve-pound shot, the weight used in high school competition. A sixteen-pound shot is used in collegiate events.

Using the smaller shot, Herman let 'er fly. Up the line the judges watched the shot land at the fifty-three-foot marker. "Lord a mercy!" exclaimed one of the judges. "He's broke the world's record!" And he had broken it, by about two feet, but now Herman lost his poise and began laughing, and the deception was revealed.

Titanic Thompson, a sportsman and gambler out of Texas, once made a bet of five thousand dollars that he could drive a golf ball over five hundred yards. A New York gambler happily took the wager. Thompson then proceeded to a hill overlooking a lake, which was frozen over. He teed up, gave the ball a smack, it hit the ice and rolled well over six hundred yards. The sucker paid off.

Norman Ross, distance swimming star of the 1920 Olympics, did some of his training in Lake Michigan. One afternoon he was swimming far out in the lake, off the Chicago beaches. As he made his way in toward the shore, a crowd began collecting. He arrived in shallow water, stood up and yelled to the crowd.

"What city is this?" he wanted to know.

"Chicago!" they yelled back at him.

"Oh, hell!" he called out. "I wanted Milwaukee!"

With that he turned, dived into the water and swam away.

24

A Dozen for the Road

The Loch Ness monster is the most famous of the sea serpents, but there have been many others, and some of them have been the invention of practical jokers. Fifty years ago a monster began appearing in Lake George, a New York State summer resort. The Lake George serpent was no hallucination and kept vacationists in a state of terror; nobody would go bathing in the lake and few would even venture out in boats. The "serpent" vanished the following season and then, after a lapse of thirty years, the secret was revealed. Harry W. Watrous, a noted artist who had a place on the lake, confessed that the monster was actually a huge log, which he had painted to resemble a hideous creature, and which he manipulated from the shore by means of ropes and pulleys.

John Hays Hammond, Jr., inventor and engineer whose experiments have advanced the techniques of radiodynamic control, was conducting a series of tests in the ocean near his home at Gloucester. Mr. Hammond brought in Dr. Lee De Forest as a consultant on the project which had to do with a radio-controlled torpedo. The two men were having some difficulty about a floating antenna. One morning Dr. De Forest told Mr. Hammond that he had had a terrible nightmare about a sea serpent and that the dream had furnished a solution to the problem. His sea serpent had been shaped like an immense doughnut. So they sent off to the Goodrich Company and had a huge inner tube made to carry their antenna on the surface of the water.

Immediately it was put in use, Gloucester fishermen began reporting having sighted it, and a few ventured the opinion that it was alive. In a sense, Dr. De Forest's dream had come true. He and Mr. Hammond set to work and painted the monster, giving it a set of eyes that would scare the paint off a battleship. From then on the local fishermen were kept in a high fret, until word got around that the beast was "one of them scientificals."

All this is by way of introduction to a scheme Mr. Hammond devised years ago for the purpose of enlivening the visits of week-end guests. He proposed to construct a house embracing features which would drive such a guest to the borders of insanity. He had the blueprints all drawn but when he found out what the thing would cost, he abandoned it.

One feature of the house was the "elevator bathroom." While a guest was in the bathtub, the entire room could be moved from floor to floor, so silently that he would never notice it. Emerging from the tub, he would open the door which he believed led back into his bedchamber, and walk into the downstairs drawing room, which of course would be full of people.

The Hammond house would also feature a revolving spiral stairway. The guest would learn that his room was directly opposite the top of the stairs. But on his next trip up the spiral stairway, he'd walk into another room on a different floor, perhaps with embarrassing results.

A third feature would be the room that changes its own furniture overnight. The host would escort the guest to his bedroom and take pains to point out certain details of the furnishings, indicating fine antiques and valuable pictures. After the guest had gone to sleep, quiet mechanisms would be set in motion. The walls would swing around on turntables and when the guest awoke in the morning, he'd find himself in a room done completely, perhaps, in modernistic style—new furniture, the fireplace gone, a whole new set of pictures.

Ira L. Smith remembers the time when his friend Dr. Pat Devlin walked into the Washington Press Club and asked Mr. Smith to accompany him on a brief journey. It was around ten o'clock in the evening and Dr. Devlin took Mr. Smith for a long walk, refusing any information as to its purpose. At last they arrived the hellandgone at a park in which stood a huge brick structure, known as the Pensions Building (it now houses the General Accounting Office).

All the way around this building, between the first and second floors, runs a terra cotta band showing, in relief, a series of Civil War scenes.

Dr. Devlin said to Mr. Smith: "See that art work running all the way around? Now, do you know what the sculptor said when he finally finished that job?" Mr. Smith said he didn't know. "He said," declared Dr. Devlin, " 'What a great relief!' "

James Warner Bellah recalls the time in the First World War when a group of submarine officers visited an American flying base. The pilots took several of the submarine men aloft and, just for the hell of it, put them through a series of spine-tingling dives and loops. The submarine men didn't like it but said nothing. They invited the airmen to visit their temporary base and take a dive in one of their pigboats. The fliers accepted. Came the day when they climbed into the sub. "The hatch was secured," Mr. Bellah relates, "orders were shouted, lights winked, gongs bonged, and somebody pulled the circuit breaker, plunging the boat into darkness. At which moment the cook threw a pail of cold salt water on the pilots. They went into complete tizzies." And they were still in those tizzies when they climbed out of the submarine, into the sunlight. The sub had never left its dock.

* * *

Max Schuster, the book publisher, is the champion memo-writer of modern times. Most of his memos are written to himself. He starts the day with a supply of paper slips in the left pocket of his jacket. All day long he jots down maxims, ideas, bits of conversation, book ideas, clever phrases, and so on, transferring the written memos to the right-hand pocket of his coat. At the end of the day he studies his supply of memos, and files them away. It is said that he contemplates producing, someday, a huge history of the world's wisdom.

One afternoon Max Eastman was in Mr. Schuster's office. He managed to sneak a slip of paper from the publisher's left-hand pocket. On it he wrote a single word, "Dinkelspiel." Then he slipped it into Mr. Schuster's right-hand pocket.

That night Mr. Schuster stayed up late, puzzling over the one-word memo. He was unable to remember why he had written it. He couldn't go to sleep. He worried about it for days, repeating it over and over to himself, sometimes aloud, confusing people in his office by pacing up and down the floor and saying, "Dinkelspiel, Dinkelspiel, Dinkelspiel." After about a week he gave it up, choosing to lose that bit of wisdom rather than drive himself mad.

Twenty-odd years ago Gene Fowler wrote an autobiographical pamphlet for the now extinct publishing firm of Covici, Friede. In it he told of an episode out of his Denver school days. I reprint it here with Mr. Fowler's permission:

Mr. Fowler's enemy in the scholastic scramble was a janitor with a *Police Gazette* mustache. He was in the habit of stealing Mr. Fowler's beer, up to and including an incident that was vulgar but dramatic.

Mr. Fowler and several of his companions purchased Coor's beer at fifteen cents a quart during noon recess. Surplus beer was stored in the school toilet, there to be swallowed between classes. God knows a little beer is of infinite help before one begins to translate the boasts of Julius Caesar!

For a month or so, bottles of beer were emptied by a mysterious raider. One day Mr. Fowler skipped his Latin class to lie in wait for the marauder. Mr. Fowler was not stingy. He would have shared his beer with anyone, but it hurt something inside him to see the janitor slink in, clutch the bottle and fit it to his black mustache. It was rape; nothing less.

The next day, Mr. Fowler removed the crown of a beer bottle, drank the beer, and then, with the assistance of a lad named Eddie Sullivan, filled the bottle with something which resembled beer in color, but presumably not in taste.

Several lads cut class to spy on the beer-raid. They saw the janitor come in, almost drooling with passion for beer. They saw him pry off the crown and lift the natural but immodest fluid. He toped lustily; then his eyes began to bulge with wonderment.

Mr. Fowler made the mistake of laughing (how many times he has made that mistake!) and the janitor captured him. In the office of the school principal, the janitor displayed the bottle and charged Mr. Fowler with being a beer drinker.

"This hurts me more than I can tell," said the good and grave-faced principal. He took the bottle from the janitor's hand, shook it and sniffed. "This hurts. Yes, Mr. Fowler, it is a sad hour for me."

Mr. Fowler possibly should have been an attorney. He clamored for proof. "It's not beer," said Mr. Fowler.

The principal was even more saddened by what he fancied an Ossa of falsehood piled on a Pelion of brew. "Not *beer*? How can you stand there and say that, when I have *this* in my hand? Shame, Mr. Fowler!"

"It's not beer. It's a beer bottle. But there's no beer."

The principal lifted it to his nose. Then he put it to his lips. The janitor was terrified. He begged the principal not to quaff the liquid. The principal was a stern, purposeful man.

"Jackson," said the principal. "We'll see about this. I never drink beer, but I know the taste."

"Please," said Mr. Jackson.

"Silence," said the principal. "I hate to hear a boy lie. It hurts me."

"It's not beer," said Mr. Fowler.

The principal puckered for the test. "I suppose you know this means expulsion, Mr. Fowler." He took a swig. Then he began to choke and gag. He waved the bottle with frantic futility. The janitor retrieved it from the trembling hand. The principal spewed and spat like any ten asthmatic patients. He glared. He was unable to speak. Mr. Fowler feared the worst.

When the belching, coughing, retching, gargling, the belly-bouncing and the diaphragmatic cataclysm subsided, the principal sat weakly, like a dog that has been vivisected. Mr. Fowler expected dismissal, but the spectacle was worth any price.

When speaking-breath re-entered the pedagogue's clay, he lifted a hand sadly. "Gentlemen, not a word of this. Go to the engine room, Jackson." Jackson backed out, bewildered. The principal bowed above his desk and studied two medals that were to be awarded in the forthcoming essay contest on the subject: "Did Bacon Write Shakespeare's Plays?" Then he spoke, as though addressing the gold medal, which was first prize: "Go to your class, Mr. Fowler. I trust you implicitly. Not a word of this . . . for the sake of the school."

George Dixon, the Washington columnist who often concerns himself with the muddleheadedness of people in the nation's capital, once made a remark that a crowd would show up at a cocktail party without any knowledge or understanding of what the affair was all about. Someone disputed him. Mr. Dixon promptly set to work to prove his point.

He hired a hotel ballroom and a caterer. Then he sent out announcements, inviting governmental figures as well as Washington correspondents to a party for the purpose of meeting Mr. Titus Oates.

The ballroom was packed. Few if any of the guests expressed any wonder about the identity of Mr. Titus Oates. They simply stood around and drank cocktails and ate canapés. Mr. Dixon let it go for a while, and then quietly took his departure, after engaging a couple of page boys to pass among the guests with printed cards which said:

"Mr. Dixon regrets to announce that Mr. Titus Oates died in England in 1705."

Harry Rice, Sr., was a widely known Chicago newspaperman in his day. He had a little trick which he employed whenever he could locate a victim occupying the proper setting. The man had to be in a plush office in which he was surrounded by other employees, preferably women. Given such a man, Mr. Rice would telephone him and identify himself as the friend of a friend.

"I'm a writer," Mr. Rice would say, "working on a magazine article, and I've come up against a grammatical problem that has bothered me for years. I never seem to be able to get it straight. Our friend Charlie says you're pretty good at grammar and that you might be able to set me straight."

The victim is flattered. "Well, let's hear it," he would say.

"My problem," Mr. Rice would say, "involves the use of the verbs 'is' and 'are.' I want to use the sentence, 'Is souls affected by good music.' Or should it be 'are'?"

"It should be 'are souls,'" the victim would say.

"I beg your pardon," Mr. Rice would say. "I'm in a phone booth and the streetcars are passing outside and I can't hear you very well. Would you repeat that, a little louder?"

"Are souls," the man would say louder.

"I'm sorry, I still didn't hear you. The noise here is terrible. A little louder please."

"Are souls. *Are souls!* ARE SOULS!" the victim would yell into the phone, while all about him the little stenographers and file girls blushed and covered their pretty ears.

There isn't much room for practical joking in the serious business of aviation, yet the crews who fly the commercial airlines have been known to engage in occasional pranks. There was one pilot, for example, who'd wait until his ship got into bumpy weather, then he'd stroll back through the cabin with a book under his arm, the title clearly exposed: *How to Fly in Twenty Easy Lessons.*

The classic airline joke involves a new stewardess on her first assignment. She is going about her routine business when the pilot speaks to her over the intercom: "Please send the co-pilot forward." She looks around, but can find no co-pilot, and so informs the pilot. He bawls her out for having closed the door at the take-off before the co-pilot came aboard and she is emotionally disturbed by her blunder.

The co-pilot is actually in the cockpit, having entered through the cargo hatch. When the plane lands at the next stop, he slips out of the hatch a couple of minutes before the stewardess opens the passengers' door. When she does open it, she hears a shout and, glancing to the rear, sees the missing co-pilot running along the field at top speed. Breathing heavily, he arrives at the doorway and exclaims to the girl, "My God! What a race! I thought I'd *never* catch up with you!"

An author told me this story, and authors are to be believed, so it must be true. In the Southwest there is a towering plateau rising out of the desert to an immense height. Many years ago certain scientists developed a special interest in this tower of stone. Its sheer walls had never been scaled, but aviators passing over it had reported that the flat plain on top was covered with some kind of vegetation. The scientists concluded that they might find something interesting, perhaps in the way of seeds, at the top and they worked out a technique for scaling it. It was a long and laborious job, and dangerous, but at last they made it to the summit. They found the grassy plain, all right, but scattered over it were empty beer and Coca-Cola bottles, paper plates, and remnants of sandwiches. A joker had secretly flown back and forth across the plateau, dropping these items just to add zest to the scientific discovery.

When Robert W. Wood, the physicist, was a student at Johns Hopkins, he usually walked from his home to the laboratory and back. The shortest route led him past a ramshackle store where a group of Negroes usually sat on the porch, sunning themselves. One day Mr. Wood noticed that there was a hole in the street directly in front of the store, and this hole was usually full of water. An idea occurred to him. He knew that when sodium is thrown into water, it explodes, creating a fierce yellow flame, a shower of sparks and then great clouds of yellow smoke.

One day at the laboratory he fixed up a little ball of sodium and carried it with him on his walk home. Arriving in front of the store he suddenly stopped, cleared his throat loudly, and spat into the puddle of water, at the same time dropping the sodium ball into it.

The resulting explosion is probably still talked about in that neighborhood, for it sent the porch loafers scrambling in all directions, convinced that Old Satan himself had appeared before them, spitting fire and brimstone.

The Viscountess Rhondda was vacationing one summer at a seaside resort on the island of Guernsey. One sunny afternoon she took a book and wandered down to a section of the beach which was spotted with small dunes. She stretched out in the sand, back of one of these dunes, and prepared to enjoy her book. Then she saw a man arrive on the beach. He looked all around, and she recognized him as being a clergyman. He was carrying a camera but now he decided this would be a fine spot for him to have a swim.

He disrobed down to his underwear, carefully placing his clothing in a little pile and putting the camera on top of the clothing. Then he went into the water and swam out some distance, disappearing behind a neck of land. At this point Countess Rhondda became aware of another presence. From behind a neighboring dune came two young women, quite attractive and shapely. They had been sunbathing in the nude and they were nude now as they went galloping down to the water's edge. They saw the little pile of clothes, and the camera, and shrieked some, but on looking around saw no sign of human life. One of them picked up the camera and the other posed, full figure, stripped to the buff. Then they changed places, and a picture of the second naked girl was taken. They replaced the camera on the pile of clothes, returned to their dune, put on their dresses and departed.

If, in this compendium, there has been no adequate defense of the practical joke, let us here at the end consider the case of Marvin Pipkin.

Whenever a green engineer was hired at the General Electric plant, the old-timers of the establishment had a routine joke they played on him. They'd assign him the impossible task of frosting light bulbs on the inside. It was explained to the newcomer that a frosted bulb would diffuse more light, and he would go to work on the job with great eagerness, and continue at it until the joke was revealed.

Came the time when Marvin Pipkin went to work at the plant, and was given the frosting assignment. He not only discovered a method for frosting the insides of light bulbs; at the same time he devised a treatment which strengthened the bulbs so that they would last much longer. Owing to his discovery, consumers today get brighter and sturdier light bulbs at less than half the cost of the pre-Pipkin product.

The Day of the Practical Joker

This is the time in England for whipping the cat, while in Scotland the day is spent Hunting the Gowk. The French practice what they call *espièglerie*, their term for a roguish frolic. It is the day of the simplistic prank and the more intricate practical joke. It is April the First—the Feast of the Ineffable Fools.

It is the moment for the exploding cigar, the wallet-on-a-string, the comical phone call. It is a day when, if you are callow of heart and the weather is fierce, you may be sent on sleeveless errands, instructed to bring back a pail of black whitewash, a left-handed monkey wrench, a bucket of steam, a bottle stretcher, a can of bugle oil, some bumblebee feathers, a four-foot yardstick, a dozen buttonholes, some pigeon's milk, or a bottle of striped ink.

On this magic mystifying day we might take stock and find that the practical joke is more than holding its own, largely because of the vast strides that have been made in such fields as electronics, television, honeymoons, chemicals, rocketry, female bosoms, household appliances, short-sheeting, and everyday living.

The chief hindrance confronting this broad and lively aspect of American life is lack of governance, and a strong movement is afoot to rectify the clog. It has been suggested that a Czar of Practical Jokery is sorely needed, a High Commissioner corresponding to the Czars we have had in the movies, in major sports, and in assorted industries. If the practical joke is to stand on a high level of dignity and social acceptability, the practical jokers must be kept in line, subjected to stern controls. There are many more of them functioning in our land than there are in baseball and motion pictures combined. So why not a Czar?

First, to establish the nature of their operations, let us consider Charlie Coker, an elderly resident of a small California town north of San Francisco. Whenever someone asks Charlie Coker how it's going, he often replies, "Things is gettin' a little too smug around here." He is a dedicated foe of pomposity, and since there is an ample supply of it around, he keeps his mind occupied with toils and stratagems directed against its entrenchments.

Not long ago a local grocer got a little too smug with Charlie, and Charlie decided to give the man a spell of the worries. He bought a dozen eggs from the grocer. He took them home, removed them from the carton, and hard-boiled every one of them. Then he replaced them in the carton, went back to the grocery store, and when no one was looking, slipped them in with the other eggs.

Charlie Coker's little maneuver doesn't seem on the surface to be either heroic or villainous, yet it's a little of both. To appreciate its potential it is necessary to sit down and think about it for a while. Let's visualize a housewife who, by chance, takes home that carton of eggs. On the following morning she gets her frying pan hot, cracks one of the eggs, holds it over the pan and flicks off the shell. A dull, grease-spattering *thump*. It could be a startling experience, even a shocking one, to a lady with delicate nerves. Or, taking it from another direction, she might boil one of the eggs for three minutes and serve it to her husband in an egg cup, evoking a domestic scene highlighted by the employment of strong language and the shattering of dishware.

The next progression in the drama, of course, is the return of the housewife to the grocery store, bearing the eggs. She accuses the grocer of vile and unpardonable trickery. The grocer utters an indignant disclaimer. Never in all his life has he sold solid eggs to a customer. In the first place, *why* would he do such a thing? And in the second, *how*? He has no stove in his store. Nevertheless, insists the lady, he did it, causing her embarrassment and mental anguish. The grocer by now has worked himself into a lather (keep in mind that he's smug) and accuses the lady of hard-boiling the eggs herself in a scheme to ruin his reputation and put him out of business. There could be shouting, and the dispute might very well end up at the police station, or in the civil courts.

Meanwhile, what of Charlie Coker? He may or may not know of the multifarious disruptions brought on by his little egg maneuver. He is content to sit back and ruminate on all the possible ructions he may have inspired. He knows that he has struck a blow against smugness.

Charlie Coker's artifice may be properly defined as a practical joke. As soon as it is so defined, then Charlie is in for widespread condemnation. In the eyes of a great many of our citizens a practical joker is an imbecile bucking for idiot who should be disenfranchised and whipped at the post. The fact stands, however, that the practical joke is as solid an American institution as the French poodle, vodka, *quiche Lorraine*, or the Volkswagen.

Years ago I compiled a sizeable book in which I made an attempt to describe all the most famous, as well as the most infamous, practical jokes in history. During the intervening years there has been a steady flow of mail from readers indicating that I barely nicked the surface. In addition, scarcely a day passes without an account of some practical joke or hoax appearing in the press. There is no way of estimating the vast numbers of people who indulge in this frisky form of recreation and revenge. Recently I spent a pleasurable afternoon going through a pile of letters, notes, and clippings that have accumulated over the years.

The file includes several articles by psychiatrists. They are devout enemies of the practical joke. Periodically they issue statements condemning all practical jokers as human polliwogs—immature misfits clamoring for attention by making other people appear to be foolish. They say a practical joker is a fellow who never really grew up and who has the mentality of a thrip. In so saying they are calling Mark Twain immature, and also Franklin D. Roosevelt, Thomas A. Edison, Benjamin Franklin, H. L. Mencken, Abraham Lincoln, Sir Osbert Sitwell, Harry Truman, Richard Brinsley Sheridan, Lord Halifax, James Thurber, Richard Nixon, Anatole France, and a host of other celebrated characters who give the impression of having achieved adulthood. T. S. Eliot, who appeared to be the most solemn of men, enjoyed dropping a device onto a chair just before some elegant lady, or stuffy old gentleman, sat down. The contrivance gave forth a noise of a most vulgar nature. And the late T. Coleman duPont liked to play little store-bought tricks on his friends. His favorite was the Exploding Bouquet. He'd present his victim with a small package, no bigger than a deck of cards; when it was opened it banged out a series of explosions and then shot forth a couple of dozen paper flowers. It jarred people.

I write of these matters because of the proposal that we have a Czar to rule over the practical joke. As somewhat of an authority on the art-sport, I was asked to nominate candidates.

All potential candidates were occupied elsewhere, and so the Czardom was offered to me. It is required that I set down my qualifications, and that is what I am doing now. I must be able to distinguish between a practical joke that is high comedy without harm to the victim, and a practical joke that is wantonly cruel. Not long ago Marie Collier, Australian opera singer, was telling someone that opera stars play hideous tricks on one another; a fairly common one is to put ground glass in a singer's cold cream. As Czar I would jail such a villainous prankster. In the other direction, consider the lady singer who appeared on stage carrying a muff. In the course of her singing she thrust both hands into the muff, and promptly went into a wild dervish-like, arm-flapping dance. Someone had put a peeled and overripe banana in the muff. I feel that this one might get my official sanction, especially if the muff-lady was mean and rotten toward her associates, and secretly put ground glass in their cold cream.

Another plank in my platform insists that books about practical joking, including my own, should be kept out of the hands of persons under twenty-five. I once spoke of this to a man named John Lewellen in Chicago and he agreed most ardently. He recalled how one evening he tried to light a cigarette with one safety match after another, drawing no flame; he then learned that his daughter, having read my book, had embarked upon a career as a practical joker—she had carefully burned the heads off all the matches in the pack and then replaced them with red paint.

A Czar of Practical Joking would need to keep abreast of contemporary developments in his field. The major changes in the art in recent years have been technological. Computers, and all their mechanical brothers and sisters and cousins in the business world, plus the swift progression of the electronic age, have evolved new exercises and praxes and perpetrations.

Employees of technological plants commit some jokes of a complicated scientific nature, but not as frequently as one might suppose. When I talked to employees of an electronics lab, I learned that they were plotting against one of their superiors who was off on a trip. They were installing metal springs and magnets on the back panels of his desk drawers. Whenever he would open a side drawer, it would promptly slide shut. Whenever he unlocked the middle drawer, it would shoot outward and slam him one in the belly button. These electronics lads told me of a fellow employee who smoked a vile-smelling tobacco in his pipe. They decided to make it viler. They got hold of his tobacco pouch and

mixed in some shredded rubber bands. When he undertook his next pipe he scowled a bit and then said, "It's getting so tobacco doesn't taste right to me any more." Forthwith he threw away his pipe and quit smoking.

Two men in the computer plant were spending hours at
work on a trick pepper mill, which they planned to get into
the hands of a company executive who was inclined to bore
people with endless gabble about the superiority of freshly
ground pepper. This pepper mill was about a foot high and
operated by battery. The pranksters were changing the gears
in it, a difficult and rather expensive procedure, and they
were searching for some way of activating it by remote
control. One moment it would be standing quiescent on
the dining table in the executive's home, then suddenly it
would begin to tremble as if having a chill, after which it
would start giving little jumps, and then execute a wild
tarantella up and down the table, possibly knocking over
wine glasses and assaulting the asparagus, clacking and
whirring like a mad thing. That's what the boys hoped for,
and they visualized handsome women guests clutching at
their bosoms and swooning, while the more masterful of the
gentlemen would be trying to flog the thing to death with
silver candlesticks.

It appears that the most common practical joke around
the computer and electronic plants involves simple smoke.
Nothing, apparently, is so disconcerting to a scientist as
smoke coming out of machinery. A new man is assigned to
work on a certain machine. He no more than gets started
when wisps of smoke come drifting out of the mechanism,
or even billows of smoke. A burning cigarette produces the
wisps, a smoke bomb the billows. I've heard of a playful
chemist in a major chemical plant who has an ambition to
load the water cooler with LSD, but thus far he has not
been able to unchicken himself. And there is a top chemical
executive who has fun with weekend guests, especially
pretty women. At his estate he has a large swimming pool,
and he furnishes his guests with bathing attire. As soon as

they get into the water the suits vanish. He has had them made up from yarns spun from a water-soluble plastic.

It is almost possible to believe that today's machines have learned to think and scheme so efficiently that they have begun to play practical jokes on people. The late Corey Ford remarked that "about the only thing a computer can't do is breed more computers." It wouldn't surprise me greatly if we soon have a breakthrough on this front. It would surely be a peak point in scientific history, and noisy.

Occasionally we hear of a computer guggling out a monthly paycheck for $5,750,000 when it should be $575. There is the story of the man in Idaho who, on a single day, had two truckloads of renewal notices from a national magazine delivered to his home; the automated addressing machinery had taken down with a stuck needle.

The technological rib is steadily on the increase, but it is worth remark that those jokes that are simple in concept can be more effective than the ones requiring forethought, long preparation, and complicated equipment. I've been told of a lady in Pasadena whose next-door neighbor was continually borrowing staples—soap, sugar, flour, bread, eggs —and rarely paying any of it back. For three weeks in a row this borrower asked for soap flakes to use in her washing machine, always laughing fit to kill over her forgetfulness in not buying her own supply. When she arrived for the fourth time, asking for soap flakes, the lady of the house excused herself and went to the basement. She emptied most of the soap from the box and replaced it with biscuit flour, baking powder, salt, and cornstarch. The two no longer speak.

More simplicity: Goodman Ace was visiting a hospital with a friend one afternoon. The two men spent a pleasant half hour riding up and down in crowded elevators, with Ace exhibiting a pair of hands that were trembling violently, and asking, "You think I'll be able to operate today, Doctor?"

Another without any great adornment was devised by

schoolchildren in a small Kansas town. On the first day of school the teacher asked each pupil to sign his or her name to the class roll. One boy signed "Herbie Hind." When the list was complete, the teacher read off the names and the designated pupils would stand. Teach would call out "Herbie Hind" three or four times before the giggles and howls from the class put her wise.

The hateful practical joke acquires a tiny measure of prestige from the fact that it has often been popular around the White House and has always been given indulgent consideration in the halls of Congress. In former times a freshman member of Congress was usually subjected to a hazing, especially if he exhibited more than average symptoms of stupidity. Veteran legislators recall the new member from a Midwestern state who, on the final day of his first term, was approached by several fellow members. "Got your crate made yet?" they asked him. What crate? Why, the crate for his desk. It was customary, they told him, for a first-term Congressman to make off with the desk he used on the floor of the House. Crate it and take it home. In short, steal it. He should go to the basement and arrange to have the desk crated and then haul it away. The new boy did go to the basement but he could find no facilities for crating desks. So he simply engaged a truck and a couple of men, and he had the desk halfway down the Capitol steps before someone set him straight on the facts of legislative life.

And Skitch Henderson tells of the time he sat down at the piano in a concert hall, intent upon achieving long-haired aplomb; he raised his hands dramatically over the keyboard and then began to play and what came out was a series of sharp explosions. Someone had installed little dynamite caps under each of the piano's keys. Mr. Henderson intimated that he was quite shook.

From that venerable usually reliable source I have the saga of Miss Veronica Long and the chest ointment. Miss Long (not her true name) is a widely prominent singer of ballads and she had been going through a period of mental anguish brought on by dissatisfaction with her own chest measurements—this at a time before bicycle pumps were brought into use. She knew that girls with enormities were getting all the big play and she confided in her friends that she would be ecstatic if she were just slightly larger in the brisket. Word of her ambition reached the ear of Michael Harmon, an actor friend of some renown. He seen his opportunity and he soze it. He bought a large jar of cold cream. He had a friend in Paris send him a fancy label, printed in French. In translation it may have said "Cough Medicine" or "Gorse and Bracken Fertilizer." No matter. Mr. Harmon knew that Miss Veronica Long had no French. He pasted the label on the jar of cold cream and took it to the girl singer. He spoke of this great medical discovery, this ointment of almost magical properties, which would enlarge a woman's chest until, as the saying goes, she resembled a bureau with the top drawer pulled out. To clinch the deception Mr. Harmon had another actor, just returned from Europe, happen along and inform Miss Long that the new unguent was the rage from Oslo to Calabria—that all over Europe women were standing in queues in order to get the stuff and slather it over their pectoral equipment. Miss Long was, of course, almost deliriously happy, and while there were no actual witnesses, it seems probable that her foretop was cold-creamed from that hour onward, at least until the jar was empty. She remains as before.

Any joke that exposes human greed and cupidity surely should be permitted. I know of a New York taxi driver who owns his own cab. He lives on Long Island where he finds it unnecessary to subscribe to a garbage collection service. Each morning he wraps his accumulated garbage into a neat package and ties it up with a ribbon. He places this package on the back seat of his cab and sets out on his day's work. He swears that if his first customer doesn't steal the package, his second is certain to do so.

Among the old standard practical joke there are few that have not been extended and improved upon. Wedding-night duggery, skul or otherwise, is as old as matrimony itself, and the most common of these perpetrations today is the secret installation of a microphone in the nuptial chamber. I have had a letter from an executive in a large eastern corporation describing what seems to be a constructive improvement on the microphone plant. A close friend of the bride and groom draws them aside and whispers, "The boys are going to hide a mike in your room. Take care." There is actually no mike, but the happy couple will likely spend most of the night ripping their room apart, searching for the infernal installation.

Put-ons are often spontaneous. There was the case of Shelton Bank, a bright young New Yorker majoring in chemistry at a local college. In the course of a chemical experiment Mr. Bank got his hands covered with a hard crust of a translucent material that wouldn't wash off. His professor told him to take a piece of sandpaper and abrade the stuff away. Mr. Bank was in a hurry to get home so he boarded a subway, took a seat, and began sandpapering his hands. A woman across the aisle watched him with great interest for a while and then could no longer resist making inquiry. She finally asked him what on earth he was doing.

"Oh," said Mr. Bank casually, "I got a pair of Christmas gloves that are too small, so I'm sanding my hands down to size."

Among the gags long popular in college as well as in the armed forces is the practice known as short-sheeting. The top sheet is removed from the bed and the bottom sheet is folded upward so that a shallow sack is formed—a frustrating and startling thing when the feet are rammed into it. A man who describes himself as a direct-mail consultant in St. Louis had told me of the unhappy consequences attending a job of short-sheeting he performed after he got out of the Army. When he returned from the wars he got married and on his wedding night, short-sheeted his young bride. She didn't complain, but neither did she split her sides. Three years later she sued for divorce, saying, "I knew that first night when you short-sheeted me that it wasn't going to work out."

People have been playing little practical jokes on dogs and other pets for centuries. The latest example of this form of foolery involves ducklings and could be considered an exercise in experimental ecology. Not, however, by the baby ducks. It has been determined that the moment a duckling emerges from the egg, the first thing it sees it believes to be its mother. If it sees a man, that man is Mama and the duckling will follow him around and yearn for him as long as he lives. Having established this duck trait, the experimenters have been tricking the ducklings, arranging that the first thing they see on hatching would be a motorcycle, or a milk bottle, or a sphygmomanometer. I confess I don't quite know how to Czar this one.

A correspondence *coup de main* guaranteed to shatter nerves appears to have come into being several years ago. A man receives the second page of a letter, the suggestion being that the writer failed to enclose the first page. One such goes this way:

2. (Wm. R. Graney)

so the IRS men finally acted as though they were satisfied. I tell you, I've never been so thoroughly grilled before. They certainly seemed familiar with all your activities, extracurricular included.

I hope you won't let this affect our friendship, whether you get things cleared up or not. I was on the spot. What could I do?

Good luck, buddy,

Gene

A lawyer in Denver sent me several additional samples of second pages, and any man receiving any one of them would lose some sleep. His name at the top of the page makes it positive that the letter was meant for him, but he can't think of anybody named Gene who might have sent it, so he has no way of checking. His back is to the wall, he is onfakalized and he is bedumbed.

Jay Marshall, a professional magician with a Jim Moranic sense of humor, sometimes carries a trick water faucet with him on his travels, a faucet equipped with a rubber suction cup on the back. Mr. Marshall gets on a plane, takes a window seat, and quietly fastens the faucet to the wall near his elbow. Then he summons the stewardess and asks, "What on earth is this faucet for?" The girl contemplates the thing with startled eyes, then hurries forward to speak to the captain. He advises her that she has mislaid her marbles, but she talks him into having a look. He arrives at Mr. Marshall's seat, glances at the wall, and says, "Okay, where's the faucet?" And Mr. Marshall, twitching his eyebrows upward, responds, "What faucet?"

A sportive California press agent named Allen A. Arthur revived an old gag involving "money pads" that was once popular among nomadic vaudeville performers. Mr. Arthur improved upon it considerably. He knows that most people are strangely suspicious of a two-dollar bill. He visited several banks to acquire a hundred of them, all crisply new. He took them to a binder and had them gummed together at one end, to make a sort of coupon book. His first foray was against the box office of a movie theater. He pulled out his pad of two-dollar bills, casually ripped one off, and handed it to the girl. Her eyes bugged, and she summoned the manager, and there was a lengthy discussion before Mr. Arthur convinced the man that his currency was legit. Later, in a liquor store, the proprietor had his clerk quietly summon the cops, and again Mr. Arthur had an enjoyable talkfest. To his credit it must be said that Mr. Arthur had his money pad constructed with imagination. It bore a stiff cover with the lettering: "Specially printed for Allen A. Arthur." And about ten bills from the bottom, a yellow insert saying, "Time to reorder."

I must confess that I am not a practical joker; I have been tempted at times, but the true spirit is not in me. I used to live on the edge of a Westchester forest where the wild bird watchers roamed. The Audubon Society's chapter in my neighborhood was strong enough to make or break a politician. As you must know, birds of a similar aspect are often identifiable, one from another, by tiny touches of color on the head, the neck, the breast, or the wing tips. I long wanted to capture a dozen or so birds and fix them up with bright paints—little spots of red or pink or yellow or blue—and then turn them loose for the purpose of confounding the bird watchers. There are three reasons why I didn't do it: I didn't have the courage, I didn't have the energy, and the damn birds wouldn't hold still long enough to be captured and painted.

On my first day as Czar of Practical Jokery I will draw up a Code, a body of law Napoleonic in concept, starting off this way:

Article I: Pulling a chair out from under a person who is about to sit upon it is forbidden, except in cases where the victim is a member of Royalty.

Article II: Goosing is sempiternal and therefore legitimate, except on cliffs, the roofs of high buildings, or in chemical plants or factories where the goosee might leap into vats or large machines.

Article III: Explosives attached to the starting mechanism of automobiles are outlawed.

One additional stipulation: for my expertise in the vibrant, adventuresome, and kooky world of the practical joke, I expect the pay to be right.

Selected New Stories

Fred Back tells in *To Hell with Golf* of a Practical Joke worked up by a few members of the old Rancho Club in Hollywood. Purpose—to startle weisenheimers. A special effects man from one of the studios went to great pains to extract the guts from a dozen golf balls through holes drilled with precision instruments. He then replaced the ball stuffing with an explosive that would detonate on impact. Each of the balls was carefully rewrapped in the original cellophane and all twelve balls were secreted in twelve different "unopened" cartons in the club golf shop. Over a period of several weeks the occasional explosion would be heard, leaving tensed-up victims standing on the tee, visibly shaken.

In the days of silent movies there was a vaudeville deadpan comic named Tommy Dugan. He would go into a theater alone and begin reading the titles in a loud voice. People all around tried to shush him into silence, but he kept it up, and when they grew threatening he would explain, "I don't know how to read to myself—I have to read them out loud so I'll understand the picture. I paid my money and I'm an American citizen, and you can't stop me."

Then, turning back to the screen, he'd read in a loud voice: "I long to kiss your lovely lips, my sweet."

My own definition of a practical joke: a hoax that is funny, and really hurts only those who have it coming— egocentric smart asses. A good practical joke is one that deflates a stuffed shirt.

Some of the jokes in this book might be classified as hoaxes, but in spite of all dictionary definitions, we tend to think of a hoax as a swindle, a con game, or a big journalistic put-on, such as Edgar Allan Poe's hoax. In this connection I have been honestly and deeply resentful over the persistent use of the term "hoax" as describing the colossal swindle perpetrated by the nasty con man Clifford Irving on the McGraw-Hill Publishing Company, with a fraudulent book about Howard Hughes. Almost every publication in the country, even to this day, when recalling the dirty affair, speaks of it as the Clifford Irving-Howard Hughes *hoax*. God damn it, as a man who has spent more than fifty years earning my living as a writer, I resent it. It was an outright swindle, a fraud, and a crime.

In August of 1967, Merriman Smith told of a practical joke on Eisenhower. Smith was playing golf with Ike at Gettysburg. Ike went into the rough, and made a bad shot near a wall, and uttered cusswords. Beyond the wall was a seminary. Smith got hold of the seminary's stationery and wrote a note to Eisenhower, purportedly from the head of the seminary, objecting to the profanity overheard by the divinity students. The note was received by Ike's press secretary, James Hagerty. He and his staff debated, and decided to keep it from Ike. They felt he'd really blow his top if he saw it, but they worried about it, and got in touch with George Allen and showed him the letter. He decided to communicate with the president of the seminary. And found out the whole thing was a hoax.

* * *

Herb Caen of San Francisco told of an Oakland citizen with a scientific-mechanical bent who had a gadget on his car which extinguished the headlamps one minute after the ignition was switched off. One evening he parked his car in front of his house and started up the walkway. A lady passing by called out, "Hey, mister, you left your lights on!" The Oaklandite, a man with a good sense of timing, turned around, drew in a deep breath, held it for a few moments, then leaning forward, blew out the headlights at a distance of fifteen yards.

Once when James Thurber was in London, Mr. and Mrs. E. B. White came to town for a few days. Thurber phoned White and, putting on his sharp British manner and accent, identified himself as a reporter; he wanted an interview. White, a shy man, said he had no time for it. The reporter all but begged for the interview but White was adamant in his refusal. Then the reporter asked if he might get simply a picture of the couple, to be used with a simple caption and no text. White said that sounded all right. The reporter then said there was one small matter to be settled: the kind of pose he could expect. White asked him what he had in mind. "Why," said the reporter, "I think a shot of Mrs. White leapfrogging naked over you." White was momentarily indignant before realizing that he was being given the old ranikaboo, and that the ranikabooer was his old pal Thurber.

Alan King tells of a harmless but hilarious prank which he and a friend played on a neighbor who had just purchased a new Volkswagen. It involved filling the Volkswagen's gas tank with gas each night, making the owner believe he was getting hundreds of miles to the gallon. Then, after a period of time and discussions with the dealer, whom King and his friend convinced that the owner was a bit flaky and needed humoring, they began siphoning gas out of the tank each night until the owner could but drive a few blocks before running out of gas.

Sometimes a practical joke with an element of cruelty in it may backfire pleasantly for the victim. In 1941 a girl named Anna, 13, West Virginia, wrote FDR congratulating him on his birthday, which was the same as hers. The White House sent a polite reply, but the letter was intercepted by Anna's brother Steve, a joker, who typed an addition to it, saying, "We would like to have you come to the White House and meet the President." Anna somehow managed to make it to Washington, where the Secret Service men told her to get lost and took her to a Police Receiving home.

Roosevelt heard about the incident and ordered that she be brought to the White House the next day. He put her up in an elegant hotel suite, spent some time chatting with her, had her taken out to look at Mount Vernon, and that night she was the guest of the Roosevelt family at the birthday ball. When Anna got home she said to her brother that she had a message for him from the President of the United States. The message to Steve was: "The joke's on you."

In 1964 the Democratic governor of Georgia, Carl E. Sanders, sent out twelve thousand Christmas cards. A Christmas tree was the principal feature of the card and hidden among the branches, in tiny script, was the name "Goldwater." At the time, Barry Goldwater was a candidate for President. When the prank was discovered, an art student at the University of Georgia confessed all. How he got access to the cards was not revealed in the account that I read. He said he thought he had put Goldwater's name into the picture so small that nobody would notice it. Some people did, and today, the story goes, the card has become a collector's item.

According to an early friend of Marlon Brando, before he

made the grade as an actor he lived in a shabby apartment next door to Leon & Eddie's nightclub in Manhattan. Brando had a habit of pausing in front of the club and inspecting the photographs of scantily dressed girls which were on display outside the club. The doorman objected to this crummy bum hanging around outside the club entrance, and called a cop, and the cop gave the future star a few whacks across the butt with his nightstick. Marlon protested to the police department, but got nowhere. So he walked all the way to the First Avenue slaughterhouses, occupying the site where the United Nations building now stands. He filled a large cardboard box with dried manure, carried it back, and made his way to the roof of Leon & Eddie's. The club had a roof that rolled back so the clientele could dine under the stars. Brando peered down into the bistro, assuring himself that it was crowded as usual, then cried out in his loudest voice: "Beware of the Flying Red Horse!" and let go with the contents of the box, sending a shower of manure down upon the merrymakers. After which he went home to bed, contented.

The English will go to any lengths in their pranking. It is recorded somewhere that one day at Windsor Castle the King, James I, was told that the Earl of Pembroke had a phobia about frogs—couldn't even stand to look at one. So the King sent for a frog and when Pembroke was woolgathering, slipped it down his neck. Pembroke all but threw a conniption fit and said to himself, well, by God, I don't care if he is the King, nobody can pull a stunt like that on *me*. He knew that King James despised swine, was horrified by sows, and so he turned one loose in the royal bedroom. That's all I know about it.

South Carolina produced Elliott White Springs, fun-loving owner of a cotton-mills empire in South Carolina, Springs Cotton Mills. He was a World War I flying ace and author of several good books, a man described by *Fortune* as "an unreconstructed business rebel." He first attracted attention with unorthodox advertising: scented cotton cloth for girls who want to avoid "dancer's diaphoresis" and the "steatopygic stance." Practical jokes were a common part of his life. Let's look at one:

He sent out a large Christmas card, purporting to show scenes around his main plant. One photo showed a barefoot child standing by a loom, and another pictured a haggard woman, also barefoot. He gave the card wide circulation and was soon being denounced from coast to coast, and fell into the hands of the Labor Department. Whereupon Springs announced that the child was his own, the unkempt woman his wife. To one customer who had sent the card to the Labor Department, Springs wrote:

"The latest available statistics show that 74.6 percent of all the cards I mailed out have already been forwarded to Washington. As for the loss of your business, you and I both know that if Iscariot & Co. offered you the original 30 pieces at a sixteenth below the market, you would ground-loop your revolving chair reaching for the sales note."

It grieves me to add that Elliott White Springs died in 1959.

Lucius Beebe, the gourmet, boulevardier, connoisseur of fine wines, newspaper columnist, fop, and all-around gay dude (dedicated snob, railroad buff, man of property, author) —the only man exhibiting all these high qualities ever to come within my own personal circle of friends—was a practical joker during his college days. He was canned out of Yale for "proving too vivacious for the faculty" and then went to Harvard. In his Yale days he was a prankster of the dynamite and planted bomb breed, and loved nothing more than spending a night touring the outer fringes of New Haven and blowing up privies. One of his stunts was directed against Professor Henry Hallam Tweedy, who was in charge of the Divinity School, a prude-in-depth and a staunch opponent of the Demon Rum. Beebe wrote an essay attacking prohibition and it appeared in one of the school papers. Professor Tweedy condemned it, publicly. Soon afterward Beebe got back at the enemy. During a performance at the Hyperion Theatre, a tall man with a long beard and severe attire arose in one of the boxes, wavering on his feet and brandishing an empty whisky bottle. He interrupted the performance and cried out, "I am Professor Tweedy of the Yale Divinity School!" Then he flung the bottle onto the stage and fell to the floor, disappearing from sight. He was gone from the premises by the time the theater management arrived.

Leonard Lyons, the New York gossip columnist, wrote once about a composer named Robert Stoltz, victim of a rather complex practical joke. Lyons said that Stoltz had composed fifty-two operettas and eighty-nine film scores. He quoted Stoltz as saying he had written 1,420 songs and 700 of them were hits. Leonard Lyons had been known to fall into error, sometimes quite often, so I must state that I have been unable to find any Robert Stoltz in books about music, operettas, film scores. I have never heard Mr. Lyons accused of making up his anecdotes, so I'll ride along with him on this one.

Stoltz told Lyons that when he was eighteen he conducted operettas in Brünn, Czechoslovakia. Then one afternoon he was informed that he would be conducting a full-fledged opera that evening—Verdi's *Il Trovatore*. Stoltz expressed pleasure that he would now be working with real singers "rather than the operetta crowd." Some member of the operetta crowd overheard the remark, and there was bad feeling. That night when he went on stage he saw a man who looked exactly like Giuseppe Verdi, bearded and wearing nineteenth-century clothing, and looking baleful, sitting in one of the boxes. Stoltz didn't know that Verdi had died in

1901, and was understandably upset when, during the opera, the Italian stamped out of the box and slammed the door hard. When the opera was over, Stoltz went to his dressing room and found a coffin, with Verdi in it. As soon as Stoltz walked into the room Verdi turned over in his coffin. It was soon established that he was an operetta clown made up as the great composer.

Everyone has heard of the Neiman-Marcus store in Dallas. The head of the firm, Stanley Marcus, has his fey moments. Once Mrs. Marcus mentioned that she had to go to the dentist for an extraction. He was a new dentist recommended to her by a friend. Merchant Prince Marcus made an arrangement. He had himself disguised, practiced a change of voice, and took the place of the dentist. After Mrs. Marcus had been escorted to the chair, the dentist entered, and placed on the tray in front of her face a pair of rusty slip-joint pliers, a coarse, large file of the type used by blacksmiths to pare down the hooves of horses, and a veterinarian's hypo needle, almost as big as a ball bat.

A London doctor was blackballed by the Royal Society. The doctor struck back. There had been a discussion of the uses of pitch, including certain medical substances in the tar-like stuff. The blackballed medico wrote to the Royal Society: "A sailor having broken one of his legs, the idea occurred to me of bringing the two parts together and joining them with pitch. The result of this treatment has been marvellous." He posed as a country doctor.

The savants of the Royal Society were astonished. The letter was read to the membership and a long discussion ensued. It was voted to publish the entire discussion, as of interest to the public as well as the medical profession. Before that happened, however, a second letter came from the country doctor. He wrote: "Excuse me, but I forgot to say that the sailor's leg was a wooden one."

* * *

The classic story out of Dartmouth concerns the time when the Hanover City Council voted to compel all Dartmouth students to pay city taxes. The students outnumbered the townies, and this ruling made them legally citizens of the community. In the next election the undergraduates elected a new mayor and council from their own number. The Council then proceeded to enact legislation for such items as the building of a town hall an inch square and a mile high, construction of a superhighway to Vassar and a railroad to Smith, and establishing free plane service to other New England campuses. It took the state legislature to get the matter straightened out.

Yucca Salamunich was a sculptor with a studio in Hollywood. My old friend Desmond Slattery tells fine stories about Yucca and one of my favorites concerns the sculptor's manner of handling requests from his friends for free examples of his work. It was Salamunich's custom to save up these letters, advising the friends that he would send them some statuary when he got something that was worthy. Then at Christmastime he would rake up broken chunks of stone and plaster, large and small, put the detritus into neat holiday packages—to give the impression that a work of art had been shattered in transit—and send them off to his pestiferous friends.

List now to the harrowing experience of Lejaren Hiller, who was one of New York's leading commercial photographers. It is a tale I had from Mr. Hiller's own lips.

Mr. Hiller went one day to the home of a prominent citizen, Mr. L., in Greenwich Village. Mr. Hiller wanted to photograph Mr. L. for a testimonial advertisement. Mr. L., a dignified man, told Mr. Hiller that he never went in for that sort of bosh, but desired that there be no hard feelings, and proposed that they have a drink together.

The two men had their drink and then another and more after that and then Mr. L. called up a lot of his friends and urged them to come over and join the party. Mr. Hiller then called a couple of his.

Soon the joint was jumping, and soon also, Mr. Hiller passed out cold. When he opened his eyes it was morning and he was lying on a divan in Mr. L.'s living room. He was somewhat dazed and bewildered, but made his way to the street and took a taxi to his home. There he collapsed on the bed without even bothering to take off his clothes.

Later in the day the telephone awakened Mr. Hiller. It was one of his friends who had been at the party. The friend was excited.

"Didn't you hear?" he cried. "Mr. L. committed suicide this morning!"

Mr. Hiller threw some cold water on his face and hurried over to Mr. L.'s house. Sure enough, Mr. L. had done away with himself, and the house was swarming with cops. Mr. Hiller sat down and told them his story and then went home.

Arriving back at his own apartment, Mr. Hiller decided it was about time he took a shower. He was removing his shirt when he saw something that shocked him to attention. There was writing of some kind all over his bare chest and the upper part of his belly. Mr. Hiller got a couple of mirrors and fixed them so he could read the writing.

Someone had used India ink and a brush to write on Mr. Hiller. He almost fainted when he read it. It was Mr. L.'s last will and testament, and it was signed by two witnesses— men who had been at last night's party. Mr. Hiller gathered up his galloping thoughts and called a friend who was a lawyer. The lawyer said, "Good God! Never heard of such a thing! Stay right there and I'll be over."

The lawyer came over and examined the chest writing. Mr. Hiller said he'd like to wash it off and forget about it forever.

"You can't do that," said the lawyer, pointing out that witnesses had signed the epidermal testament. So they got in touch with a surrogate and went to his chambers, where Mr.

Hiller peeled off his shirt. The surrogate was duly impressed by the chest testament and, after studying it for a while, said to Mr. Hiller:

"Were you a witness to this will?"

"No, Your Honor," said Mr. Hiller in all truth.

The situation was without precedent but the surrogate handled it nicely. He had a photographer called in, Mr. Hiller bared his chest (and belly) and the last will and testament of Mr. L. was photographed. After that Mr. Hiller rendered an affidavit, telling his story, and the surrogate said he could go home and wash off the will.

Mr. Hiller told me that he learned the torso testament started out to be a joke; his friends said Mr. L. himself wrote the will and appeared to be having a lot of fun doing it. Had he already decided to kill himself? Or did the idea of suicide come to him after he had written the will? Mr. Hiller didn't know the answer.

Conchita Jurado, who had been a charwoman for sixty years in Mexico City, died. Conchita spent the first sixty years of life scrubbing floors. She saved money, and when she reached sixty decided to have fun during her remaining years. She had the capabilities of a fine actress, and so in 1926 she changed her identity. She became a man. She assembled a disguise, the haberdashery of an elegant but slightly eccentric gentleman, a black slouch hat, and a false black moustache. Then she went forth into Mexico City's top social circles as Don Carlos Balmori, a wealthy grandee with vast estates and castles in Spain. "Don Carlos" mixed with the top people of Mexico and always seemed to want to help them, to contribute money to their causes; they included one ex-president of Mexico, generals who thirsted for high public office, women who wanted fine haciendas, artists and musicians who yearned for advancement, bankers who sought power. After she had written a check for whatever these people required, she would immediately reveal her little gambit, and swear them to secrecy, and admit them to her society of the greedy and gullible.

It was said that almost all of her victims were enchanted with her duplicity, and it was reported further that in the course of her five years as Don Carlos, she married more than a hundred women.

Ukie Sherin's profession in Hollywood was playing piano in hotels and clubs. His avocation was practical jokery. Years ago he played a disturbing joke on Spade Cooley, ballroom proprietor in Santa Monica.

Came the day when Spade Cooley called in Ukie and signed him up to play a date at Cooley's Santa Monica ballroom. Ukie signed a thirteen-week contract to play in the "M Room" at the Santa Monica spot. Ukie wanted to know about the "M Room" and Cooley told him it was one of the nicest niches in the ballroom, and one of the most frequented.

When he turned up for his first evening's work Sherin was escorted to the men's room where, on the door, was the sign: "Ukie Sherin Now Appearing in Person." He shrieked and bellowed and protested, and then took his case to the musicians' union. They couldn't help him—his name was on the contract. Ukie decided to try to sit down and reason with Spade Cooley, but the only satisfaction Spade could give him was: "You shouldn't be griping like this. After all, if you give them a good show you might go right up the ladder—you might even get an engagement to play the men's room at Ciro's."

And so there was music amidst the vitreous china installations.

The office of the president of Northwestern University at Evanston received a phone call from a "secret service" man saying Prince Charles III of Belgium was in Chicago and wanted to visit the university. Arrangements were made, the young man arrived, was given the red-carpet treatment. Among other things he asked to see the dormitories where the girls lived, and on being taken there he began making passes at the co-eds. People grew suspicious. The "Prince" was arrested and it was revealed that he was Jules Stern, a seventeen-year-old son of a Chicago salesman. Stern told the authorities he got the idea from reading the original version of this book, in which he seems to have been impressed by the Jim Moran caper in Hollywood.

There have been several non-artists as well as artists who have played tricks on the art critics as well as the art-loving public, by haphazard slapping of paint onto canvas and passing the result off as superb modern art. One of the best examples of this duplicity was engineered by Paul Jordan Smith, author, teacher, and literary critic in Los Angeles for many years. Mr. Smith was an avowed ferninster when it came to Dadaism, impressionism, cubism, surrealism, and other "modern" methods of painting pictures which are not pictures at all and, in fact, are not much of anything at all.

Mr. Smith's wife was a painter and some of her portraits, which were true pictures, were attacked by distortionist critics as being "distinctly of the old school." What a condemnation!

Mr. Smith was irritated. He had never drawn so much as a Crayola apple, but now he seized brushes and canvas and quickly ran up a modernist painting of a savage holding a couple of bananas. He titled the painting, "Yes, We Have No Bananas."

Shortly afterward a young art critic happened to visit the Smith home and was shown the painting and was told that it represented Paul Jordan Smith's commentary on futuristic art. The young man said that, actually, "Bananas" had merit, was meaningful, and when Mr. Smith said it was rotten, the critic said that "one had no right to judge unless one knew what was in the soul of the artist."

Whereupon Paul Jordan Smith became Pavel Jerdano-witch, and changed the title of his picture to "Exaltation" and sent it in, handsomely framed, to an art exhibit in Los Angeles. It was close to being a sensation, and art people in Paris got interested. There followed exhibitions in other cities of Jerdanowitch paintings—his masterpiece, which he called the quintessence of the Disumbrationist school, was hung at the Marshall Field galleries in Chicago, and drew raves, and was titled "Aspiration." Nothing but blobs and smears. Then his "Adoration" and his "Illumination" were exhibited at the Waldorf-Astoria in New York, to great acclaim—slap-dab daubs a four-year-old child would have disowned.

Smith-Jerdanowitch kept up the joke for three years and then confessed, in 1927. The following year his four paintings were hung in the Vose Galleries in Boston; the catalog for this exhibition described them as being "for those who realize that real art depicts not what we see but what we feel, hear and smell . . ." It is likely that Mr. Smith conceded the truth in the word "smell."

My old friend Alton Cook was sojourning in Italy a long time back. Riding a bus from the Milan airport to the railroad station, Alton found himself sitting next to an attractive young thing, like himself a resident of New York. In transit the girl remarked on the beauty of a large and ornate building they were passing.

"That," said Alton, "is the Palazzo di Grasso, famed in Italian history and famed, in fact, throughout world folklore because of one small incident."

"What was the incident?"

"Back in Renaissance times," Alton told her, "the palazzo was erected and the Di Grasso family organized a great ball. You see, my dear, even the Italian aristocracy enjoys a good housewarming. Well, one of the Di Grasso boys more playful than the others, decided to enliven the proceedings. He reversed one of his spurs, fastening it to the toe of his boot, rather than the heel. Then he gently prodded the backside of a female guest. Do you mind my use of the word backside, child?"

"No," said the demure young thing, "not as long as it's history."

"The female guest so prodded," Alton continued, "was elderly and of noble bloodlines, and she leaped two feet off the ballroom floor when the spur caressed her behind. The merriment evoked among the company was great, and so at the next ball in the palazzo, the same young man obtained the head of a golden goose and fastened it to the toe of his boot, and went about indiscriminately prodding the ladies in the same sensitive area. There was much leaping and squealing that night, you may be sure. It became a tradition after that, for many years, to have one member of the family wear the golden goose on his boot, and the prodding gesture became known as the rite of the *oca*. And this, my dear, was the origin of the little gesture which we call the goose."

The young lady gave no indication of knowing about the goose, and goosing, and did not ask for a definition, and they arrived at the railroad station and did not see each other again. Alton Cook worried some for a while. He was a student of history and he knew that history sometimes gets distorted by just such small incidents as his Di Grasso story. The girl, he felt, might spread the tale as the true origin of the goose, and it would go into the books. It might even wind up in the pages of Volume V of Will Durant's grand series, *The Story of Civilization.*

Lord Byron wrote poetry, but he also indulged in practical jokes, and over the years had more mistresses than Edgar Guest had hairs on his head. Died at thirty-six. Good going for a man who died at thirty-six. His final illness came at Missolonghi in Greece, where he was helping the Greeks fight against the Turks. He took down with a fever and while on his deathbed he learned that his physician was dreadfully afraid of earthquakes. Byron had some soldiers gather up a couple dozen cannonballs and put them in a room above the bedchamber where he was lying. The cannonballs were stacked in a pyramid. When Byron's doctor returned and was in the patient's room, a signal was given and the cannonballs were dislodged so that they thundered and crashed and bounced about overhead, scaring the hell out of the doctor. It was the celebrated poet's last act of any consequence before he died.

Hugh Troy never sought publicity for his operations, but he did chicken out once, and kept silent about an exploit which he later referred to as "My one bid for sainthood." This one may be difficult of belief, but in all the years I knew him I never knew him to lie. It concerns his taking snakes to Ireland.

One of his friends gave me a rather vague account of it, and when I was preparing the original edition of this book I asked him about it. He said, "Forget about it—it didn't happen."

Long after the book was published he relented. He wrote me from Washington, D.C., where he lived during his final years. He said he actually *did* take those snakes to Ireland.

He said that he learned one day that a country can't really do without snakes, wherefore St. Patrick had done Ireland a disservice in driving the vipers into the sea. Hugh went to call on an old friend, Raymond Ditmars, eminent zoologist and probably the greatest authority on reptiles in the world. Hugh told Dr. Ditmars that he wanted to take some snakes to Ireland and quietly turn them loose.

Dr. Ditmars fell in with the plot. He chose the most useful and harmless varieties, snakes that would likely thrive in the island's climate. And he smoothed the way for Hugh to get his box of serpents past the snake subdivision of the Customs Department. Thus it came about that on St. Patrick's Day in 1932, Hugh arrived beside the River Shannon where his grandmother had been born, and on that spot he released the serpents. In his letter confessing all, years afterward, Hugh said that snakes are prevalent again throughout a large section of Ireland, and doing much good at keeping nature in balance.

The psychiatrists are forever issuing pronouncements from on high saying practical jokers are fellows who have never grown up, who yearn for attention from their friends and associates. There is little that can be done, say the shrinks, to help him out of his condition. I have a pronouncement. Psychiatrists are people who have never grown up, and yearn for attention, and there is little that can be done for them. If psychiatrists are so god damn smart, if they know *everything*, why the hell ain't they runnin' the country?

The practical joke is almost as old as time, and we even find an example of the backfiring joke as having occurred a long long time ago, maybe even before our Civil War, for it is narrated in *The Arabian Nights' Entertainments*.

A prince of the great Barmecide family in Bagdad, feeling sportive, asked a poor, starving wretch named Schacabac, to come to the Barmecide palace for a good dinner. Once Schacabac was seated at table, the servants began setting a series of empty plates before him.

"How do you like the soup?" the prince would ask.

"Excellently well," replied the bewildered Schacabac.

"Did you ever see whiter bread, my man?"

"Never, honorable sir."

"And you must have some wine," said the prince, whereupon a servant brought an empty glass and an empty bottle.

"But I am already drunk," said the wretch and, rising from his chair, knocked the prince flat on his ass.

U.S. Navy midshipmen, during their summer cruises, were victimized by regular sailors—always. The only difference between a gob's uniform and a midshipman's was the hat. The midshipman's hat is the same white article worn by the gobs, save for a dark blue band. For many years it has been a custom, during these cruises, for the first sailors ashore in any foreign port to spread the word among the local girls that a blue band on the hat signifies that the wearer is under treatment for venereal disease.

I have been told by George S. McMillan of certain exploits of a boy named Quent Beecham, who lived in a big house on the Hudson River north of Yonkers. The boy's father was interested in steamboating and was friendly with many people in that business. There was a maiden aunt, of powerful opinions, who came to visit the Beechams and always sat in the same chair in the parlor. Quent did not care for her. He managed to borrow a steamboat whistle, which he rigged to the safety valve of the furnace in the cellar, placing the whistle directly below the chair which his aunt always occupied. He bored a small hole in the floor and snaked a wire through to the safety valve, so he could open it by giving the wire a jerk. Then on a Sunday afternoon, with his aunt gabbing away in her favorite chair, he activated his mechanism. The blast sent her a foot and a half off the chair.

When the boy Beecham grew older, he devised a method for driving the family touring car from the back seat. He hooked a pair of reins onto the steering wheel, and used a long pole with a loop of wire on the end to shift gears. He startled many citizens of Hudson River communities, who were not accustomed to seeing automobiles coming along without a driver.

Mrs. Winston Churchill, visiting at the White House, asked FDR when he was going to England. He said he dearly loved England and her people but that he sometimes delayed his visits when he took to thinking about Brussels sprouts. The English simply didn't know how to cook them. One of those common arguments over English cookery ensued, and FDR finally said he'd come over to London if he could get assurance that he would not be served Brussels sprouts that had been boiled. Mrs. Churchill grew mildly indignant, demanding to know how else could sprouts be cooked—she had never heard of an unboiled Brussels sprout. FDR improvised—boil, bake, roast, fry, make a soup or a soufflé out of them. *Never* boiled!

Back home Mrs. C. called in the American ambassador, John Winant, and asked him for the recipe for broiled Brussels sprouts. Winant said he had never heard of broiled sprouts. Then Mrs. C. told him what FDR had said. He told her he would make an effort to get the recipe for her. The next time he saw FDR (by this time he knew it was a joke) he said he had to have a leave, to take the course at Cordon Bleu.

Jokers sometimes slip a bill through the legislature and it gets past the governor and becomes law. In Arizona it is against the law to score a touchdown against the University of Arizona in any game played within the city limits of Tucson. Another joke-law was passed by city authorities in Los Angeles, declaring that a resident may grow as tall as he desires.

A Mexico City magazine, *Mexico This Month*, told the story of the long-enduring practical joke practiced in the state of Yucatan. The procedure is called the *cultivo*, in which the victim is cultivated. The whole community sometimes participates and always there are scores of Yucatecans involved in the conspiracy. In the *cultivo* an elaborate fake buildup is undertaken to make the victim believe that he has suddenly sprung into great importance. In one case a small-scale storekeeper, known for his blustering vanity, was persuaded that he would make a good governor of the state. Slowly, at first, he was told that it was not an impossibility, and then street-corner rallies were organized and speakers lauded the storekeeper as a great political thinker, and after that the candidate began to make personal appearances, delivering speeches, which were greeted with loud applause; campaign literature was issued, and almost everyone in the city of Merida was in on the joke, including the legitimate candidates. The victim of the hoax, of course, would find out eventually that he was being had—but he could not walk away from it; he was in too deep. He knew that he had made a fool of himself, but would be a bigger fool to acknowledge it.

An AP dispatch came out of Somerville, New Jersey, one day, telling how Stanley Dudeck, a private flier, had thrown a life-size dummy out of his plane while high over Franklin Township. Residents of the area saw the falling body and sounded an alarm. Police and firemen spent two hours searching the woods before they found the dummy. Someone had recognized the plane as belonging to Dudeck and he was given a summons. "It was just a gag," he told the magistrate The judge didn't think it was funny but he couldn't find anything in the law books forbidding the tossing of dummies out of aircraft. So he fined Mr. Dudeck fifty dollars and costs for violating the township dumping ordinance.

Otto Witte, an eighty-seven-year-old trapeze artist and sword-swallower with a European circus, was King of Albania for five days in 1913.

Witte and a couple of circus friends were in Albania when a revolution broke out. One of his friends remarked that Witte bore a striking resemblance to Prince Halim Eddin of Turkey, who was scheduled to take over. The circus men found a secondhand store carrying military uniforms; they bought an outfit made for a Turkish general, together with an array of medals and a handsome sword. Wearing these habiliments, Otto Witte turned up, having previously sent a message to the commander-in-chief of the Albanian Army saying that Prince Halim Edin was en route to take command of all troops in Albania. Much to his astonishment, he was escorted to an unoccupied castle and on February 15, 1913, crowned King. Five days later he was chased off the throne after a telegram came from the real Prince Halim Eddin, saying Witte was an imposter. Witte left town hastily, and resumed the business of swallowing swords and eating fire.

FDR sometimes went on cruises aboard Vincent Astor's palatial yacht, the *Nourmahal*. Usually Astor himself was along, as well as some of his friends—most of them wealthy New York bluebloods, and Republican conservatives. Each day on the *Nourmahal* a summary of news dispatches came by radio and was published in a mimeographed bulletin. One day FDR decided that the news report was running dull and he undertook to revise it, to juice it up, as he later put it. He inserted an item saying the U.S. Supreme Court had invalidated all quickie divorces granted in western states, thus casting doubts on remarriages made in the wake of such decrees. Consternation ensued, because several of the prominent passengers had been placed in the position of being bigamists. FDR and Vincent Astor let them suffer for several hours before revealing the truth. Another item invented by the President involved Justice Frederic Kernochan of New York, who was on the *Nourmahal*. The State Supreme Court, said the fake dispatch, had reversed all decisions made by Justice Kernochan, and the "discredited jurist" was being investigated by the State Bar Association, with a view to disbarment.

Several books could be filled with collegiate pranks. Let us take note of one, involving an impersonation. A young man who was a freshman at Yale named Robert L. Hathaway was approached by an old friend who was an undergraduate at Harvard. Coming up at Harvard was an election to choose the chairman of the Freshman Jubilee, a big Harvard spring weekend. Young Hathaway's friends proposed that he, Hathaway, become a candidate for the chairmanship. The prepossessing name of "Lamont Dupont" was chosen for the candidate, and elaborate plans were schemed. A brisk campaign was launched. Hathaway was furnished with a top hat, morning coat, and walking stick. His slogan was chosen: "Vote for Lamont Dupont—he owns us all anyway." He had cabled his acceptance from Government House in Jamaica, where he was on a diplomatic mission for Her Majesty's government and having a go at his favorite sport, falconry. Several Harvard students were participants in the affair, and they had a limousine ready for him when he arrived at Cambridge for a ceremony on the steps of Widener Library. Several thousand students attended the rally, cheering for Lamont Dupont. He responded, saying, "In spite of the vulgarity which has characterized the campaign of my opponents, I will not be deterred. No time for snobbery, this." He was easily elected. His chief opponent, one Oliver A. Yabook, tried to tell the electorate that Lamont Dupont was really a Yale student, but Yabook was shouted down and pelted with soggy vegetables and fruits. Dupont did not assume office, being busy at the time attending his classes at New Haven.

The Amboy Volcano is a landmark about halfway between Needles and Barstow in California, visible from the town of Amboy. It is a flattish cone rising several hundred feet from the desert floor, surrounded by vast acres of black lava flow.

A group of schoolboys in Amboy decided it would be fun to fake a volcanic eruption. They collected old automobile tires and other combustible junk, spending several nights secretly carrying the stuff out to the crater, a mile and a half distant from the town. When the pile had reached suitable proportions, the boys set it afire. The villagers of Amboy awoke to see great billows of smoke, and flickers of flame, rising from the crater. The schoolboys thought the whole enterprise would be good for a community laugh. They were astonished at what happened. There was a great scurrying about, and much shouting; preparations were under way for a general exodus out of the town; word was sent to Los Angeles requesting a special train to evacuate the populace (under one hundred souls). Citizens were loading their possessions into Model T Fords and lighting out across the desert. The culprits, by this time, were frightened and couldn't bring themselves to confess. One Los Angeles newspaper sent a reporter and photographer by plane, and now the hoax was discovered. The plane flew over the crater and it was apparent that the smoke and flames were not coming out of the cone. When the Needles *Desert Star* recounted the story in 1963, the writer did not specify what punishment, if any, was inflicted on the schoolboys.

John Duffie of Toronto remembers hearing about a super-hot-foot played on a member of the Elks Club who was sprawled out asleep in a clubroom chair. The boys shoved a pool cue up each pants leg and then gave him a double hot-foot.

W. C. Fields, for several seasons in a row, gave his closest friends a special kind of Christmas present—a heavy, bulky package which contained a thick, handsomely bound volume embossed with gold lettering that said: "Places Where I Am Not Wanted. W. C. Fields." Inside the elegant binding was the Los Angeles phone book.

Stanley Marcus of the far-famed Neiman-Marcus store in Dallas once acquired a painting by Saul Schary, the New York artist. It was a large picture of a nude girl, as seen from the rear. Marcus was quite fond of the painting and kept it hanging, for years, halfway up the main staircase in his home.

On a Christmas Eve when the tree trimming had been completed in the living room, Marcus started up the stair-

way for his bedroom. Midway he halted, staring at the
Schary painting. *The naked girl had turned around and
was facing him!*

An expensive jest, but then Marcus had expensive ten-
dencies. Several of his well-off friends had arranged with
Saul Schary to do the head-on view of the same model.

Among the more poignant legends of Hollywood is the
story of Buster Keaton's last years. He had been up there
with Chaplin and Harold Lloyd in his prime years, but
then he faded from view and was upstaged by family and
friends. He was a lonely man in his final years—nobody
ever invited him anywhere. He had a small trailer and on
occasion he would drive it up and park it in front of a
Beverly Hills mansion. He'd take out a bridge table and
set it up at the curb, cover it with a red-checked tablecloth,
put out some eating tools, and then serve himself dinner.
If anyone came out and asked him why he was doing this,
he would just look sad and go on eating.

During one of the low points of the recession-depression
in 1975, *Newsweek* went searching for businesses which
were enjoying prosperous times—shoe repair shops, dealers
in parts for broken appliances, processors of macaroni
products, sellers of home-gardening tools. In Chicago they
found The Funny Farm, a store dealing in joke novelties.
The proprietor said his business was up 45 percent over the
previous year and then, in common with the average American, he turned psychiatrist-sage for a moment—he said that
in hard times people get rid of their frustrations by playing
practical jokes.

The old-time jazz musicians were usually great practical
jokers. One who built up a big reputation as a gagster was
Joe Venuti, the great jazz violinist. One gloomy day in
Los Angeles, Venuti sat in his hotel room, unable to think
of anything interesting to do. He stood at the window of

his corner room and looked down at the busy intersection. He dug out a copy of the musicians' union directory for Los Angeles. He telephoned every bass-fiddle player in the book, identifying himself as a union official; he had a good-paying one-shot job for a bull-fiddle man; the guy would be picked up on the corner below Venuti's window that afternoon. About thirty-five showed up, with fiddles.

In Westchester County I once knew a pleasant elderly man who had been proprietor of a popular restaurant in Manhattan. He was a great hand to fart. His daughter and her family lived nearby and his four-year-old grandson often came to his house to play and to hear rat-killing stories from Grampaw. Now and then the grandfather would hold out his hand, middle finger extended, and say to the child: "All right. Pull on that finger again." The boy would seize the finger and give it a tug, whereupon Grampaw would deliver himself of a thundersprake. The little boy always reacted glowingly—he was a person of definite achievement.

Hiram Maxim was one of this country's leading inventors back in the heyday of Thomas Edison and, in fact, very nearly beat Edison to the electric light bulb. His name is best known, perhaps, as inventor of the Maxim machine gun (his son invented the Maxim silencer). Hiram Stevens Maxim got sore at his native land because the government would not accept his inventions; the British did accept them, and made important use of them, and Hiram moved to England for good—he eventually was knighted by Queen Victoria. He was an incorrigible practical joker.

One example should suffice. Life with Father Maxim was forever eventful, according to his son Hiram Percy Maxim. When Hiram Percy was a small boy a neighborhood storekeeper in Brooklyn had a dog that the boy coveted. The storekeeper said he would give the animal to little Hiram in exchange for a penny with heads on both sides. Big joke. Some days later the boy mentioned this offer to his father, saying he had been unable to locate a penny with heads on both sides. The following day Papa went into his factory and used a lathe to shave down the thickness of two pennies, then cemented them together to create a penny with two heads. He then accompanied his son to the store and confronted the merchant, demanding the dog in exchange for the penny. A cyclonic argument ensued, with threats of lawsuits and talk of punches in the nose. In the end Father was satisfied with administering a solemn lecture, cautioning the storekeeper against taking advantage of little boys.

Harry Houdini, the greatest of all escape artists, devoted the later years of his life to investigations of psychic science. He seemed to regard all spiritualistic mediums as palpable frauds and mountebanks, and he exposed hordes of them.

Houdini died in 1926. After hundreds of harrowing and hair-raising escapes from death, he met his end in a most commonplace manner. To demonstrate the strength of his stomach muscles he invited a student in Montreal to hit him in the stomach as hard as he could. The blow ruptured Houdini's appendix and he died a few days later.

One of his most devoted admirers was a newspaper editor named Meyer Solmson who, in 1927, was in charge of editorial operations at the New York *Morning Telegraph*. In the autumn of that year Solmson received a notice of the unveiling of a Houdini monument in a Brooklyn cemetery. Solmson remembered that he had once heard the escape artist say that, after death, he might play possum for a while and then emerge from the tomb. The thing began to chew on Solmson's mind and it occurred to him that this ceremony on the first anniversary of Houdini's death might be the very occasion for The Return. The editor called in Johnny O'Connor, one of his best reporters and a Broadway iconoclast. Solmson told O'Connor of his hunch, and O'Connor suggested that the entire matter be forgotten, lest the people of New York put them down as lunatics. Solmson insisted that Johnny O'Connor be present at the ceremony in the cemetery.

Johnny didn't bother. Instead he attended his usual poker game on Saturday night and slept most of the next day, arriving at his office in the evening. A wire-service dispatch told him that the Houdini affair had come off without incident. He was about to write his own second-hand account of the ceremony when someone told him that Meyer Solmson had been trying, excitedly, to get him on the phone all day. So O'Connor told his boss that he had been delayed in the graveyard *because Harry Houdini had escaped from his casket.*

"My God!" cried Solmson over the phone. "This is the greatest story since the first Easter! I'll be right down!"

At the *Telegraph* the editor took charge of the story as Johnny O'Connor pounded out the copy, snatching the sheets from the O'Connor typewriter and all but dancing up and down in his excitement. It was a graphic and overpowering story O'Connor wrote and Solmson fired it, sheet by sheet, to the printers in the composing room.

There were a few actual facts in it. Mayor Walker had been present, and William Randolph Hearst, and Mrs. Houdini, of course, and assorted political and ecclesiastical bigwigs.

In the O'Connor account, the most prominent of the guests marched with the widow to the mausoleum, and as they reached the entrance three doves flew from the interior and soared skyward. Mrs. Houdini shrieked and fainted. When she was brought around, the ceremony proceeded and the group entered the tomb.

O'Connor was now writing . . .

Suddenly, from within the casket, came the sound of a gong. It registered twelve distinct bells, and was followed by a low voice which said, "Twelve O'clock and I am ready."

It was exactly midnight now. Those close to the casket began to show the strain. A series of rappings from within the box followed. A light suddenly appeared from elsewhere, spotting the head of the casket and lighting up a circumference of about eight inches. Slowly, the lid began to rise. A deep voice calling for assistance was recognized as Houdini's by those who had known him. The magician's head came through the opening . . .

At this point Meyer Solmson descended on O'Connor and said that the printers were yelling for a close-out; Solmson grabbed the last sheet, announcing that they'd have to cut the story at that point. He congratulated O'Connor on the story, removed his eyeshade, took a few deep breaths, put on his coat, and went home—a gleam in his eye, denoting his satisfaction over a job well done. He didn't know, of course, that everyone else in the building knew the story of Houdini's Resurrection had been made up, word for word and line for line, by the capable Johnny O'Connor, and not a word of it appeared in the *Telegraph* when the paper hit the streets a short while later. Editor Solmson did not, as was expected, fire Johnny. When he arrived at the office next day he clapped O'Connor on the back and, with a hollow sort of laugh, said, "I was wise to the whole thing, Johnny, the minute you started writing."

I do not vouch for the truth of any part of this tale, but I got it from the files of Gene Fowler, who succeeded Meyer Solmson on the *Telegraph* the following year. Mr. Fowler, one of the great men of American journalism, said it was all true. I ride with Ole Gene.

Late in his life Robert Benchley made his home in a cottage at the Garden of Allah, a Hollywood complex popular with the leading movie stars. The great humorist shared his cottage with his old friend, the actor Charlie Butterworth (there was no faggotry involved here). One season Benchley took down with pneumonia and his doctor prescribed some of the new sulfa drugs, warning him that there might be certain side effects and urging Benchley to report any such developments. The next time the doctor called at the cottage Benchley was in bed. Had he taken the miracle drugs? Religiously, said Benchley. The doctor pulled down the sheet and inspected the Benchley chest carefully. Nothing amiss. "Are you sure," asked the doctor, "that you've experienced no side effects?" Benchley replied, "None that I've noticed . . ." then a nervous hesitation, and ". . . but, Doc, I don't quite know what to make of this." He pulled the sheet back to reveal that from the waist down, his body was covered with chicken feathers. He and Butterworth had fastened them on with library paste.

Benchley enjoyed strong drink, and the waters sometimes led him into strange adventures. Once in that Garden of Allah cottage he put in a long-distance call to the ex-Kaiser Wilhelm, who was living in exile at Doorn, Holland. Be-dogged if he didn't succeed in getting Kaiser Bill on the phone. "I just wanted to find out how you're feeling," said Benchley, "and practice my German." He was unable to report, later, on what Wilhelm II said in response.

While studying at Harvard, Benchley and a student friend crossed the river one day and went wandering through the sedate precincts of Louisburg Square, home of some of the stuffiest Boston Brahmins. On impulse, Benchley led his friend to the front entrance of a fine old house and sounded the knocker. A maid responded. "We've come for the davenport," said Benchley. The maid hesitated, then let them in. They picked up a davenport and carried it out, crossed the square, rang another bell, and Benchley said, "We've brought the davenport. Where shall we put it?" They deposited it in the living room and resumed their little journeyings.

Carole Lombard, at the height of her fame as a picture star and as the wife of Clark Gable, was a client of the

Hollywood agent Myron Selznick. He told her that as a formality they ought to have a contract. She went out and had one printed up, in the form of a standard agent's contract, signed it, and took it to Selznick. He didn't bother to inspect it but put it away in his safe. Then one day Miss Lombard's lawyer telephoned, demanding to know where the money was. It turned out that as a gag the actress had devised a contract under which Selznick was to pay her 10 percent of all his earnings. ●